McCall's Best Recipes

1991

Oxmoor House®

Library of Congress Catalog Number: 88-43142
ISBN: 0-8487-1034-7

Manufactured in the United States of America
First printing 1991

Published by arrangement with Oxmoor House, Inc.
Book Division of Southern Progress Corporation
P.O. Box 2463, Birmingham, AL 35201

McCall's

  Editor-in-Chief: Anne Mollegen Smith
  Executive Editor: Lisel Eisenheimer
  Managing Editor: Leslie Smith

  Food Editor: Marianne Langan
  Senior Associate Food Editor: Mary B. Johnson
  Test-Kitchen Supervisor: Holly Sheppard
  Associate Food Editors: Pamela M. Berger,
    Claudia Gallo, Lynne Giviskos,
    Donna Meadow, Sarah Reynolds,
    Karen Sethre White, Marianne Zanzarella
  Assistant Food Editors: Carmen McLeod, Ines Reyes
  Executive-Dining Room Chef: Melva Victorino
  Photographer: Victor Scocozza
  Additional photography by Kenro Izu, pages
    214–215, 216–217, 219; Matthew Klein,
    pages 157, 158–159, 160–161, 168, 172, 173,
    193, 194–195, 196–197; Philip Laurent, pages
    224, 225, 226; Michael Mazzeo, pages
    208–209; Judd Pilossof, pages 152, 186–187;
    Aaron Rezny, pages 175, 176–177, 178–179,
    188, 189, 191

Oxmoor House, Inc.
  Executive Editor: Ann H. Harvey
  Director of Manufacturing: Jerry R. Higdon
  Art Director: Bob Nance

McCall's Best Recipes 1991

  Senior Editor: Olivia Kindig Wells
  Editor: Cecilia C. Robinson
  Copy Chief: Mary Ann Laurens
  Copy Editor: Melinda E. West
  Editorial Assistants: Carole Cain, Leigh Anne Roberts
  Senior Designer: Cynthia Rose Cooper
  Production Manager: Rick Litton
  Associate Production Manager: Theresa Beste

Cover: *Three-Chocolate Mousse, page 153.*

Back cover: *(Clockwise from top right) Chicken Brochettes, page 71; Curly-Top Marble Pound Cake, page 34; Savory Spaghetti Pork Roast, page 149; Strawberry Floating Island, page 37.*

To subscribe to *McCall's* magazine, write to *McCall's*, P.O. Box 3178, Harlan, IA 51537-0369.

Contents

McCall's
Annual Collection

McCall's *food staff includes (back row, left to right) Melva Victorino, Executive-Dining Room Chef; Carmen McLeod, Assistant Food Editor; Lynne Giviskos, Associate Food Editor; Claudia Gallo, Associate Food Editor; Sarah Reynolds, Associate Food Editor; (center row, left to right) Marianne Zanzarella, Associate Food Editor; Ines Reyes, Assistant Food Editor; Marianne Langan, Food Editor; Mary B. Johnson, Senior Associate Food Editor; (center) Holly Sheppard, Test-Kitchen Supervisor. Not pictured, Pamela M. Berger, Associate Food Editor; Donna Meadow, Associate Food Editor; Karen Sethre White, Associate Food Editor.*

This has been a truly constructive year at *McCall's*—a new owner, *The New York Times*; a new editor, Anne Mollegen Smith; and a new address, complete with brand-new, fully-equipped test kitchens.

In September, the magazine staff moved to Manhattan's lower Fifth Avenue into a marvelous renovated building. The food department's latest home is completely up-to-date and sparkling clean, a true joy to our professional staff and a source of personal pride to our treasured housekeeper. The transition has been especially welcome since our previous facilities were designed over 40 years ago! Now, with our modern test kitchens to inspire us, we look forward to creating even more delicious and attractive recipes for you to savor and treasure.

Editorially, this has been an exciting year as well. Building on the great success we have had with our Lite Eating page, this September we introduced yet another feature geared to modern cooking. Our innovative "Masterpiece" series is dedicated to the woman of today who is eager for fresh and different recipes to expand her entertaining menu. The Masterpiece dishes, tantalizing both visually and gastronomically, are intended to dazzle guests. Lavish and worthy of their preparation time, they offer gourmet cooking that does not require great experience to reproduce, whether the cook chooses to duplicate the dish entirely, or in part.

This collection includes recipes that are economically smart as well as the special-occasion splurges guaranteed to impress. The ever-practical family-style casserole and weekend roast, along with fast-fix suggestions that take busy schedules into account, are an important part of this cookbook. The result is an inventive mix of dishes ranging from the more involved recipes to ones with short ingredient lists that are easy and quick to prepare.

As always, our recipes are developed by our staff, drawing on our experiences in the restaurants we frequent, the many trips we take, the cookbooks we constantly peruse and the inspirations we draw from friends and family. Each recipe is tested four times or more before it is published and rechecked by a member of our staff not involved with the initial development. The recipes are meticulously edited to provide careful directions that, when followed precisely, will result in dishes as attractive as the photographs and as delicious as when our staff prepares them.

We hope you enjoy our latest edition and will continue to be inspired by our recipes. Food plays an important part in all of our lives, and we at *McCall's* are proud of the varied and creative meal ideas we share with you.

Marianne Langan, Food Editor

January

Impress your guests with our company recipes, all listed below and photographed for three holiday parties. A festive wine and appetizer get-together is pictured here, followed by a stunning buffet starring a crown of pork spareribs. The final celebration shows a do-ahead dessert party.

Piña Colada Saga   Mexican Wontons

Ricotta-Sausage Strudel

Shrimp Curried Eggs   Tempura Tempters

Crown of Spareribs   Pearl-Onion Confit

Chicken Scarparella

Savory Steak on Garlic Bread

Marinated Pepper Salad

Cranberry-Pear Pastry

Eggnog Bread Pudding

Amaretti-Cheese Pie   Orange-Pecan Loaf

Gala Holiday Cookbook

Plan now to celebrate the new year with a party, starting with these party-special recipes.

Piña Colada Saga
(pictured, page 7)

²/₃ **cup honey-roasted macadamia nuts, coarsely chopped**
¼ **cup flaked coconut**
2 **tablespoons light-brown sugar**
2 **cans (8-ounce size) crushed pineapple, drained**
1 **(9- to 10-inch) round Saga blue cheese (2¾ pounds)**
Crackers or sliced French bread

1. In small bowl, combine nuts, coconut, sugar and pineapple. Mix well; set aside.
2. Place cheese on serving platter. With long serrated knife, slice cheese in half horizontally. Remove top layer; set aside.
3. Spread half of pineapple mixture over cut side of cheese on platter; top with remaining half of cheese, cut side down. Spread remaining pineapple mixture over top of cheese to within ½ inch of edges. Serve cheese with crackers or sliced French bread.

Makes 20 servings.

Page 7: (Counterclockwise from top) Piña Colada Saga, Mexican Wontons, Ricotta-Sausage Strudel, Shrimp Curried Eggs, Tempura Tempters.

Pages 8 and 9: (Clockwise from top left) Crown of Spareribs, Pearl-Onion Confit, Chicken Scarparella, Savory Steak on Garlic Bread, Marinated Pepper Salad.

Pages 10 and 11: (Clockwise from top left) Cranberry-Pear Pastry, Eggnog Bread Pudding, Amaretti-Cheese Pie, Orange-Pecan Loaf.

Ricotta-Sausage Strudel
(pictured, page 7)

1 **container (15 ounces) ricotta cheese**
⅓ **cup grated Parmesan cheese**
1 **package (10 ounces) frozen chopped spinach, thawed and squeezed dry**
¾ **pound sweet Italian sausage, casings removed**
1 **medium onion, chopped**
½ **teaspoon dried basil leaves, crushed**
1 **jar (6 ounces) roasted red peppers, drained and chopped**
½ **cup coarsely chopped black pitted olives**
2 **large eggs**
12 **sheets phyllo pastry**
¾ **cup butter or margarine, melted**
1 **cup Italian-seasoned fine dry bread crumbs**

1. In large bowl, combine ricotta, Parmesan and spinach; set aside. Preheat oven to 375°F.
2. In large skillet, over medium heat, cook sausage, onion and basil until sausage is browned and onion is tender, about 5 minutes, breaking up sausage with spoon. Using slotted spoon, transfer sausage mixture to bowl with cheese mixture. Stir in red peppers, olives and eggs until well mixed; set aside.
3. On work surface, place 1 sheet phyllo; cover remainder with plastic wrap or damp kitchen towel. Brush phyllo sheet with some melted butter; sprinkle with 1 tablespoon bread crumbs. Repeat, layering 5 more sheets phyllo over first sheet. Reserve remaining phyllo, butter and crumbs.
4. With kitchen shears, cut prepared phyllo layers in half crosswise. Spread 1¼ cups cheese mixture over pastry along cut side of each half to within 3 inches of cut edges and 1½ inches of short edges. Fold short sides of phyllo over filling; beginning with long side with filling, roll up each strudel, jelly-roll fashion. Place both strudels on jelly-roll pan. Set aside. Make 2 more strudels, repeating procedure beginning with step 3. Brush all strudels with melted butter, and sprinkle with remaining bread crumbs, dividing evenly. Bake 20 minutes, or until golden brown. With serrated knife, cut strudels crosswise into 1-inch-wide slices.

Makes 32 servings.

Mexican Wontons

(pictured, page 7)

Salsa
3 Italian plum tomatoes or 1 large tomato, finely chopped
½ can (4-ounce size) chopped green chiles, drained
2 tablespoons minced red onion
1 tablespoon minced cilantro (fresh coriander) leaves
⅛ teaspoon salt
1 teaspoon lime juice

Wontons
1 pound ground beef
1 medium onion, chopped
1 medium clove garlic, crushed
2 teaspoons chili powder
½ can (4-ounce size) chopped green chiles, drained
2 tablespoons chopped cilantro (fresh coriander) leaves
1 teaspoon salt
⅛ teaspoon ground red pepper
½ cup water
¼ cup tomato paste

16 egg-roll wrappers
Salad oil

1. Make salsa: In small bowl, combine salsa ingredients. Cover; set aside until serving time.

2. Make wontons: In large skillet, over medium heat, brown ground beef. With slotted spoon, remove meat from pan; set aside. To hot drippings in pan, add onion and garlic; over medium-high heat, sauté until onion is tender, about 3 minutes. Add chili powder; cook 1 minute. Return meat to pan; add chiles, cilantro, salt, red pepper, water and tomato paste. Cook, stirring, until thickened, about 5 minutes.

3. On work surface, place 2 egg-roll wrappers on top of each other (keep remaining wrappers covered with damp paper towel). Spoon scant ¼ cup beef mixture onto center of wrappers; brush edges with water. Gather edges together; pinch above filling to seal, making little packages. Repeat with remaining filling and wrappers.

4. Line plate with paper towels; set aside. In medium saucepan or deep-fat fryer, heat 3 inches oil to 375°F. Fry wontons, two at a time, until golden, about 3 minutes. With slotted spoon, remove wontons to prepared plate. Serve with salsa.
Makes 4 servings.

Tempura Tempters

(pictured, page 7)

½ pound cleaned fresh or frozen (thawed) squid
½ pound large shrimp
1 medium acorn squash
1 medium yam
1 medium zucchini
½ pound green beans
1 small head cauliflower
1 small red pepper
1 cup parsley sprigs
Salad oil

Batter
1¾ cups unsifted all-purpose flour
2 teaspoons cornstarch
¼ teaspoon salt
2 large eggs
1 can (12 ounces) cold beer

Japanese Dipping Sauce (recipe follows)
½ cup fresh lemon juice
½ cup soy sauce

1. Slice squid body crosswise into ½-inch-wide rings; cut tentacles into several pieces if they are large. Cover; refrigerate. Clean and devein shrimp, leaving tails intact. Cover; refrigerate. Cut squash in half; remove seeds. Slice into ¼-inch-thick wedges; with paring knife, remove skin. Pare yam; cut crosswise into ¼-inch-thick slices. Cut zucchini in half crosswise; cut each half into ¼-inch-thick sticks. Trim green beans. Cut cauliflower into flowerets. Cut red pepper in half; remove seeds, and cut into 1-inch-wide strips. Rinse parsley; pat dry. Chill vegetables.

2. Preheat oven to 200°F. Line baking sheet with paper towels. In 5-quart Dutch oven or deep-fat fryer, heat 2 inches oil to 375°F.

3. Meanwhile, make batter: In large bowl, mix flour with cornstarch and salt. Whisk in eggs and beer just until blended.

4. Working with a few pieces at a time, dip seafood and vegetables into batter; drain slightly. Gently drop into oil; fry until lightly browned, about 2 minutes, turning with slotted spoon or tongs. Remove from oil; drain on baking sheet. Keep warm while preparing remaining seafood and vegetables. Arrange tempura on warm platter; serve with Japanese Dipping Sauce, lemon juice and soy sauce.
Makes 12 appetizer servings.

Japanese Dipping Sauce

2 tablespoons grated daikon (white Japanese radish; see *Note*)
2 teaspoons grated ginger root
1 cup water
¼ cup mirin (sweet rice wine)
¼ cup soy sauce

In small saucepan, combine all ingredients. Over medium heat, cook until very hot; keep warm.
Makes ½ cup.
Note: Available in Oriental food markets and specialty food areas of some supermarkets.

Gala Holiday Cookbook

Shrimp Curried Eggs

(pictured, page 7)

3 cups water
2 tablespoons dry sherry
1¼ teaspoons salt
1 pound small shrimp, shelled
  and deveined
12 large hard-cooked eggs
¼ cup parsley sprigs
1 teaspoon dry mustard
½ teaspoon curry powder
½ teaspoon paprika
½ teaspoon pepper
⅓ cup mayonnaise
2 tablespoons milk

1. In large saucepan, bring water and sherry to boiling. Add 1 teaspoon salt and the shrimp; cover. Cook 1 minute, or until shrimp are pink and cooked. Drain; rinse with cold water until cool. Pat dry with paper towels. Set aside 24 shrimp; place remainder in food processor.

2. Shell eggs; with crinkle cutter, slice in half lengthwise. Place yolks in food processor; add parsley, dry mustard, curry powder, paprika, remaining salt, the pepper, mayonnaise and milk. Process until blended. Spoon mixture into egg whites, mounding slightly. Garnish each with a reserved shrimp.

Makes 12 appetizer servings.

Savory Steak On Garlic Bread

(pictured, pages 8 and 9)

Marinade
1 medium clove garlic, crushed
½ cup bourbon
½ cup low-salt soy sauce

2-pound flank steak

Garlic Bread
1-pound long loaf Italian bread
½ cup butter or margarine,
  melted
1 large clove garlic, crushed

1. In small glass measure, combine marinade ingredients. Place steak in shallow baking dish; pour marinade over steak. Cover with plastic wrap; let stand at room temperature 30 minutes.

2. Meanwhile, make garlic bread: Slice bread into ¼-inch-thick slices. In small bowl, combine butter and garlic; brush mixture over one cut side of bread. Arrange on baking sheet; set aside.

3. Drain steak, reserving marinade; place on rack in broiler pan. Broil 6 inches from heat 5 minutes. Turn steak over; broil 5 minutes longer. Place steak on carving board; let stand 10 minutes.

4. Meanwhile, place marinade in small saucepan. Bring to boiling; simmer 5 minutes. Brush steak with some hot marinade; pour remainder into sauceboat.

5. Broil garlic bread until lightly browned, about 1 minute. Thinly slice steak across the grain. Serve with garlic bread; pass sauce separately. If desired, garnish with parsley and cherry tomatoes.

Makes 18 appetizer servings.

■ To make a cherry-tomato flower, cut through skin at top of tomato, dividing it into thirds. Carefully pull open, separating skin from center. Make a thin strip of cucumber skin 1 inch long. Twist into a circle; place in center of tomato. Chill, covered with a damp towel.

■ With a rolling pin, roll dried apricots and dried apples until flattened. Coil each kind of fruit into a flower shape; pinch at one end to hold "petals" together.

■ For a green-onion flower, trim white part to 2 or 3 inches. Make several crosscuts, ½ inch deep, in each end. Place in bowl of ice water; ends will open and curl in about 1½ hours.

Crown of Spareribs

(pictured, page 8)

2 (2-pound) racks pork
  spareribs
Salt
Pepper

Stuffing
1 pound bulk country-style
  sausage
3 tablespoons butter or
  margarine
1 cup sliced celery
1 cup chopped onion
1 package (8 ounces)
  cornbread stuffing mix
1 package (6 ounces) assorted
  dried fruit, chopped
¾ teaspoon salt
¼ teaspoon freshly ground
  pepper
1¼ cups water

**Sweet 'n' Sour Sauce (recipe
  follows)**
**Pearl-Onion Confit (recipe
  follows)**

1. Preheat oven to 325°F. Line large roasting pan with aluminum foil; set aside.

2. Form racks of spareribs in a ring; secure with kitchen string or poultry pins. Place in prepared pan, bone tips up; lightly sprinkle spareribs with salt and pepper. Roast, uncovered, 2 hours.

3. Meanwhile, prepare stuffing: In large skillet, crumble sausage. Over medium-high heat, cook sausage, stirring, until browned. With slotted spoon, remove from pan. Drain; place in large bowl.

4. In hot drippings in skillet, melt butter; add celery and onion. Over medium-high heat, sauté until vegetables are tender, about 5 minutes. Transfer vegetables to bowl with sausage; add stuffing mix, fruit, salt, pepper and water.

5. Remove ribs from oven. Fill center with stuffing; brush ribs with some Sweet 'n' Sour Sauce. Bake 30 minutes, or until stuffing is heated

through and meat is tender. Arrange stuffed crown of spareribs on serving platter; if desired, garnish with mâche (lamb's lettuce) and dried-fruit flowers. Pass additional sauce and the confit separately.

Makes 6 servings.

Sweet 'n' Sour Sauce

½ cup sugar
2 teaspoons dry mustard
½ cup white vinegar
¼ cup water
1 large egg, lightly beaten
¼ cup apricot preserves

In top of double boiler, combine sugar and mustard. Whisk in vinegar, water and the egg. Over gently boiling water, cook mixture, stirring frequently, until mixture thickens, about 10 minutes. Stir in preserves; heat through. Keep warm, but do not boil.

Makes 1⅓ cups.

Pearl-Onion Confit
(pictured, pages 8 and 9)

2 pounds pearl onions
3 tablespoons butter or
    margarine
4 medium cloves garlic,
    crushed
¼ cup firmly packed
    light-brown sugar
1 teaspoon salt
¼ teaspoon pepper
¼ cup raisins
1 cup white wine
⅓ cup red-wine vinegar
2 tablespoons tomato paste

1. Peel onions. Quarter large onions; leave small onions whole. In 12-inch skillet, over medium heat, melt butter. Add onions, garlic, sugar, salt and pepper. Cook, uncovered, 15 minutes, or until liquid evaporates.
2. Stir in raisins, wine, vinegar and tomato paste. Cook confit over low heat, uncovered, 30 minutes,

stirring occasionally, until liquid evaporates and onions are soft and glazed. Serve with pork.

Makes 2 cups.

Marinated Pepper Salad
(pictured, page 8)

1 pound carrots
2 cups boiling water
½ teaspoon salt
1 can (16 ounces) wax
    beans, drained
1 small green pepper
1 small red pepper
4 green onions
¼ cup minced chives

Marinade
3 tablespoons sugar
1 teaspoon salt
¼ teaspoon ground white
    pepper
½ cup white-wine vinegar
¼ cup salad oil
2 tablespoons water
1 tablespoon prepared
    mustard
1 tablespoon soy sauce

Lettuce leaves, washed and
    crisped

1. Pare and trim carrots; with crinkle cutter, cut crosswise into ¼-inch slices. In boiling water in medium saucepan, cook carrots with salt, covered, until tender-crisp, about 5 minutes. Drain; immediately place carrots in large bowl of ice and water. Let stand until carrots are thoroughly chilled.
2. Meanwhile, place wax beans in large mixing bowl. Cut peppers into ½-inch pieces; cut green onions, including tops, into 1-inch pieces. Add peppers, green onions and chives to bowl with beans; set aside.
3. Make marinade: In 2-cup jar with tight-fitting lid, combine marinade ingredients. Shake until mixture is blended and sugar dissolves.

4. Drain carrots; place in bowl with vegetables. Pour marinade over vegetables; toss well. Cover with plastic wrap; refrigerate at least 4 hours and up to 3 days, stirring occasionally. To serve, line bowl with lettuce leaves. Spoon salad over greens.

Makes 6 to 8 servings.

Bring on the Buffet

■ Easy on both the hostess and guests, buffet-style parties involve fewer last-minute hassles than a sit-down dinner and more flexibility for people to pick and choose what they want without feeling self-conscious. Also, you can often invite more guests to a buffet than to a formal dinner.

■ Place flatware, napkins and beverages at the end of the line so that guests won't be encumbered with them while trying to serve themselves.

■ Two-sided buffets are better for large groups, with one side of the table setting mirroring the other. You needn't set out separate serving dishes for each item; just be sure to have appropriate utensils on each side of the table.

■ If guests will be balancing plates on their laps or standing while eating, avoid foods that require cutting. Be sure plates and napkins are large and sturdy enough to guard against spills on clothing or furniture.

■ For your enjoyment and for food-safety reasons, plan a menu that isn't temperature-critical.

■ Select music that is lively and appeals to all tastes. Although classical tunes may suit the dinner hour, they can also subdue spirited conversation.

Chicken Scarparella

(pictured, page 9)

1 small bunch arugula
¼ cup olive or salad oil
1 red pepper, julienned
2 medium cloves garlic,
　crushed
2½ pounds chicken, cut into
　serving pieces
1 pound sweet or hot Italian
　sausage links, cut crosswise
　in half
¾ pound mushrooms, sliced
1 medium onion, sliced
½ teaspoon salt
¼ teaspoon dried rosemary
　leaves, crushed
⅛ teaspoon pepper
1 cup chicken broth
½ cup dry white wine
1 package (8 ounces) linguine
2 tablespoons all-purpose flour
¼ cup water

1. Rinse arugula well; pat dry. Reserve half of the arugula for garnish; discard tough stems from remainder. Thinly slice prepared arugula; set aside.

2. In large skillet, heat 2 tablespoons oil over medium-high heat. Add red pepper; sauté until tender. Add prepared arugula and half the garlic; sauté until arugula is wilted. Transfer vegetables and pan drippings to bowl.

3. In same skillet, heat remaining oil. Add chicken and sausage in batches; brown on all sides, removing pieces to plate as they brown. Discard all but 2 tablespoons drippings from pan. To hot drippings in pan, add mushrooms, onion and remaining garlic; sauté until tender. Return chicken and sausage to skillet. Add salt, rosemary, pepper, broth and wine. Bring to boiling; simmer, covered, until chicken is tender, about 25 minutes.

4. Meanwhile, prepare linguine as package label directs. Drain; return to pan. Add red-pepper mixture; heat through. Toss to combine. Cover; keep warm.

5. Remove chicken and sausage from skillet; arrange on warm serving platter. Skim fat from mixture in skillet. In small glass measure, mix flour with water until blended. Stir into liquid in skillet. Bring to boiling, stirring constantly; boil 1 minute, stirring, until mixture thickens. Spoon sauce mixture over chicken and sausage. Arrange pasta on platter with chicken. Garnish with reserved arugula.

Makes 6 servings.

Cranberry-Pear Pastry

(pictured, page 10)

1½ cups butter
1¼ cups cranberries
¾ cup sugar
1 tablespoon lemon juice
2½ pounds ripe pears, cored
　and pared (about 5 large)
2 tablespoons instant tapioca
10 sheets phyllo pastry
¼ cup finely ground nuts

1. In medium saucepan, over medium heat, melt 2 tablespoons butter. Stir in cranberries, 7 tablespoons sugar and the lemon juice. Bring to boiling; simmer, stirring occasionally, 3 minutes or until berries pop. Remove from heat. In large bowl, combine cranberry mixture, pears and tapioca; set aside.

2. Preheat oven to 375°F. Unfold phyllo sheets onto flat surface; cover with damp towel to prevent phyllo from drying out. Remove 2 sheets. Cut sheets in half crosswise; cut each piece in half crosswise to make 8 rectangles. Cover with plastic wrap; set aside.

3. Melt remaining butter; grease 9-inch pie plate with some melted butter. Place 1 sheet uncut phyllo on clean surface. Brush with some melted butter; sprinkle with 2 teaspoons sugar and 1 tablespoon ground nuts. Place phyllo, sugar side up, in prepared pie plate. Repeat with 3 more whole sheets phyllo,

placing each sheet in pie plate at a slight angle to other sheets so that edges are not over each other and hang over edge of dish.

4. Spread pear mixture over phyllo in pie plate. Bring overhanging sheets up and over filling. Brush 1 whole sheet of remaining phyllo with melted butter; sprinkle with 2 teaspoons sugar. Place phyllo, sugar side up, over filling. Repeat with 2 whole sheets phyllo, placing sheets at an angle over each other as above. Cover pie with remaining whole sheet phyllo; do not brush top with butter or sprinkle it with sugar.

5. Tuck overhanging edges of phyllo sheets under and then down into side of pie plate. Cut 3 or 4 steam vents into phyllo on top of pie. Bake 45 minutes, covering loosely with foil if pastry browns too quickly. Let cool 40 minutes before cutting.

6. Meanwhile, make phyllo bows: Brush each reserved cut phyllo sheet with some of remaining butter. Cover each of 4 prepared sheets phyllo with 1 prepared sheet phyllo; pinch each set of sheets in center of long sides to make 4 bows. Sprinkle each bow with remaining sugar, dividing evenly. Place on baking sheet; bake 8 minutes, or until golden brown. Place on top of cooled pastry; if desired, garnish with sugared cranberries.

Makes 8 servings.

Orange-Pecan Loaf

(pictured, page 10)

⅔ cup sugar
¼ cup butter
2 large eggs
2 cups unsifted all-purpose
　flour
1 tablespoon baking powder
Dash of ground nutmeg
½ teaspoon salt
1 cup pineapple-orange juice
½ teaspoon vanilla extract
⅔ cup chopped pecans

Glaze
1 to 2 tablespoons orange juice
1 cup confectioners' sugar

8 pecan halves

1. Preheat oven to 350°F. Grease 9-by-5-by-3-inch loaf pan; set aside.

2. In large bowl of electric mixer, at medium speed, beat sugar with butter and eggs until smooth; set aside. On waxed paper, combine flour, baking powder, nutmeg and salt; set aside. In small glass measure, combine 1 cup juice with vanilla; set aside. Alternately add flour mixture and juice mixture to sugar mixture, beginning and ending with flour mixture and beating well after each addition. Stir in nuts.

3. Pour batter into prepared pan. Bake 1 hour, or until cake tester inserted in center of loaf comes out clean. Remove loaf from pan; place, right side up, on wire rack. Cool completely.

4. Make glaze: In small bowl, add enough juice to confectioners' sugar to make thick but pliable consistency. With glaze in pastry bag fitted with number-1 tip, using photograph as a guide, drizzle glaze over loaf. While glaze is still wet, arrange pecan halves over top. If desired, serve loaf with a mixture of equal parts orange marmalade and butter.

Makes 1 loaf.

Amaretti-Cheese Pie
(pictured, page 11)

1 container (15 ounces) whole-milk ricotta cheese
1 cup finely crushed bittersweet almond-flavored Italian cookies
1 cup unsifted all-purpose flour
½ cup cold butter or margarine
4 large eggs
½ cup golden raisins
¾ cup sugar
½ teaspoon grated lemon peel

1. Place ricotta in sieve set over bowl. With back of spoon, press cheese to squeeze out excess liquid. Set aside.

2. In medium bowl, combine cookie crumbs with flour. Add butter; with pastry blender or 2 knives, cut in butter until mixture resembles coarse crumbs. In custard cup, with fork, beat 1 egg until blended; stir into crumb mixture until mixture forms a ball. Remove ½ cup pastry; form into a disk. Reshape remaining pastry into a ball; flatten to a ½-inch-thick disk. Wrap each disk in plastic wrap; refrigerate 30 minutes.

3. Preheat oven to 400°F. On lightly floured surface, with lightly floured rolling pin, roll out larger portion of pastry to an 11-inch round. Transfer pastry to 9-inch pie plate; ease pastry to fit around side. Flute edges; freeze 10 minutes.

4. Bake pie shell 10 minutes. Cool slightly. Reduce oven temperature to 375°F. On baking sheet, roll out remaining pastry to a 7-inch round. With fluted pastry wheel, cut round into 1-inch-wide strips; place baking sheet with strips in refrigerator while preparing filling.

5. Place raisins in small bowl; cover with boiling water. Let stand 5 minutes.

6. Meanwhile, in large bowl of electric mixer, at high speed, beat remaining eggs until thick and lemon-colored. Gradually beat in sugar. At low speed, beat in ricotta and lemon peel. Drain raisins; stir into cheese mixture. Pour filling

---

■ Try this easy, no-mess method for decorating pastries: Fill a plastic sandwich bag with frosting, softened cream cheese or whipped cream; then cut off a small piece of one corner and squeeze out the contents. Simply throw the bag away when you're finished.

---

into prepared pie crust. Arrange reserved pastry strips in lattice fashion over filling. Bake 30 minutes. Cool completely on wire rack. If desired, garnish with whipped cream and small bittersweet almond-flavored Italian cookies.

Makes 8 servings.

Eggnog Bread Pudding
(pictured, pages 10 and 11)

¾-pound loaf egg bread (challah), cut into 1-inch cubes
1 cup coarsely chopped green and red candied cherries
½ cup raisins
½ cup firmly packed light-brown sugar
6 large eggs
½ teaspoon ground nutmeg
4 cups eggnog
2 cups half-and-half
2 tablespoons brandy
2 tablespoons butter or margarine

1. Preheat oven to 325°F. Grease 13-by-9-by-2-inch baking dish; set dish aside.

2. Place bread cubes in roasting pan. Bake 10 minutes, stirring occasionally, until toasted; place in prepared baking dish. Stir in cherries and raisins.

3. In large bowl, whisk sugar and eggs until blended. Stir in nutmeg, eggnog, half-and-half and brandy until blended. Pour eggnog mixture over bread-cube mixture; dot with butter. Set baking dish in roasting pan; place on oven rack. Fill roasting pan with enough hot water to come halfway up sides of baking dish. Bake 50 minutes, or until knife inserted in center comes out clean. If desired, serve with whipped cream or ice cream and sprinkle with additional ground nutmeg.

Makes 12 servings.

Quick-Fix Skillet Suppers

Turkey Patties 'n' Potatoes

¾ cup stuffing mix
2 tablespoons butter or
 margarine, melted
½ cup whole-berry cranberry
 sauce
1 pound ground turkey
2 tablespoons salad oil
1 package (5.5 ounces) au
 gratin potato mix
2⅓ cups water
⅔ cup milk
1 package (10 ounces) frozen
 sugar snap peas
4 green onions, thinly sliced

1. In medium bowl, combine stuffing mix, butter and cranberry sauce; let stand 2 minutes, until stuffing mix absorbs liquid. Stir in turkey until mixed. Form mixture into oval patties.

2. In large skillet, heat oil over medium-high heat. Add patties; cook until browned, about 3 minutes on each side. Remove patties; keep warm. Remove and discard drippings in skillet. In same skillet, combine potato slices and seasoning packet from au gratin mix, water and milk. Bring to boiling; simmer, covered, 10 minutes. Stir in peas and green onions. Return mixture to boiling; arrange patties on top. Simmer, covered, 15 minutes, or until patties are cooked. If desired, serve with orange slices, sautéed squash and a mixed-green salad with hearts of palm.

Makes 4 to 6 servings.

Clockwise from top left: Kielbasa Stew, Mexicali Franks, Turkey Patties 'n' Potatoes, Pepperoni Frittata.

Mexicali Franks

2 tablespoons salad oil
1 pound frankfurters,
 quartered lengthwise
1 medium onion, chopped
1 large clove garlic, crushed
1 can (1 pound) whole
 tomatoes
1 can (15 ounces) pinto beans
⅔ cup uncooked long-grain
 rice
2 teaspoons chili powder
1 cup chunky salsa
½ cup water
1 cup (4 ounces) shredded
 Monterey Jack cheese with
 jalapeño
Cilantro (fresh coriander)
 leaves

1. In large skillet, heat oil over medium-high heat until hot. Add frankfurters; sauté until browned. With slotted spoon, remove from pan; place on one side of serving platter. Keep warm.

2. To drippings in skillet, add onion and garlic; sauté 2 minutes. Add tomatoes and their liquid, beans and their liquid, rice, chili powder, salsa and water. Bring to boiling; simmer, covered, 15 minutes, or until rice is cooked.

3. Spoon rice mixture next to frankfurters on platter. Sprinkle cheese over rice. Garnish with cilantro leaves.

Makes 6 servings.

■ To release a garlic clove from its skin, place the clove on a flat surface and press down with the flat side of a chef's knife. You also can place the clove in hot tap water for a few minutes; this will make the skin slide off.

Kielbasa Stew

1 package (1 pound) kielbasa
2 large celery stalks
1 large onion
1 package (6 half ears) frozen corn
1 tablespoon salad oil
1 can (10¾ ounces) cream-of-celery soup, undiluted
1 cup water
1 package (10 ounces) frozen whole baby carrots
1 package (10 ounces) frozen peas
½ teaspoon dried thyme leaves, crushed

1. Cut kielbasa diagonally into ½-inch pieces; set aside. Cut celery into ½-inch pieces; set aside. Cut onion into wedges; set aside. Cut corn crosswise in half; set aside.

2. Heat oil in large deep skillet, over medium-high heat, until hot. Add kielbasa, celery and onion; sauté 2 minutes. Add soup; gradually blend in water. Add corn, carrots, peas and thyme. Bring to boiling; simmer, covered, 12 minutes, stirring and turning corn occasionally.
Makes 4 to 6 servings.

Pepperoni Frittata

6 large eggs
¼ cup milk
¼ teaspoon dried basil leaves, crushed
½ teaspoon salt
⅛ teaspoon pepper
3 tablespoons salad oil
1 package (24 ounces) frozen O'Brien potatoes with onion and pepper
¼ pound pepperoni, thinly sliced
½ cup (2 ounces) shredded mozzarella cheese
2 medium tomatoes, cut into wedges

1. In medium bowl, beat eggs with milk, basil, salt and pepper until mixed; set aside.

2. In 10-inch nonstick skillet, heat oil over medium-high heat until hot. Add potato combination; sauté 5 minutes. Add pepperoni; mix well.

3. Pour egg mixture over potato mixture. Over low heat, cook frittata until eggs set. With spatula, lift frittata to allow uncooked eggs to flow underneath. Cover; cook 15 minutes. Remove pan from heat; sprinkle cheese around top edge of frittata. Let stand, covered, 2 minutes, or until cheese melts. Arrange tomato wedges on top.
Makes 6 servings.

Flounder Florentine

1 package (10 ounces) frozen chopped spinach
1 small Kirby cucumber
¾ teaspoon salt
⅜ teaspoon pepper
¼ cup mayonnaise
2 teaspoons prepared horseradish
3 flounder fillets (1¾ pounds)
2 tablespoons fresh lemon juice
2 tablespoons salad oil
1 large onion, chopped
1 large clove garlic, crushed
1 can (1 pound) whole tomatoes
¼ cup white wine
1 package (4.2 ounces) risotto-with-mushrooms mix

1. Thaw spinach; squeeze dry. Place in small bowl. Pare cucumber; remove and discard seeds. Finely chop cucumber; place in bowl with spinach. Add ¼ teaspoon salt, ⅛ teaspoon pepper, the mayonnaise and horseradish. Mix well, and set spinach mixture aside.

2. Cut flounder fillets lengthwise in half; sprinkle with lemon juice and remaining ½ teaspoon salt and ¼ teaspoon pepper, dividing evenly. Spread ¼ cup spinach mixture over dark side of each fillet. Starting from narrow end of each fillet, roll up, jelly-roll fashion. Secure each roll with wooden pick.

3. In large skillet, heat oil over medium-high heat until hot. Add onion and garlic; sauté 2 minutes. Add tomatoes and their liquid, the white wine and risotto-with-mushrooms mix. Bring to boiling; add fillets, placing open side down. Cover; simmer 20 minutes, or until flounder is cooked and rice is tender.
Makes 6 servings.

■ To make onion garnishes, use red, yellow and green onions. For red and yellow flowers, select firm, well-rounded onions. Peel each one, leaving the root intact. With a sharp knife, cut each onion into quarters to within ½ inch of the root. Be careful not to cut completely through the onions. Continue cutting between the original cuts until no more cuts can be made. Place onions in bowl of hot water for 5 minutes, then in bowl of ice water; cover bowl, and refrigerate until onions open.

■ To make leek flowers, wash well; trim away the green part and the root. Lay the leek on its side, and cut to within 1 inch of root end. Cut many times. Place leeks in bowl of hot water for 5 minutes, then in bowl of ice water; cover bowl, and refrigerate until leeks open.

■ To make a tomato rose, cut a ½-inch-wide strip of skin from a firm red tomato. The longer you make the strip, the bigger your rose will be. Starting in center, wrap tomato strip, skin side at bottom, with toothpick. Arrange tomato rose with cucumber peel leaves. Refrigerate, covered with damp towel.

Lite Eating: Heavenly Desserts

Clockwise from top: Jamocha Cheesecake, Orange-Chocolate Ice, Pumpkin-Snap Mousse.

Jamocha Cheesecake

Nonstick cooking spray
15 chocolate-wafer cookies
1 container (15 ounces)
 part-skim ricotta cheese
¼ cup European-style
 unsweetened cocoa powder
Dash of salt
¼ cup sugar
1 envelope unflavored
 gelatine
½ cup double-strength coffee
¾ cup skim milk
1 teaspoon rum extract
1 teaspoon vanilla extract
1 container (8 ounces) frozen
 nondairy whipped topping,
 thawed

1. Grease 8-inch springform pan with cooking spray. Crush all but 2 cookies; sprinkle 1 tablespoon crumbs over pan bottom. In food processor, blend cheese, cocoa and salt. In saucepan, combine sugar, gelatine and coffee; soak 1 minute. Heat over low heat until clear. Off heat, stir in milk, extracts and cheese mixture. Place pan in bowl of ice and water; stir until thickened. Fold in all but ½ cup whipped topping; pour into springform pan. Cover, and refrigerate at least 4 hours.

2. Remove pan side. Pat remaining cookie crumbs onto cake side. Using photograph as guide, cut reserved cookies into 5 pieces. Garnish with reserved topping and cookie pieces.

Makes 12 servings, 162 calories each.

Pumpkin-Snap Mousse

Nonstick cooking spray
1 package (1.08 ounces)
 low-calorie vanilla-flavored
 pudding mix
2 envelopes unflavored gelatine
1 cup skim milk
1 can (30 ounces) pumpkin-pie
 filling
½ teaspoon vanilla extract
1 container (8 ounces) frozen
 nondairy whipped topping,
 thawed
1 cup coarsely chopped
 gingersnaps

Grease 8½-by-4½-by-2-inch loaf pan with cooking spray. In saucepan, combine pudding mix and gelatine; gradually whisk in milk, and bring to boiling. Off heat, whisk in pumpkin and vanilla. Place pan in bowl of ice and water; whisk until cool. Whisk in all but ¾ cup topping. Pour half into pan; sprinkle with ¾ cup gingersnaps. Top with remaining mousse. Cover; chill at least 4 hours. Unmold; garnish with remaining topping and gingersnaps.

Makes 12 servings, 163 calories each.

Orange-Chocolate Ice

2 large egg whites
¾ cup sugar
1 cup semisweet-chocolate
 pieces
2 cups water
¼ cup orange juice
1 tablespoon grated orange peel

1. Preheat oven to 250°F. Line baking sheet with parchment paper. In bowl of electric mixer, beat egg whites until frothy. Beat in ¼ cup sugar until stiff peaks form when beaters are raised. Place in pastry bag fitted with star tip; pipe 48 stars onto parchment. Top each with a chocolate piece; cover with a star of remaining meringue. Bake 50 minutes. Turn off oven; cool meringue stars in oven 2 hours.

2. In saucepan, stir remaining ½ cup sugar, the water and orange juice until boiling. Simmer 5 minutes. Off heat, stir in ⅔ cup chocolate pieces and the orange peel until smooth. Freeze in ice cream freezer. Serve with meringue stars.

Makes 8 servings, 163 calories each.

Micro-Way: Holiday Gifts in a Hurry

Applesauce-Spice Cake

¾ cup butter or margarine
2½ cups unsifted all-purpose
   flour
2 teaspoons baking soda
1 teaspoon ground cinnamon
½ teaspoon ground allspice
1½ cups granulated sugar
2 large eggs
2 cups applesauce
¾ cup chopped pecans or
   walnuts
½ cup chopped candied
   cherries
½ cup golden raisins
2 tablespoons brandy

Glaze
2 tablespoons butter or
   margarine
¾ cup confectioners' sugar
½ teaspoon vanilla extract
Milk

1. Grease and flour 12-cup micro-wave-safe Bundt pan. On waxed paper, soften butter on LOW, about 1 minute. On waxed paper, mix flour with baking soda and spices. In bowl of electric mixer, at medium speed, cream butter and sugar. Beat in eggs, one at a time; beat in apple-sauce. In bowl, mix pecans, fruits, brandy and ½ cup flour mixture. Stir remaining flour mixture into butter mixture. Stir in fruit mixture. Pour mixture into pan. Place on inverted microwave-safe cereal bowl. Cook on MEDIUM 10 minutes, rotating after 5 minutes. Cook on HIGH 10 minutes, rotating every 3 minutes. Let stand 15 minutes.

2. Make glaze: In glass bowl, melt butter on HIGH 30 seconds. Stir in sugar, vanilla and enough milk to make spoonable. Invert cake onto plate; drizzle with glaze. If desired, garnish with pecan halves and candied cherries.

Makes 24 servings, 1 cup glaze.

Saltwater Taffy

2 tablespoons plus about 2
   teaspoons butter
2 cups sugar
1 teaspoon salt
1 cup light corn syrup
1 cup hot water
1 teaspoon vanilla extract
Green or red food color

Lightly butter jelly-roll pan. In 3-quart microwave-safe casserole with high sides, mix sugar, salt, syrup and hot water. Cook on HIGH until boiling, about 8 minutes. Stir. Cook until mixture reaches 260°F on candy thermometer, about 15 to 20 minutes. Remove mixture from oven. When bubbling stops, stir in 2 table-spoons butter, the vanilla and food color. (If desired, divide mixture into two parts and tint each a different color.) Pour taffy into prepared pan. Cool about 5 minutes. Lightly butter hands; gather one-sixth of taffy into a ball. Pull until taffy holds its shape in a ½-inch-thick strand. With buttered shears, cut taffy into 1-inch lengths. Wrap each taffy piece in plastic wrap. Repeat with remaining taffy.

Makes 1½ pounds.

Coco-Nut Balls

1 package (12 ounces)
   semisweet-chocolate pieces
¼ cup butter
⅓ cup evaporated milk
2 large eggs
1 teaspoon vanilla extract
2 cups sifted confectioners'
   sugar
1¾ cups flaked coconut
1½ cups chopped blanched
   almonds

In glass bowl, melt chocolate and butter in milk on HIGH about 1 minute. Stir in eggs; cook on ME-DIUM 4 minutes, stirring every minute. Add vanilla and sugar; mix well. Stir in ¾ cup coconut and ½ cup almonds. Chill until just firm. On waxed paper, combine remaining coconut and almonds. Roll tea-spoonfuls of chocolate mixture into balls; coat with coconut mixture. Chill until firm.

Makes about 5 dozen balls.

Macadamia-Orange Fudge

½ cup butter
1½ cups sugar
1 can (5 ounces) evaporated
   milk
2 cups miniature marshmallows
1 package (6 ounces)
   semisweet-chocolate pieces
¾ cup macadamia nuts,
   chopped
1 tablespoon orange-flavored
   liqueur

With aluminum foil, line 8-inch square pan. In glass bowl, melt butter on HIGH 1 minute. Stir in sugar and milk. Cook mixture on HIGH 8 minutes, stirring every 3 minutes. Add marshmallows and chocolate; stir until melted and mixture is smooth. Stir in nuts and liqueur. Pour into pan. Cut into pieces; chill.

Makes 2 pounds.

Clockwise from top: Saltwater Taffy, Applesauce-Spice Cake, Coco-Nut Balls, Macadamia-Orange Fudge.

February

Take our cross-country tour of scrumptious cakes, flavorful pies and other tasty treats that represent the special American way with desserts. Start out with the rich chocolate cake spotlighted here and try all of the regional delicacies listed below and pictured on the following pages.

Peanut Lover's Pie   Decadent Fudge Cake

Bananas and Papayas Foster

Orange-Cream Gingersnaps

Light and Luscious Jelly Doughnuts

Two-Tone Tapioca   Cran-Pear Cobbler

Mississippi Mud Cakes

Cinnamon Churros   Tangy Lemon Drops

Chocolate-Cream Snowballs

Curly-Top Marble Pound Cake   Margarita Pie

Orange-Toffee Cream Puffs   Poppy-Seed Cake

All-American Dessert Cookbook

For a taste of American diversity, sample this outstanding collection of luscious desserts.

Peanut Lover's Pie

(pictured, page 25)

¼ cup strawberry or raspberry jam
9-inch graham cracker crust
1 package (8 ounces) cream cheese, softened
1 cup chunky peanut butter
1 cup confectioners' sugar
1 teaspoon vanilla extract
2 cups heavy cream
Additional heavy cream, whipped
Peanuts

1. Spread jam over bottom of pie crust; set aside. In large bowl of electric mixer, at medium speed, beat cream cheese and peanut butter until blended. Beat in sugar and vanilla until smooth.

2. In small bowl of electric mixer, at high speed, beat 2 cups heavy cream until stiff peaks form when beaters are raised. With rubber spatula, fold whipped cream into cream-cheese mixture until no white streaks remain; pour mixture into pie crust. Refrigerate until firm, about 2 hours. Garnish with additional whipped cream; sprinkle cream with peanuts. If desired, cut a large strawberry lengthwise into thin slices attached at the hull; use to garnish pie.

Makes 8 servings.

Page 25: Peanut Lover's Pie, Decadent Fudge Cake, Bananas and Papayas Foster.

Pages 26 and 27: (Clockwise from top right) Light and Luscious Jelly Doughnuts, Two-Tone Tapioca, Cran-Pear Cobbler, Cinnamon Churros, Mississippi Mud Cakes, Tangy Lemon Drops, Orange-Cream Gingersnaps.

Pages 28 and 29: (Clockwise from top left) Chocolate-Cream Snowballs, Curly-Top Marble Pound Cake, Margarita Pie, Orange-Toffee Cream Puffs, Poppy-Seed Cake.

Bananas and Papayas Foster

(pictured, page 25)

4 medium bananas
1 large ripe papaya
½ cup dark rum
1 cup pecan halves
¾ cup firmly packed light-brown sugar
½ teaspoon ground cinnamon
Dash ground ginger
¼ cup butter, softened
1 quart vanilla ice cream

1. Peel bananas; pare, halve and seed papaya. Cut fruit into 1-inch chunks; place in medium bowl. Add rum; toss to coat. Cover with plastic wrap; set aside to marinate 20 minutes. Meanwhile, in small bowl, combine pecans, sugar, cinnamon and ginger; with fork, cut in butter until well blended. Set aside.

2. Preheat oven to 400°F. Drain fruit over bowl, reserving marinade. Place fruit in 1-quart shallow baking dish; sprinkle butter mixture over top. Bake until bubbly, about 10 minutes. Broil 4 to 6 inches from heat until browned, 2 or 3 minutes.

3. In small saucepan, heat ¼ cup reserved marinade; carefully ignite. Pour over fruit mixture, stirring to blend. Spoon ice cream into 8 dishes; top with warm fruit mixture. Serve immediately.

Makes 8 servings.

■ If your ice cream pie recipe calls for a graham-cracker crust, freeze the crust before adding the ice cream; this will prevent crumbs from getting mixed into the filling.

■ To make greasing a baking pan effortless, invert and run hot water over the bottom for several seconds. This will heat the pan so that butter or shortening can be spread easily and evenly over the inside surface.

Decadent Fudge Cake

(pictured, page 25)

Fudge Sauce
½ cup European-style cocoa
   powder
½ cup sugar
½ cup hot water
¼ cup light corn syrup
1 teaspoon vanilla extract

Cake
2 cups unsifted all-purpose
   flour
⅔ cup European-style cocoa
   powder
2¼ teaspoons baking powder
1 teaspoon salt
1 cup butter or margarine,
   softened
2 cups sugar
4 large eggs, at room
   temperature
1½ teaspoons vanilla extract
1 cup milk
¼ teaspoon baking soda

Glaze
1 package (12 ounces)
   semisweet-chocolate pieces
⅛ teaspoon salt
1 cup sour cream

Sweetened whipped cream
**Chocolate Leaves (recipe
   follows)**

1. Make fudge sauce: In small heavy saucepan, mix cocoa with sugar. Gradually stir in water until blended; stir in syrup. Over low heat, cook, stirring frequently, until mixture is almost boiling; simmer 2 minutes, stirring constantly. Off heat, stir in vanilla. Cool.

2. Preheat oven to 350°F. Grease and flour 12-cup Bundt pan; set pan aside.

3. Make cake: On sheet of waxed paper, combine flour, cocoa, baking powder and salt; set aside. In large bowl of electric mixer, at medium speed, beat butter until smooth; gradually beat in sugar until mixture is light and fluffy, about 5 minutes. Beat in eggs, one at a time, beating well after each addition; beat in vanilla. At low speed, alternately beat in flour mixture and milk until blended, beginning and ending with flour mixture.

4. Pour two-thirds of batter into prepared pan, spreading evenly. Stir baking soda into fudge sauce; blend sauce into remaining cake batter. Pour fudge-sauce mixture over batter in pan (do not stir mixtures together). Bake 1 hour and 10 minutes, or until cake tester inserted in center comes out clean. Cool in pan on wire rack 10 minutes; invert cake onto wire rack to cool completely.

5. Make glaze: In top of double boiler, over hot, not boiling, water, melt chocolate pieces. Remove pan from heat; whisk in salt and sour cream until blended. Place cake on serving dish; cover with glaze. Decorate cake with whipped cream and Chocolate Leaves.
Makes 12 servings.

Chocolate Leaves

12 mint or lemon leaves
Salad oil
**1 tablespoon butter or
   margarine**
**½ cup semisweet- or
   milk-chocolate pieces**
1 tablespoon light corn syrup

Wash mint leaves; pat dry with paper towels. Brush with oil. In top of double boiler, over hot, not boiling, water, melt butter and chocolate. Add corn syrup; stir until smooth. Brush thick layer of chocolate mixture on back of each leaf; place on waxed paper. Chill until firm. When ready to serve, peel leaves from chocolate; garnish cake.
Makes 12 chocolate leaves.

Two-Tone Tapioca

(pictured, page 27)

½ cup sugar
¼ cup quick-cooking tapioca
3½ cups milk
1 large egg, beaten
¼ teaspoon almond extract
¼ teaspoon vanilla extract
1 package (10 ounces) frozen
   raspberries in light syrup,
   thawed
¼ cup shelled pistachios,
   chopped
1 cup heavy cream
1 tablespoon sugar
Tangy Lemon Drops (page 32)

1. In medium saucepan, combine ½ cup sugar, the tapioca, milk and egg; let stand 5 minutes. Bring to boiling, stirring constantly. Remove from heat; stir in almond and vanilla extracts. Let stand 30 minutes, stirring occasionally; pour into 6 individual serving dishes. Chill.

2. Meanwhile, drain raspberries, reserving ¼ cup syrup. Puree berries and reserved syrup in food processor or blender. Pass through sieve; discard seeds. Reserve 1 tablespoon nuts; stir remainder into raspberry puree. Spoon mixture over pudding in dishes, dividing evenly.

3. In small bowl of electric mixer, at high speed, beat heavy cream until soft peaks form when beaters are raised. Beat in 1 tablespoon sugar until stiff peaks form. Place whipped cream in pastry bag fitted with star tip; garnish puddings with cream. Sprinkle cream with reserved pistachios, dividing evenly. Serve with Tangy Lemon Drops.
Makes 6 servings.

Orange-Cream Gingersnaps
(pictured, page 26)

Gingersnaps
2 cups unsifted all-purpose flour
2 teaspoons baking soda
1 teaspoon ground cinnamon
1 teaspoon ground ginger
½ teaspoon ground cloves
¾ cup butter or margarine
¾ cup granulated sugar
¼ cup molasses
1 large egg

Orange Cream
2¼ cups confectioners' sugar
¼ cup crystallized ginger
½ cup butter or margarine, cut into pieces
2 tablespoons orange marmalade

1. Make gingersnaps: On sheet of waxed paper, combine flour, baking soda and spices; set aside. In medium saucepan, melt butter. Remove from heat; stir in sugar and molasses until sugar dissolves. Beat in egg until blended; stir in flour mixture until dry ingredients are moistened. Transfer to medium bowl; cover with plastic wrap. Refrigerate overnight.

2. Preheat oven to 375°F. Form rounded teaspoonfuls dough into 1-inch balls; place 2 inches apart on nonstick baking sheets. Bake 8 minutes, or until golden brown. With spatula, flatten cookies slightly. Cool a few minutes on sheets on wire rack; remove cookies to wire rack to cool completely.

3. Make orange cream: In food processor, process sugar with ginger until ginger is minced. Add butter and marmalade; process until smooth.

4. Spread rounded teaspoonful orange cream onto flat side of half the cookies. Top with remaining cookies, flat side in.

Makes 28 filled cookies.

Light and Luscious Jelly Doughnuts
(pictured, pages 26 and 27)

3½ cups unsifted all-purpose flour
⅓ cup sugar
2 envelopes fast-rising or regular dry yeast
1 teaspoon salt
⅓ cup butter or margarine
½ cup milk
½ cup water
3 large egg yolks
1 large egg white, lightly beaten
Salad oil
Strawberry, raspberry or currant jelly
Additional sugar

1. In large bowl of electric mixer, combine 1 cup flour with ⅓ cup sugar, the yeast and salt. Set aside.

2. In small saucepan, heat butter, milk and water until hot, 120° to 130°F. In bowl of electric mixer, at medium speed, beat hot milk mixture into flour mixture until blended, about 2 minutes. Beat in egg yolks and 1 cup flour, beating until blended. With wooden spoon, beat in remaining 1½ cups flour until blended; dough will be soft.

3. Cover bowl with plastic wrap and then a kitchen towel; let dough rise in warm place (85°F), free from drafts, until double in bulk, 1 to 1½ hours. Punch dough down; turn out onto lightly floured surface. Knead about 10 times, or until dough is smooth. Divide dough in half.

4. With floured rolling pin, roll out one-half dough to ¼-inch thickness. With floured 3-inch round cookie cutter, cut into 12 rounds. Brush top edge of 6 rounds with some egg white; cover each with a remaining round. Sprinkle large baking sheet with flour; arrange dough rounds on sheet. Repeat with remaining dough and egg white; reroll scraps to cut additional rounds. Cover doughnuts with a clean kitchen towel; let rise in warm place (85°F), free from drafts, until double in bulk, 30 to 45 minutes.

5. Meanwhile, in deep-fat fryer or Dutch oven, heat 2 inches oil to 350°F on deep-fat thermometer. Line baking sheet with paper towels; set aside. Gently drop doughnuts, 3 at a time, into hot oil. Fry, turning as doughnuts rise to surface and again as they brown, until golden brown on all sides, about 4 minutes in all. (Break one open to test for doneness; adjust frying time, if necessary.) With slotted spoon, remove doughnuts to prepared baking sheet. While doughnuts are warm, with jelly in icing bag fitted with number-3 tip, fill each doughnut with about 1 teaspoon jelly; sprinkle on all sides with additional sugar.

Makes 12 to 14 doughnuts.

Tangy Lemon Drops
(pictured, page 26)

5 tablespoons butter, at room temperature
¾ cup unsifted cake flour
¼ cup confectioners' sugar
1 teaspoon grated lemon peel
Additional confectioners' sugar

1. In medium bowl, mix butter with flour, ¼ cup confectioners' sugar and the lemon peel until combined. Divide dough in half; on floured surface, roll each half to a 6-inch-long cylinder. Wrap each half in plastic wrap; refrigerate 1 hour.

2. Preheat oven to 325°F. Grease large baking sheet. Cut each roll of chilled dough crosswise in ½-inch-thick slices. Place cookies, cut side up, on prepared baking sheet. Bake 12 minutes, or until tops of cookies are firm to the touch and bottoms are lightly browned. With spatula, remove to wire rack; cool. Sprinkle cookies with additional confectioners' sugar before serving.

Makes 2 dozen.

Cran-Pear Cobbler
(pictured, page 27)

⅓ cup butter or margarine
⅔ cup sugar
1 large egg yolk
¾ cup unsifted all-purpose
    flour
½ cup uncooked rolled oats
    (not quick-cooking)
½ teaspoon baking powder
1 package (12 ounces)
    cranberries
1 teaspoon ground cinnamon
1 teaspoon grated orange
    peel
1 cup maple syrup
2 tablespoons cornstarch
2 tablespoons orange juice
5 ripe pears, pared, cored and
    sliced (2½ pounds)
1 cup chopped pecans or
    walnuts
Ice cream

1. In small bowl of electric mixer, at medium speed, beat butter and ⅓ cup sugar until light and fluffy. Beat in egg yolk. Stir in flour, oats and baking powder; shape dough into a disk. Cover dough with plastic wrap; refrigerate.

2. In medium saucepan, combine cranberries with remaining sugar, the cinnamon, orange peel and maple syrup. Bring to boiling; simmer, stirring occasionally, until berries pop, about 3 minutes. Remove from heat.

3. Preheat oven to 375°F. In large bowl, blend cornstarch with orange juice. Add pears, nuts and cranberry mixture; mix well. Spoon mixture into 2-quart shallow baking dish.

4. On lightly floured surface, roll dough to an 11-inch round. Cut into twelve ¾-inch-wide strips; arrange strips, lattice fashion, over fruit mixture, trimming pastry ends to fit. If desired, reroll pastry scraps and cut leaf shapes to arrange on pastry strips. Bake until pastry is golden and filling is bubbly, about 40 minutes. Serve warm, with ice cream.
Makes 8 servings.

Chocolate-Cream Snowballs
(pictured, page 28)

1 package (about 19 ounces)
    devil's-food cake mix

Filling
⅓ cup butter or margarine,
    softened
3½ cups sifted confectioners'
    sugar
3 tablespoons warm milk
1 teaspoon rum extract or
    brandy flavoring

Marshmallow Frosting
2 envelopes unflavored gelatine
½ cup cold water
½ cup granulated sugar
⅔ cup light corn syrup
2 teaspoons vanilla extract

1 package (7 ounces)
    sweetened flaked coconut

1. Prepare cake batter and bake as package label directs for 24 cupcakes, using paper liners to line cupcake pans. Cool completely. Remove and discard paper liners.

2. In small bowl of electric mixer, at high speed, beat butter with sugar, 2 tablespoons milk and the rum extract until light and fluffy. If filling is stiff, beat in remaining milk.

3. Place filling in large pastry bag fitted with ⅜-inch-wide plain tip. Insert tip into top of cupcake; squeeze about 1½ teaspoons filling into cake. Place, filling side down, on baking sheet; repeat with remaining cupcakes and filling. Refrigerate cupcakes.

4. Make frosting: In top of double boiler, sprinkle gelatine over water; let stand 5 minutes. Place over simmering water; stir until gelatine dissolves. Add sugar; stir until sugar dissolves. Pour mixture into large bowl of electric mixer; add syrup and vanilla. At high speed, beat until light and fluffy, about 5 minutes.

5. With metal spatula, cover tops and sides of cakes with ⅛-inch-thick coating of frosting, beating teaspoonfuls of warm water into frosting if it becomes too stiff to spread. Cover each snowball with coconut, dividing evenly. Store in an airtight container.
Makes 24 snowballs.

Cinnamon Churros
(pictured, page 26)

¼ cup butter or margarine
1 cup plus 1 tablespoon sugar
½ teaspoon salt
1 cup water
½ cup white cornmeal mix
½ cup unsifted all-purpose
    flour
3 large eggs
2 teaspoons ground cinnamon
Salad oil

1. In medium saucepan, heat butter with 1 tablespoon sugar, the salt and water to boiling. Remove pan from heat; immediately add cornmeal and flour all at once. Over low heat, cook mixture, stirring constantly, until dough forms a ball, about 1 minute. Remove from heat; let stand 5 minutes. Beat in eggs, one at a time, beating vigorously after each addition until dough is smooth.

2. Line baking sheet with paper towels; set aside. In paper bag or in large bowl, mix remaining sugar with cinnamon; set aside. In deep heavy skillet or Dutch oven, heat 3 inches oil until oil registers 375°F on deep-fat thermometer. Spoon dough into pastry bag fitted with number-6 tip. Pipe 5-inch lengths of dough into hot oil; fry until browned on both sides, about 1½ minutes per side. With slotted spoon or tongs, remove churros to prepared baking sheet to drain; while hot, place in bag or bowl and coat with sugar mixture. Repeat with remaining dough and sugar mixture. Serve immediately.
Makes about 2 dozen.

All-American Dessert Cookbook

Mississippi Mud Cakes
(pictured, page 26)

Cakes
1 cup butter or margarine
1½ cups granulated sugar
½ cup unsweetened cocoa
   powder
4 large eggs
1½ cups unsifted all-purpose
   flour
1 tablespoon vanilla extract
1½ cups chopped pecans

Chocolate Frosting
2 cups confectioners' sugar
3 tablespoons unsweetened
   cocoa powder
½ cup butter or margarine,
   melted
1 teaspoon vanilla extract
1 to 2 tablespoons milk

1. Preheat oven to 350°F. Line 13-by-9-by-2-inch baking pan with aluminum foil, extending ends of foil 1 inch over sides of pan. Grease and flour foil. Set aside.

2. Make cakes: In medium saucepan, melt butter; stir in sugar and cocoa powder. Remove pan from heat; beat in eggs, one at a time, until blended. Stir in flour and vanilla until blended. Stir in 1 cup pecans. Pour into prepared pan; bake 25 minutes, or until cake tester inserted in center comes out clean. Cool in pan on wire rack.

3. Meanwhile, make frosting: In medium bowl, combine sugar and cocoa powder; beat in butter and vanilla until smooth. Beat in enough milk to make frosting fluffy and spreadable.

4. Using ends of foil, lift brownie layer from pan. Spread top with frosting; sprinkle with remaining pecans. Cut into squares. Remove foil; place cakes on serving platter.
   Makes 15 servings.

■ Substitution for 1 cup heavy cream: ¾ cup milk plus ⅓ cup butter or margarine.

Curly-Top Marble Pound Cake
(pictured, pages 28 and 29)

Ganache
1½ cups heavy cream
6 squares (1-ounce size)
   semisweet chocolate, finely
   chopped

Chocolate Curls
1 package (12 ounces)
   semisweet-chocolate pieces

Cake
3 squares (1-ounce size)
   unsweetened chocolate
4¾ cups unsifted cake flour
2 tablespoons baking powder
1 teaspoon salt
1 cup butter or margarine,
   softened
3 cups sugar
6 large eggs, at room
   temperature
2 teaspoons vanilla extract
1½ cups milk

1. Day before serving, make ganache: Over medium heat, in large heavy saucepan, heat cream to simmering. Remove from heat; whisk in chopped chocolate until chocolate is partially melted. Let stand 20 minutes; whisk until blended. Pour into bowl; cover with plastic wrap. Refrigerate until very cold, 12 hours or overnight.

2. Meanwhile, make chocolate curls: In top of double boiler, over hot, not boiling, water, melt chocolate pieces. With aluminum foil, line 5-by-2½-by-2-inch loaf pan, extending ends of foil 1 inch over sides of pan; pour melted chocolate in pan. Let stand at room temperature overnight until hardened, or refrigerate 1 hour and allow loaf to stand at room temperature 1 hour. Grasping foil ends, remove chocolate loaf from pan. Remove and discard foil. With vegetable parer, peel long, curly strips of chocolate from top of loaf, turning loaf and peeling from sides of loaf until all chocolate is

used. If necessary, curl chocolate strips around finger as they come off the loaf; chocolate will become more pliable as it warms to room temperature. If chocolate is too firm to curl, place chocolate loaf on a piece of foil in a warm place, or hold chocolate in hands. Place curls on baking sheet; refrigerate until ready to use.

3. Make cake: In top of double boiler, over hot, not boiling, water, melt unsweetened chocolate. Let cool. Preheat oven to 325°F. Grease and flour 10-inch tube pan; set aside. In small bowl, mix flour with baking powder and salt; set aside. In large bowl of electric mixer, at medium speed, cream butter and sugar until light and fluffy, about 5 minutes. Beat in eggs, one at a time, beating well after each addition. Beat in vanilla. At low speed, alternately beat in flour mixture and milk, beginning and ending with flour mixture and adding ⅓ of milk at a time.

4. In medium bowl, mix about one-third of batter with melted chocolate until blended. Spoon plain and chocolate batters into prepared pan, alternating spoonfuls in pan and being careful not to blend batters. With metal spatula or knife, cut through batters, forming a "Z" pattern around pan with chocolate batter. Bake until cake tester inserted in center of cake comes out clean, about 1 hour and 20 minutes. Invert cake onto wire rack; cool completely.

5. Place cooled cake on serving plate. With wooden spoon, stir ganache to make a thick, spreadable consistency; with metal spatula, spread ganache over top and sides of cake. Cover with chocolate curls. Store in refrigerator.

   Makes 24 servings.

■ Bake and freeze cream-puff shells to fill later with small, pop-top cans of vanilla pudding.

Margarita Pie

(pictured, page 29)

1¼ cups pretzel crumbs
2 tablespoons light-brown
  sugar
½ cup butter or margarine,
  melted
2 envelopes unflavored gelatine
1 cup lime juice
4 large eggs, separated
¾ cup granulated sugar
1 teaspoon grated lime peel
¼ cup tequila
3 tablespoons Cointreau or
  other orange-flavored liqueur
Green food color
1 cup heavy cream

1. In medium bowl, combine pretzel crumbs and brown sugar. With fork, stir in butter until blended. Press onto bottom and sides of 9-inch pie plate; refrigerate.

2. In small bowl, sprinkle gelatine over ¼ cup lime juice; let stand 5 minutes to soften. Meanwhile, in top of double boiler, combine egg yolks with ½ cup sugar and the remaining lime juice. Cook over simmering water, stirring constantly, until mixture is slightly thickened, about 12 minutes. Stir in gelatine mixture and lime peel. Stir mixture until gelatine dissolves.

3. Transfer mixture to large bowl; stir in tequila, Cointreau and 3 to 4 drops food color. Place bowl in large bowl of ice and water; chill, stirring frequently, until mixture is the consistency of unbeaten egg white, about 15 minutes.

4. Meanwhile, in large bowl of electric mixer, at medium speed, beat egg whites until foamy. At high speed, gradually beat in remaining sugar until stiff peaks form when beaters are raised; set aside. In small bowl of electric mixer, at high speed, beat heavy cream until stiff peaks form when beaters are raised. With rubber spatula, fold beaten egg whites and half the whipped cream into tequila mixture until no white streaks remain. Pour mixture into prepared pie shell. Refrigerate 1 hour, or until firm. Place remaining whipped cream in pastry bag fitted with star tip; pipe whipped cream in a ring around top of pie. If desired, garnish with lime slices.

Makes 8 servings.

Orange-Toffee Cream Puffs

(pictured, page 29)

Cream Puffs
¼ cup butter or margarine
1 teaspoon grated orange peel
⅛ teaspoon salt
½ cup water
½ cup unsifted all-purpose
  flour
2 large eggs, at room
  temperature

Custard Filling
1 package (3¼ ounces) vanilla
  pudding-and-pie filling mix
  (not instant)
¾ cup milk
¾ cup orange juice
1 teaspoon grated orange peel
2 tablespoons confectioners'
  sugar
½ cup heavy cream
½ package (9-ounce size)
  miniature chocolate-covered
  toffee candy bars

Glaze
½ cup confectioners' sugar
¼ teaspoon grated orange
  peel
2 teaspoons orange juice

1. Make cream puffs: Preheat oven to 400°F. In small saucepan, bring butter, grated orange peel, salt and water to boiling. Remove from heat; immediately add flour, all at once. Over low heat, with wooden spoon, beat pastry until it leaves side of pan and forms a ball. Remove pan from heat; beat in eggs, one at a time, beating vigorously after each addition, until dough is shiny and smooth. Drop dough by rounded tablespoonfuls placed 2 inches apart on ungreased baking sheet. Bake 35 minutes, until cream puffs are golden brown and sound hollow when lightly tapped on bottom. Cool on wire rack.

2. While cream puffs bake, make filling: Prepare pudding as package label directs, except use ¾ cup milk and ¾ cup orange juice; stir in grated orange peel. Pour into medium bowl; cover with plastic wrap placed directly on surface of pudding. Refrigerate pudding until cold, at least 1 hour.

3. In small bowl of electric mixer, combine sugar with heavy cream. At high speed, beat until stiff peaks form when beaters are raised. With rubber spatula, fold whipped cream into pudding. Cut 3 candy bars in half diagonally; set aside. Coarsely chop remaining candy bars; fold into pudding. Refrigerate, covered, until ready to serve.

4. At serving time, cut off tops of cream puffs; with fork, remove and discard any uncooked pastry. Spoon ½ cup filling into each puff; replace pastry tops. In custard cup, mix glaze ingredients until blended. With spoon, drizzle glaze over cream puffs. Top each with a reserved candy triangle; if desired, garnish with an orange-peel bow. Serve soon after filling, as puffs get soggy on standing.

Makes 6 servings.

> ■ Serving up pies with luscious, flaky crusts is a source of pride for many at-home bakers. The most important step to perfect piecrust is to cut the fat into the flour as well as possible—really work it into small beads. You can't overdo! Another hint: If you think you've added a bit too much water, freeze the unbaked crust overnight before baking; this will help dry it out.

Poppy-Seed Cake

(pictured, page 28)

Cake
2¼ cups unsifted all-purpose
    flour
1½ cups granulated sugar
¾ cup butter or margarine,
    softened
¼ cup poppy seeds
1 tablespoon grated lemon peel
2½ teaspoons baking powder
1 teaspoon salt
¾ cup milk
3 large eggs
2 teaspoons lemon extract
1 teaspoon vanilla extract

Frosting
1½ packages (8-ounce size)
    cream cheese, softened
½ cup unsalted butter,
    softened
3½ cups confectioners' sugar
2 teaspoons lemon extract
2 tablespoons poppy seeds

1. Preheat oven to 375°F. Grease and flour two 9-inch round cake pans; set aside.

2. Make cake: In large bowl of electric mixer, combine all cake ingredients. At low speed, beat until well mixed, scraping bowl occasionally with rubber spatula. At high speed, beat 2 minutes longer. Pour batter into prepared pans, dividing evenly. Bake until cake tester inserted in center of cake comes out clean, about 25 minutes. Cool cakes in pans on wire rack 10 minutes; invert cakes onto wire racks to cool completely.

3. Make frosting: In large bowl of electric mixer, at high speed, beat cream cheese and butter until smooth. Beat in sugar and lemon extract until mixture is blended, about 3 minutes.

4. Place one cake layer on serving dish. With metal spatula, spread with some frosting. Cover with second cake layer; cover top and sides with remaining frosting. From cardboard, cut 1 large square and 1 small square. Place large square on cake; using photograph as a guide, sprinkle about 1 tablespoon poppy seeds around edge of square. Remove square; place small square in center of cake. Sprinkle remaining poppy seeds around edge of square; remove cardboard.

Makes 8 to 10 servings.

Chocolate Pecan Pie

1 package (9½ or 11 ounces)
    piecrust mix

Filling
3 squares (1 ounce each)
    semisweet chocolate
¼ cup butter or margarine
4 large eggs
½ cup sugar
¾ cup dark corn syrup
⅓ cup light corn syrup
⅓ cup honey
2 cups pecan halves

1. Prepare piecrust mix as package label directs for 2-crust pie. Shape pastry into a ball; flatten to 1-inch thickness. Roll on lightly floured surface to form a 12½-inch round. Fit pastry round loosely into a 10-inch pie plate (do not stretch); fold edge of pastry under ½ inch; crimp or flute edge decoratively. Refrigerate until ready to use.

2. Preheat oven to 350°F. Make filling: In medium saucepan, over low heat, melt chocolate and butter, stirring frequently; remove from heat, and cool slightly.

3. In medium bowl, with rotary beater or portable electric mixer at low speed, beat eggs well; add sugar, corn syrups and honey. Continue to beat at low speed until all ingredients are well combined. Stir in melted chocolate-butter mixture; blend well.

4. Spread pecans evenly in bottom of prepared pie shell; pour chocolate mixture evenly over pecans. Bake until filling is set in the center when pie is shaken gently, about 50 minutes.

5. Cool pie completely on wire rack. If desired, chill slightly before serving time, and garnish pie with whipped cream.

Makes 10 servings.

Pear Pie With Streusel Topping

1 (9-inch) unbaked pie shell

Streusel Topping
⅔ cup unsifted all-purpose
    flour
⅓ cup firmly packed
    light-brown sugar
⅓ cup butter or margarine

Filling
¼ cup granulated sugar
¼ teaspoon ginger
4 teaspoons flour
5 ripe Bartlett or Anjou pears
    (2 pounds)
¼ cup light corn syrup
4 teaspoons lemon juice

1. Prepare pie shell.

2. Make topping: Combine ⅔ cup flour and the brown sugar. Cut in butter with pastry blender or 2 knives until mixture resembles coarse cornmeal. Refrigerate.

3. Preheat oven to 450°F.

4. Make filling: Combine granulated sugar, ginger and 4 teaspoons flour; sprinkle about one-third of filling mixture over bottom of prepared pie shell.

5. Peel and core pears; slice thinly into bowl. Arrange half of pears in shell; sprinkle with a third of sugar mixture. Add remaining pears; sprinkle with remaining sugar mixture. Drizzle corn syrup and lemon juice over top. Cover with topping. Bake 15 minutes. Reduce oven temperature to 350°F. Bake 30 minutes.

Makes 8 servings.

Heavenly Heart Meringue

Strawberry Floating Island

6 large eggs, separated and at
   room temperature
1 cup sugar
3 cups half-and-half
1 teaspoon almond extract
1 teaspoon vanilla extract
¼ teaspoon cream of tartar
½ cup crushed bittersweet
   almond-flavored Italian
   cookies
1 pint unhulled strawberries
2 tablespoons strawberry jelly,
   melted
1 square (1 ounce) semisweet
   chocolate, melted
1 teaspoon salad oil

1. In large bowl of electric mixer, at medium speed, beat egg yolks until blended. Gradually beat in ½ cup sugar. In large saucepan, heat half-and-half until almost boiling; with mixer at medium speed, add ¼ cup half-and-half to egg-yolk mixture. Gradually beat in remainder. Pour into saucepan; over low heat, cook, stirring, until custard thickens enough to coat the back of a metal spoon, about 20 minutes. (Do not boil.) Stir in almond and vanilla extracts; pour into bowl. Cool, stirring occasionally; cover with plastic wrap placed directly on surface of custard. Chill at least 2 hours.

2. Preheat oven to 275°F. Generously grease 6-cup heart-shape mold or casserole. Set aside.

3. In clean large bowl of electric mixer, at medium speed, beat egg whites with cream of tartar until frothy. At high speed, beat until soft peaks form when beaters are raised; beat in remaining sugar, 1 tablespoon at a time, until stiff peaks form. With rubber spatula, fold in cookies; spread in mold. Place mold in roasting pan; place on oven rack. Pour enough hot water into pan to come halfway up sides of mold. Bake 1 hour and 30 minutes. Remove mold from pan; cool on wire rack 10 minutes. Invert onto serving dish with a rim. Arrange strawberries over meringue; brush with jelly. Pour custard around meringue.

Celebrate Valentine's Day with Strawberry Floating Island.

4. In small pan over hot water, melt chocolate with oil; stir until smooth. Place in icing bag fitted with small writing tip; pipe chocolate onto custard. Chill up to 1 hour before serving.

Makes 8 servings.

Quick & Easy:
Perfect Party Cakes

Cookies-and-Cream Pool Table

1 container (8 ounces) frozen
    nondairy whipped topping,
    thawed
Green food color
Unsweetened cocoa powder
½ gallon ice cream brick (any
    flavor)
1 package (7 ounces) pastry or
    sandwich finger cookies
3 orange gumdrops
9 chocolate-covered finger
    cookies
16 candy-coated gum balls
Red string licorice
2 hard-candy straws

1. Place half of whipped topping in each of 2 bowls. With green food color, tint one-half green; with cocoa powder, tint remainder brown. Set aside.

2. Unwrap ice cream; place on serving platter. Working quickly, frost sides with brown whipped topping; press pastry fingers into topping, arranging cookies vertically. Frost top of ice cream brick with green topping. Freeze 2 hours.

3. Cut gumdrops crosswise; arrange as pool-table pockets on green topping. Arrange chocolate-covered finger cookies around edge on topping, cutting cookies to fit around pockets. Arrange 15 gum balls on top of cake in a triangle; wrap licorice "rack" around balls. Place candy-straw "cues" and a white candy "cue ball" on table. Freeze until serving time.

Makes 10 servings.

Pattern for a Perfect Cake

1 can (8 ounces) almond paste
3 large eggs
1 package (about 19 ounces)
    cherry-chip cake mix
½ cup salad oil
¼ cup water
1 can (1 pound)
    vanilla-flavored frosting
1 tablespoon almond extract
1 tube (4.25 ounces) blue
    decorating icing

1. Preheat oven to 350°F. Grease and flour 13-by-9-by-2-inch baking pan; set aside. In large bowl of electric mixer, at low speed, beat almond paste with 1 egg until smooth; add cake mix, remaining eggs, the oil and water. Beat as cake-mix-package label directs. Pour into prepared pan; bake as package label directs for sheet cake. Cool cake 10 minutes in pan on wire rack; invert onto serving tray.

2. Turn cake with a short side facing you. Using photograph as a guide, mark a T-shirt outline on cake, indicating sleeve on left side only. Remove cake from under left sleeve; cut out a 4-by-6-inch parallelogram to create a right sleeve. Remove piece from neckline. Place right sleeve at right shoulder; trim as necessary to match left sleeve.

3. In medium bowl, blend frosting with almond extract; spread over cake. Using photograph as a guide, with writing tip on icing tube, decorate cake with icing.

Makes 10 to 12 servings.

Cherry Checkerboard

1 package (about 19 ounces)
    pudding-included white cake
    mix with candy bits
3 large eggs
⅓ cup salad oil
¼ cup water
3 cans (1-pound size)
    vanilla-flavored frosting
1 tube (.68 ounce) red glossy
    decorating gel
2 squares (1-ounce size)
    semisweet chocolate,
    melted
24 gumdrops (12 each of 2
    colors)

1. Preheat oven to 350°F. Grease and flour two 9-inch square cake pans; set aside. In large bowl of electric mixer, combine cake mix, eggs, oil and water; mix, bake and cool cake as package label directs.

2. Remove cakes from pans; if necessary, trim and discard rounded cake tops. Place one layer, cut side down, on serving tray; spread with 1½ cups frosting. Top with second layer, cut side down. Spread 2 cups frosting over top and sides of cake. With remaining frosting in icing bag fitted with medium star tip, outline all cake edges. With red decorating gel, using photograph as a guide, make checkerboard design on top of cake; drizzle melted chocolate into alternate squares, using wooden pick to spread into corners. Arrange gumdrop "checkers" on cake "game board."

Makes 9 to 12 servings.

Clockwise from top right: Cookies-and-Cream Pool Table, Cherry Checkerboard, Pattern for a Perfect Cake.

■ What to do if you want to decorate a cake directly on its serving plate? Slip strips of waxed paper under the edge of the cake, allowing the strips to hang over the rim of the plate. Frost the cake; then with a quick motion, pull out the paper.

Lite Eating: Northwest Fish Bounty

Basil-Scallop Linguine

1 tablespoon olive oil
2 shallots, minced
2 medium cloves garlic, crushed
2 tablespoons minced Italian parsley
2 tablespoons minced fresh basil or 2 teaspoons dried basil leaves, crushed
¼ teaspoon crushed red-pepper flakes
1 teaspoon salt
⅛ teaspoon pepper
1 can (16 ounces) tomatoes
½ cup dry white wine
2 tablespoons tomato paste
1 pound sea scallops
1 package (9 ounces) frozen artichoke hearts, thawed
1 package (8 ounces) whole-wheat linguine
2 tablespoons toasted pine nuts

1. In 3-quart saucepan, heat oil over medium heat. Add shallots and garlic; sauté 3 minutes. Add parsley, basil, pepper flakes, salt, pepper, tomatoes, wine and tomato paste. Bring to boiling. Stir to break up tomatoes. Cover; simmer mixture 20 minutes.

2. Slice scallops crosswise in half; add scallops and artichoke hearts to tomato mixture. Cook until scallops are cooked and artichokes are hot, about 5 minutes.

3. Cook linguine as package label directs; drain. On platter, toss pasta with scallop mixture; sprinkle with pine nuts. If desired, garnish with basil leaves.

Makes 6 servings, 298 calories each.

Stuffed Rainbow Trout

¾ pound fresh kale or spinach
1 carrot, pared and coarsely shredded
½ cup fine dry bread crumbs
½ cup chopped parsley
1 large green onion, minced
¾ teaspoon salt
⅛ teaspoon pepper
2 tablespoons reduced-calorie margarine, melted
1 large egg, slightly beaten
4 whole rainbow trout, boned with tails and heads left on (about 2½ pounds)
2 tablespoons lemon juice
2 tablespoons dry vermouth
Lemon wedges

1. In saucepan, in 2 cups boiling water, cook kale until tender, about 5 minutes. Drain kale; pat dry and chop. In bowl, mix kale, carrot, bread crumbs, parsley, green onion, salt, pepper, margarine and egg.

2. Preheat oven to 400°F. Grease jelly-roll pan; set aside. Sprinkle cavity of each trout with lemon juice; fill with stuffing. Secure with wooden picks. Place on pan. Sprinkle with vermouth. Cover with foil; bake until done, about 20 minutes. Remove picks. Serve with lemon wedges.

Makes 4 servings, 296 calories each.

Broiled Salmon With Tomato-Pepper Sauce

2 tablespoons reduced-calorie margarine
1 small onion, chopped
1 plum tomato, seeded and chopped
½ small green pepper, chopped
½ small red pepper, chopped
½ small yellow pepper, chopped
½ cup clam juice
1 tablespoon cornstarch
1 cup low-fat milk
¾ teaspoon salt
¼ teaspoon hot-red-pepper sauce
4 small salmon steaks, ½ inch thick (about 2 pounds)

1. In saucepan, over medium heat, melt margarine. Add onion, tomato and peppers; sauté until vegetables are tender-crisp, about 3 minutes. Add clam juice; bring to boiling. Cover; simmer 5 minutes.

2. In small glass measure, blend cornstarch with milk; stir into sauce. Bring to boiling, stirring; simmer 1 minute, until thickened. Stir in salt and the pepper sauce; keep warm.

3. Place salmon on rack in broiler pan; broil 4 inches from heat, about 4 minutes on each side. Pass sauce.

Makes 4 servings, 295 calories each.

Clockwise from top: Stuffed Rainbow Trout, Basil-Scallop Linguine, Broiled Salmon With Tomato-Pepper Sauce.

Micro-Way: Southwest Specialties

Goat-Cheese Burritos, Picadillo Cornbread Pie.

Picadillo Cornbread Pie

3 tablespoons butter
¼ cup water
2¼ cups crushed cornbread
  stuffing mix
1 large egg
1 large onion, chopped
2 cloves garlic, crushed
1 green pepper, chopped
1 tablespoon salad oil
1 pound ground beef
1 tablespoon brown sugar
½ teaspoon ground
  cinnamon
½ teaspoon ground
  cumin
1½ cups chunky salsa
1 can (10 ounces) kidney
  beans, drained
½ cup raisins
1 cup (4 ounces) shredded
  Cheddar cheese

1. In bowl, heat butter in water on HIGH 1 minute. Stir in stuffing mix and egg; press into 9-inch microwave-safe pie plate.

2. In 3-quart microwave-safe casserole, mix onion, garlic, green pepper and oil. Cover; vent. Cook on HIGH 3 minutes, stirring once. Add beef; cook on HIGH 6 minutes, stirring once. Discard fat; stir in sugar, spices and salsa. Cook on HIGH 3 minutes. Stir in beans and raisins. Spoon into crust; cook, uncovered, on HIGH 6 minutes, rotating pie plate after 3 minutes. Sprinkle casserole with cheese; let pie stand 5 minutes.

Makes 6 servings.

Goat-Cheese Burritos

½ cup chopped green onions
1½ pounds boneless chicken
  breasts, cut into ¼-inch-wide
  strips
1 large green pepper, cut into
  ¼-inch-wide strips
1 can (4 ounces) whole green
  chiles, julienned
2 cloves garlic, crushed
½ teaspoon dried cilantro
1 tablespoon salad oil
4 ounces goat cheese,
  crumbled
1 cup (4 ounces) shredded
  Monterey Jack cheese
2 tablespoons chopped
  sun-dried tomatoes
8 flour tortillas
½ cup mild chunky salsa

1. Set aside 2 tablespoons green onions. In 3-quart microwave-safe casserole, mix remaining onions, the chicken, green pepper, chiles, garlic, cilantro and oil. Cover with plastic wrap; turn back one corner to vent. Cook on HIGH 8 minutes, stirring after 4 minutes. Stir in goat cheese, ½ cup Monterey Jack and the sun-dried tomatoes.

2. Wrap half the tortillas in dampened paper towels. Warm on HIGH 30 seconds. Spoon ½ cup chicken mixture across center of each tortilla. Roll up; place, seam side down, in glass baking dish. Repeat with remaining tortillas and filling. Cover; vent. Cook on HIGH 4 minutes, rotating dish after 2 minutes.

3. Place tortillas on serving dish. Spoon salsa on top; sprinkle with remaining Monterey Jack and onions. Cover; let stand 5 minutes.
Makes 4 servings.

Santa Fe Chowder

1 large onion, chopped
1 small carrot, sliced
1 can (4 ounces) chopped
  green chiles
2 cloves garlic, crushed
2 teaspoons chili powder
½ teaspoon dried cilantro
½ teaspoon ground cumin
½ teaspoon dried oregano
1 tablespoon salad oil
¾ pound round steak, cubed
2 cans (14-ounce size) beef
  broth
1 can (14 ounces) tomatoes
1 small zucchini, diced
1 cup frozen corn, thawed

In 3-quart microwave-safe casserole, mix onion, carrot, chiles, garlic, spices and oil. Cover; vent. Cook on HIGH 4 minutes. Stir in beef. Cover; vent. Cook on HIGH 5 minutes. Mix broth with enough water to make 4 cups; stir into beef mixture. Add tomatoes. Cover; vent. Cook on HIGH 10 minutes. Stir in zucchini and corn. Cover; vent. Cook on HIGH 5 minutes.
Makes 8 servings.

■ To use a microwave without a turntable, rotate dish and stir, or rearrange food at least once.

Sante Fe Chowder.

March

You can make preparing dinner deliciously simple: Choose a recipe from the one-dish collection below. The meat and vegetables share the same pan for no-fuss family meals.

Four-Peppercorn Steak Dinner

Forum Chicken and Vegetables

One-Pan Veal Paprikash

Meat Loaves Mexicali

Glazed Ham and Sweet Potato Supper

Crustless Sausage Pizza

Turkey à la King

Spicy Scallops With Black Beans

Chicken Stir-Fry

Veal Piccata With Vegetables

Winter Pork Chops

Sausage Ratatouille

One-Dish Dinners Cookbook

Try our one-pan versions of old favorites—they're updated and easy on the cook.

Four-Peppercorn Steak Dinner
(pictured, page 45)

1 tablespoon black peppercorns
1 tablespoon green
    peppercorns
1 tablespoon pink peppercorns
1 tablespoon white
    peppercorns
1½ teaspoons salt
4 boneless shell or rib-eye
    steaks, ¾ inch thick
    (about 10 ounces each)
3 tablespoons butter or
    margarine
1 tablespoon salad oil
8 small red potatoes, unpared
    and quartered
¾ pound whole green beans,
    trimmed
½ pound whole baby carrots,
    pared
½ pound medium mushrooms,
    quartered
2 shallots, minced
½ cup dry sherry
½ pint cherry tomatoes
¼ cup brandy, slightly warmed
Watercress sprigs

1. Place peppercorns in heavy plastic bag. With rolling pin, crush peppercorns. (Or use a mortar and pestle.) Mix with 1 teaspoon salt. Rub mixture on both sides of steaks.

2. In 12-inch skillet, melt 1 tablespoon butter in oil over medium-high heat. Add steaks; sauté about 5 minutes, turning once, or until of desired degree of doneness. Remove steaks from skillet; keep warm.

3. In same skillet, melt remaining 2 tablespoons butter. Add potatoes, green beans, carrots, mushrooms, shallots and ½ teaspoon salt. Sauté 5 minutes, or until vegetables are lightly browned. Add sherry; bring to boiling. Simmer, covered, 5 minutes or until vegetables are tender.

4. Return steaks to skillet. Add cherry tomatoes; heat through. Pour brandy over steaks. Carefully set aflame with lighted match held to one side of inside edge of skillet. With long-handled tongs, turn steaks until flaming stops. Place each steak on warm serving dish with some vegetables, dividing evenly; garnish with watercress sprigs.
Makes 4 servings.

Page 45: Four-Peppercorn Steak Dinner, Forum Chicken and Vegetables.

Pages 46 and 47: (Clockwise from top left) One-Pan Veal Paprikash, Meat Loaves Mexicali, Glazed Ham and Sweet Potato Supper, Crustless Sausage Pizza, Turkey à la King.

Pages 48 and 49: (Clockwise from top right) Spicy Scallops With Black Beans, Chicken Stir-Fry, Veal Piccata With Vegetables, Winter Pork Chops, Sausage Ratatouille.

Forum Chicken and Vegetables
(pictured, page 45)

2 tablespoons all-purpose flour
1 can (about 14 ounces)
    chicken broth
½ ounce dried porcini
    mushrooms
1 red pepper
2 cups fresh spinach leaves
1 large egg
1 tablespoon water
½ cup Italian-seasoned fine dry
    bread crumbs
2 whole boneless chicken
    breasts, skinned and split
    (1½ pounds)
¼ cup butter or margarine
2 tablespoons pine nuts
2 tablespoons salad oil
1 medium onion, sliced
2 medium cloves garlic,
    crushed
1 package (9 ounces) frozen
    artichoke hearts, thawed
1 teaspoon dried basil leaves,
    crushed
¼ cup grated Parmesan cheese

1. In small cup, mix flour with ¼ cup chicken broth until blended; set aside. In small saucepan, heat remaining chicken broth to boiling. Stir in mushrooms; set aside to soften. Cut red pepper into ½-inch strips. Cut strips crosswise in half; set aside. Trim and discard stems from spinach. Thinly slice spinach leaves; set aside.

2. In pie plate, with fork, beat egg with water until mixed. Place bread

One-Dish Dinners Cookbook

crumbs on sheet of waxed paper. Dip one chicken breast into egg mixture; drain off excess. Dip in crumbs to coat both sides; shake off excess. Place on another sheet of waxed paper. Repeat with remaining chicken, egg mixture and bread crumbs.

3. In large skillet, melt 1 tablespoon butter over medium heat. Add pine nuts; sauté until golden. With slotted spoon, remove nuts to small cup; set aside. In same skillet, over medium heat, melt 2 tablespoons butter in oil. Add chicken breasts; sauté 4 minutes or until browned, lowering heat to medium-low after turning chicken. Place chicken on platter; keep warm.

4. In same skillet, over medium heat, melt remaining butter. Add the reserved red pepper, onion, garlic and the artichoke hearts; sauté 3 minutes. Add chicken broth and mushrooms, slicing larger mushrooms in half or into quarters; stir to loosen brown bits in pan. Stir in spinach and basil; simmer, covered, 2 minutes. Add broth-flour mixture; cook, stirring, until thickened. Stir in cheese. Transfer chicken to plate; spoon spinach mixture onto platter. Top with chicken; sprinkle with pine nuts.

Makes 4 servings.

■ A paper bag lets fresh mushrooms "breathe" and stay fresh longer, so when you buy a plastic package of mushrooms or purchase them loose in a plastic bag, be sure to place them in a paper bag, twisted closed, in the refrigerator. When you're ready to use the mushrooms, simply wipe them with a damp paper towel—never soak them, or they'll become soggy.

One-Pan Veal Paprikash
(pictured, page 46)

2 tablespoons salad oil
1 pound boneless veal shoulder, cut into ¼-inch strips
½ pound small whole mushrooms
1 large onion, cut into wedges
1 medium green pepper, cut into 1-inch cubes
1 large clove garlic, crushed
4 teaspoons paprika
¼ teaspoon salt
⅛ teaspoon pepper
1 can (14½ ounces) whole tomatoes
1 can (about 14 ounces) beef broth
½ cup red wine
1 tablespoon Worcestershire sauce
1 package (8 ounces) egg noodles, uncooked
½ cup sour cream
Dill sprigs

1. In Dutch oven, heat oil over medium-high heat until hot. Add veal; sauté until browned on all sides, about 6 minutes. Add mushrooms, onion, green pepper and garlic. Sauté 2 minutes. Add paprika; sauté 1 minute longer. Stir in salt, pepper, tomatoes and their liquid, beef broth, wine and Worcestershire. With spoon, break up tomatoes. Bring to boiling; simmer, covered, 20 minutes.

2. Stir noodles into veal mixture. Simmer, uncovered, stirring frequently so noodles do not stick, 12 minutes or until tender. Remove from heat; stir in sour cream. Garnish with dill sprigs; if desired, sprinkle with snipped fresh dill.

Makes 4 servings.

Crustless Sausage Pizza
(pictured, pages 46 and 47)

1 tablespoon salad oil
1 medium onion, chopped
1½ pounds bulk country-style pork sausage
½ cup fine dry bread crumbs
1 large egg
¾ cup prepared pizza sauce
½ green pepper, thinly sliced into rings
¼ cup sliced pitted black olives
1 cup (4 ounces) shredded Italian fontina cheese
¼ cup freshly grated Parmesan cheese

1. In 10-inch nonstick skillet, heat oil over medium-high heat. Add onion; sauté until tender, about 5 minutes. Transfer to medium bowl; stir in sausage, bread crumbs and egg, mixing well. Pat into bottom of same skillet to form a large patty. Over medium-high heat, brown patty 5 minutes, shaking pan frequently to keep meat from sticking.

2. Place baking sheet over skillet; turn out patty onto baking sheet. Carefully slip patty back into skillet with uncooked side down. Cook 5 minutes, or until browned and cooked through. Remove pan from heat; spoon off and discard drippings in pan.

3. Spoon pizza sauce over patty, spreading evenly to within ¼ inch of edges. Arrange pepper and olive slices on top; sprinkle with cheeses. Cover skillet handle with double thickness of aluminum foil if not heat-safe; broil pizza 5 inches from heat until cheeses are bubbly. Gently slide pizza onto serving platter; cut into 8 wedges. If desired, serve with focaccia or other herbed Italian bread.

Makes 4 servings.

Turkey à la King
(pictured, page 46)

1 medium green pepper
1 medium red pepper
2 packages (10-ounce size) frozen broccoli spears
⅓ cup unsifted all-purpose flour
½ teaspoon salt
⅛ teaspoon pepper
1½ pounds turkey cutlets (about 8)
¼ cup butter or margarine
2 tablespoons salad oil
½ pound mushrooms, sliced
3 green onions, sliced
¾ cup chicken broth
¼ cup sherry
½ cup heavy cream

1. Cut peppers into 1-inch triangles; set aside. In large skillet, bring ½ cup water to boiling. Add broccoli; cook until tender-crisp, about 3 minutes. Drain. Place on serving platter; keep warm.

2. On sheet of waxed paper, combine flour, salt and pepper. Coat turkey cutlets with flour mixture; set aside on another sheet of waxed paper. Reserve 3 tablespoons flour mixture.

3. In large skillet, over medium-high heat, melt 2 tablespoons butter in oil. Add turkey cutlets; brown on both sides, about 6 minutes. Remove to serving platter with broccoli; keep warm. In same skillet, over medium-high heat, melt remaining butter. Add peppers, mushrooms and green onions; sauté 3 minutes.

4. Add chicken broth and sherry, stirring to loosen brown bits. Boil 2 minutes. In small cup, blend heavy cream and reserved flour mixture; stir into liquid in skillet until blended. Bring to boiling, stirring constantly; simmer 1 minute or until thickened. Add turkey; cook until heated through. Serve with broccoli and, if desired, corn muffins.

Makes 4 to 6 servings.

Meat Loaves Mexicali
(pictured, pages 46 and 47)

4 green or red frying peppers
4 medium ears frozen corn
2 medium onions
1½ pounds ground beef
1 cup canned pinto beans, drained
1½ teaspoons salt
½ teaspoon chili powder
½ teaspoon ground cumin
⅛ teaspoon ground red pepper
2 tablespoons water
3 tablespoons salad oil
2 large cloves garlic, crushed
1 can (14½ ounces) stewed tomatoes
¼ cup sliced pitted black olives

1. Seed and quarter frying peppers lengthwise; set aside. Cut corn crosswise into 3-inch pieces; set vegetables aside.

2. Cut onions into thick slices. Mince enough onion slices to measure ¼ cup; set aside remaining slices. In large bowl, combine minced onion, ground beef, pinto beans, ¾ teaspoon salt, the chili powder, cumin, ground red pepper and water. Shape beef mixture into 6 oval loaves.

3. In 12-inch skillet, heat 2 tablespoons oil over medium-high heat until hot. Add meat loaves; cook about 10 minutes, or until evenly browned on both sides. Remove from skillet; set aside. To drippings in skillet, add 1 tablespoon oil. Heat over medium-high heat until hot. Add reserved sliced onions, frying peppers and the garlic; sauté 5 minutes or until browned. Add corn, tomatoes, olives and ¾ teaspoon salt. Return meat loaves to skillet; bring liquid to boiling. Simmer, covered, 20 minutes, or until vegetables are cooked.

Makes 6 servings.

Glazed Ham and Sweet Potato Supper
(pictured, page 47)

2 medium Granny Smith apples
1 medium onion
¼ cup butter or margarine
1½ pounds lean ham
1 can (2½ pounds) sweet potatoes, drained
⅓ cup firmly packed light-brown sugar
¼ teaspoon dried chervil leaves, crushed
⅛ teaspoon ground nutmeg
¾ cup orange juice
¼ cup apple juice
1 tablespoon coarse-grained Dijon mustard
1 package (8 ounces) frozen sugar snap peas
1 tablespoon cornstarch

1. Core and slice apples; set aside. Cut onion into wedges; set aside.

2. In large skillet, over medium heat, melt butter. Add ham; cook until browned on all sides. Transfer to plate; cover. Set aside. To drippings in skillet, add apples and onion. Sauté 3 minutes. Add sweet potatoes, sugar, chervil, nutmeg, ½ cup orange juice, the apple juice and mustard. Stir gently to combine. Bring to boiling; simmer, covered, 3 minutes. Add ham and sugar snap peas; cook 3 minutes longer.

3. In small glass measure, mix cornstarch with remaining orange juice until blended. Remove ham to serving plate; stir cornstarch mixture into liquid in skillet until blended. Bring to boiling, stirring constantly; simmer 1 minute or until thickened. Spoon vegetable mixture onto serving platter with ham.

Makes 4 to 6 servings.

■ Give a family-style supper a touch of country charm. Set the mood by using tattersall dish towels as place mats and napkins. A textured tablecloth and chunky candles complete the effect.

Sausage Ratatouille
(pictured, pages 48 and 49)

1½-pound coil garlic-flavored
   sausage
1 large zucchini
1 medium eggplant (1¼
   pounds)
1 medium Spanish onion
1 medium green pepper
1 medium red pepper
1 medium yellow pepper
¼ cup olive oil
2 medium cloves garlic,
   crushed
1 can (28 ounces) Italian plum
   tomatoes, drained
3 tablespoons tomato paste
¼ cup minced parsley
1 tablespoon chopped fresh
   basil or 1 teaspoon dried
   basil leaves, crushed
1 teaspoon salt
¼ teaspoon pepper
1 can (19 ounces) garbanzo
   beans

1. On flat surface, coil sausage into a tight spiral. Insert long skewer near loose end of the spiral through all coils. Insert another skewer at a perpendicular angle through all coils, to form a cross. Set aside. Cut zucchini into 1½-inch pieces; cut eggplant, onion and peppers into 1-inch pieces. Set aside.

2. Line plate with paper towels; set aside. In 12-inch skillet, heat 2 tablespoons oil over medium-high heat until hot. Add sausage; brown on both sides, about 5 minutes. With wide spatula, remove sausage to prepared plate.

3. In same skillet, heat remaining oil. Add eggplant and onion; sauté 5 minutes. Add peppers and garlic; cook, covered, 5 minutes, or until vegetables are tender.

4. Stir in zucchini, tomatoes, tomato paste, parsley, basil, salt and pepper; with wooden spoon, break up tomatoes. Return sausage to skillet; bring to boiling. Simmer, covered, 30 minutes. Stir in garbanzos; heat through. Remove skewers from sausage. If desired, garnish with fresh basil leaves, and serve with breadsticks.

Makes 6 servings.

Veal Piccata With Vegetables
(pictured, pages 48 and 49)

2 tablespoons all-purpose flour
1 teaspoon salt
¼ teaspoon pepper
4 veal loin chops, ⅓ inch thick
   (1⅓ pounds)
1 small butternut squash
   (1 pound)
1 bunch broccoli (1 pound)
2 tablespoons butter or
   margarine
2 tablespoons salad oil
3 green onions, cut into 1-inch
   pieces
1 cup chicken broth
2 tablespoons lemon juice
1 teaspoon dried thyme leaves,
   crushed
½ cup pecan halves, toasted
Lemon twists
Parsley sprigs

1. On sheet of waxed paper, combine flour, salt and pepper; coat each veal chop with flour mixture, shaking off excess. Set aside on another sheet of waxed paper.

2. With sharp knife, pare squash. Cut crosswise into ½-inch-thick slices; cut each slice in half. Set aside. Pare broccoli stalks. Cut into 3-inch lengths. Set aside.

3. In large skillet, over medium-high heat, melt butter in oil. Add veal chops; lightly brown on both sides. Arrange squash, broccoli and green onions over chops; add chicken broth, lemon juice and thyme. Cover skillet; simmer 5 minutes, or until vegetables are tender-crisp, stirring occasionally. Stir in pecans. Arrange on platter. Garnish with lemon and parsley.

Makes 4 servings.

Winter Pork Chops
(pictured, page 48)

1 tablespoon all-purpose
   flour
1½ teaspoons sugar
½ teaspoon ground cinnamon
½ teaspoon cracked black
   pepper
4 boneless pork chops, ¾ inch
   thick (about 1½ pounds)
3 tablespoons butter or
   margarine
½ head cauliflower, cut into
   flowerets
4 large carrots, pared and
   sliced diagonally
1 pint brussels sprouts,
   trimmed
½ pint pearl onions,
   trimmed
¼ teaspoon salt
1 cup apple cider
3 tablespoons ketchup

1. On waxed paper, combine flour, sugar, cinnamon and cracked black pepper. Coat pork chops with mixture.

2. In large skillet, melt 2 tablespoons butter over medium-high heat. Add pork chops; cook until lightly browned on both sides. Remove to plate; in skillet, melt remaining butter. Add vegetables. Sauté until lightly browned. Return chops to skillet. Stir in salt, cider and ketchup, scraping to loosen brown bits. Bring to boiling. Cover; simmer 20 minutes, or until pork is tender. Stir occasionally.

Makes 4 servings.

■ When choosing the freshest cauliflower for cooking, make sure the flowerets are snow white in color and the leaves are blue-green. If you are preparing the cauliflower whole, trim the leaves and hollow out the core for even heating. To prevent the head from turning gray during cooking, add lemon juice or milk to the water.

Spicy Scallops With Black Beans

(pictured, page 49)

Sauce
1 tablespoon cornstarch
2 teaspoons grated pared ginger root
¾ teaspoon crushed red-pepper flakes
¼ cup chicken broth
2 tablespoons dry sherry
2 tablespoons soy sauce

1 large Spanish onion
1 medium green pepper
1 medium red pepper
1 medium yellow pepper
2 Italian plum tomatoes
2 tablespoons butter
2 tablespoons olive oil
1 pound bay scallops
1 can (16 ounces) black beans, drained and heated
2 cups hot cooked white rice

1. Make sauce: In 1-cup glass measure, mix sauce ingredients until blended. Set aside.

2. Cut Spanish onion into 1-inch pieces; separate layers. Set aside. Cut peppers into 1-inch pieces; set aside. Seed and chop plum tomatoes; set tomatoes aside.

3. In large skillet, over medium heat, melt 1 tablespoon butter in 1 tablespoon oil. Add scallops; sauté until opaque and firm, about 4 minutes. With slotted spoon, remove to small bowl; set aside.

4. In skillet, over medium heat, melt remaining 1 tablespoon butter in remaining 1 tablespoon oil. Add onion; sauté 3 minutes. Add peppers; sauté 5 minutes longer, or until tender-crisp. Add tomatoes. Stir sauce mixture to recombine; add to mixture in skillet. Bring to boiling, stirring constantly. Boil 1 minute. Return scallops to pan; toss to coat with sauce. Serve immediately with black beans and hot rice.

Makes 4 servings.

Eggplant-and-Meat-Patties-Parmigiana Casserole

Tomato Sauce
2 tablespoons butter or margarine
½ cup chopped onion
1 medium clove garlic, crushed
½ teaspoon salt
¼ teaspoon pepper
1 can (1 pound) tomatoes, undrained
1 can (8 ounces) tomato sauce
1 tablespoon sugar
1 teaspoon dried oregano leaves
½ teaspoon dried basil leaves

1 large eggplant (1½ pounds)
¼ cup unsifted all-purpose flour
1 teaspoon seasoned salt
⅛ teaspoon pepper
Salad oil

Meat Patties
1½ pounds ground chuck
1 large egg, slightly beaten
½ cup soft bread crumbs (1 slice)
¼ teaspoon salt
¼ cup grated Parmesan cheese
½ package (8-ounce size) mozzarella cheese, sliced

1. Make tomato sauce: In hot butter in medium saucepan, sauté onion and garlic until onion is golden brown, about 5 minutes. Add salt, pepper and remaining sauce ingredients; bring to boiling. Reduce heat and simmer, uncovered, 10 minutes.

2. Meanwhile, wash eggplant. Cut crosswise into ½-inch-thick slices. Combine flour, seasoned salt and pepper; use to coat eggplant.

3. Heat 2 tablespoons oil in skillet; sauté eggplant slices, a few at a time. Add more oil as needed. Remove slices as they brown.

4. Preheat oven to 350°F.

5. Make patties: In medium bowl, combine meat, egg, bread crumbs

and salt; mix gently. Shape into 8 patties, ½-inch thick each. In large skillet, without fat, over medium heat, brown on each side.

6. Spoon half of tomato sauce into shallow round 10-inch baking dish. Arrange eggplant and meat alternately around side of dish. Spoon remaining sauce on top. Sprinkle with Parmesan cheese; top with mozzarella.

7. Bake, uncovered, 20 to 25 minutes, or just until mozzarella is melted and golden.

Makes 8 servings.

Chicken Stir-Fry

(pictured, page 49)

1 pound boneless chicken breasts, cut into ½-inch strips
2 tablespoons cornstarch
Salad oil
1 can (8 ounces) sliced water chestnuts, drained
2 medium cloves garlic, crushed
1 package (4.7 ounces) Oriental-style rice-and-seasoning mix
1 cup chicken broth
2 tablespoons soy sauce
2 red peppers, thinly sliced
¼ pound snow peas

1. In plastic bag, toss chicken with cornstarch until coated. In wok or deep 12-inch skillet, heat 2 tablespoons salad oil over medium-high heat until hot. Add one-third of chicken; stir-fry until golden brown. Remove from wok; set aside. Stir-fry remaining chicken, adding more oil as necessary.

2. In wok, heat 2 tablespoons oil until hot. Add water chestnuts and garlic; stir-fry 2 minutes. Stir in chicken, rice mix and seasoning packet, chicken broth and soy sauce; bring to boiling. Cover; simmer 10 minutes. Stir in peppers and peas; cook a few minutes, until vegetables are tender-crisp. Serve immediately.

Makes 5 to 6 servings.

Festive Easter Dinner

FRESH FRUIT CUP
*STUFFED PORK LOIN
WITH WILD BLUEBERRY SAUCE
STEAMED BABY CARROTS
*HERBED VEGETABLE SALAD
HOT BUTTERED ROLLS

*recipe given

Stuffed Pork Loin With Wild Blueberry Sauce

Stuffing
4 tablespoons butter or
   margarine
⅓ cup chopped shallots
1½ cups chopped hazelnuts
4 cups bread cubes
1 large egg, lightly beaten
¼ cup minced parsley
¾ teaspoon salt
¼ teaspoon pepper
¼ cup water

5-pound boneless pork loin
Salad oil
¼ teaspoon salt
⅛ teaspoon paprika
⅛ teaspoon pepper

Wild Blueberry Sauce
2 tablespoons butter or
   margarine
2 tablespoons chopped shallots
½ cup Marsala wine
2 tablespoons lemon juice
2 cans (15-ounce size) wild
   blueberries
1 tablespoon cornstarch
2 tablespoons sugar
1 teaspoon grated lemon peel
⅛ teaspoon salt

1. Make stuffing: In large skillet, over medium heat, melt butter. Add shallots; sauté 1 minute. Add hazelnuts; sauté until lightly browned, about 2 minutes. Remove skillet from heat; add bread cubes, egg, parsley, salt, pepper and water. Toss gently to mix; set aside.

2. Preheat oven to 325°F. Place loin on work surface. Cut along length of one long side to within ¼ inch of opposite side. Spread loin open with short side facing you; with hands, flatten slightly. Spread stuffing over right half of meat to within ½ inch of edge. Fold other side of meat over stuffing.

3. Place wooden picks along cut edges at 1-inch intervals; wrap kitchen string around picks, boot-lace fashion. Wrap string around loin to form a roll; place on rack in roasting pan. Brush lightly with oil; sprinkle with salt, paprika and pepper. Roast, uncovered, 2 hours, or until meat thermometer inserted in center registers 170°F. When pork is done, cover loosely with foil; let stand 10 minutes. Remove string and picks.

4. Meanwhile, make blueberry sauce: In saucepan, over medium heat, melt butter. Add shallots; sauté 1 minute. Add Marsala wine and lemon juice; bring to boiling. Simmer, uncovered, 10 minutes or until mixture is reduced by half. Drain 1 can blueberries; place blueberries in food processor. Puree; add to shallot mixture. Stir in cornstarch. Drain second can of blueberries; add whole berries, sugar, lemon peel and salt to shallot mixture. Bring to boiling; cook, stirring, until thickened. Keep warm.

Makes about 12 servings.

Serve Stuffed Pork Loin With Wild Blueberry Sauce as the main feature of your holiday meal.

Herbed Vegetable Salad

1 package (8 ounces) frozen
   ears of baby corn
1 package (8 ounces) frozen
   baby green beans
1 can (16 ounces) red kidney
   beans, drained and rinsed
1 can (16 ounces) white kidney
   beans, drained and rinsed
1 large red pepper, julienned
6 medium radishes, sliced
1 small red onion, sliced
2 tablespoons minced parsley
½ cup bottled Italian dressing
   with herbs

Cook corn and green beans as package labels direct; cool. Place in bowl with remaining ingredients. Refrigerate at least 4 hours to blend flavors, stirring occasionally.

Makes 8 to 12 servings.

Deluxe Dessert for Passover

Chocolate-Hazelnut Mousse.

and 2 egg yolks. Mix in remaining egg yolks, 2 at a time.

3. In bowl of electric mixer, at high speed, beat egg whites until stiff peaks form when beaters are raised; add one-fourth of egg whites to chocolate, turning processor on and off several times until mixed. Fold chocolate and ½ cup nuts into remaining egg-white mixture. Pour into dish; chill until set, about 3 hours. Remove foil; pat remaining nuts around side.

Makes 12 servings.

A History of the Haggadah

■ Each Passover, Jewish families gather to hold the seder, the ceremonial holiday meal, guided by a book call the Haggadah, the "narration." A collection of illustrated excerpts from the Bible and rabbinical commentaries, the Haggadah recalls how the ancient Israelites were liberated from slavery in Egypt, describes the many seder rituals and includes prayers and songs of thanksgiving. The earliest existing Haggadahs date to the 13th and 14th centuries. Since that time, the Haggadah has been translated into many languages. Despite small regional variations in the service, however, the Haggadah is generally the same worldwide.

Chocolate-Hazelnut Mousse

1 package (12 ounces) semisweet-chocolate pieces
¾ cup water
1 package (.3 ounce) kosher for Passover, unflavored, unsweetened jel dessert
¼ cup orange juice
9 large eggs, separated
¾ cup chopped toasted hazelnuts

1. Tape a 2½-inch-wide strip of aluminum foil around top edge of 1½-quart soufflé dish to make a high collar. In food processor, finely chop chocolate; let stand in processor while dissolving jel dessert.

2. In saucepan, bring water to boiling; remove from heat. With fork, stir in jel dessert until dissolved. Return to heat; bring to full boil. With processor running, pour in melted jel dessert. Process until chocolate melts. Mix in orange juice

Quick & Easy: Tex-Mex Quick Breads

Chile Chimichangas

3 green onions
6 (8-inch) flour tortillas
3 cups (12 ounces) shredded Monterey Jack cheese
1 can (4 ounces) chopped green chiles, drained
1 cup bottled salsa
Salad oil

1. Preheat oven to 350°F. Cut green tops from green onions; cut each top lengthwise into quarters to make 12 strips. Set strips aside.

Chop remaining white portion; set aside. Place tortillas on sheet of aluminum foil; place green-onion strips on top. Wrap tightly; heat in oven 15 minutes. Meanwhile, in large bowl, combine cheese, chiles, chopped green onions and ¼ cup salsa.

2. Tie ends of two green-onion strips together to make 6 long strips. Spoon one-sixth of cheese-chile mixture crosswise over center of each tortilla; fold sides of tortilla over cheese-chile filling. Fold ends over tortilla to make a packet; tie

one green-onion strip around each packet to secure.

3. In large skillet, heat ¼ inch oil to 375°F. Add packets; fry until golden brown, turning once, about 3 minutes. Drain. Serve immediately with remaining salsa.

Makes 6 servings.

Clockwise from left: Southwestern Kebabs, Onion Tiles, Chile Chimichangas, Jalapeño Corn Breads.

Southwestern Kebabs

Salsa
1 tablespoon olive oil
1 small onion, chopped
1 clove garlic, crushed
3 Italian plum tomatoes, chopped
1 tablespoon chopped cilantro (fresh coriander) leaves
¼ teaspoon salt
⅛ teaspoon pepper
1 tablespoon lime juice

Kebabs
1 green pepper, cut into 1-inch strips
1 red pepper, cut into 1-inch strips
¼ cup butter or margarine
1 clove garlic, crushed
2 teaspoons chili powder
¼ teaspoon ground cumin
¼ teaspoon oregano leaves, crushed
½ loaf (10-ounce size) Italian bread, cut into 1-inch cubes

1. Make salsa: In medium saucepan, heat oil over medium-high heat. Add onion and garlic; sauté until tender, about 3 minutes. Stir in tomatoes, cilantro, salt, pepper and lime juice. Cook just until heated through. Cover; keep salsa warm.

2. Make kebabs: In medium saucepan, bring 2 quarts water to boiling. Add peppers; boil 1 minute. Drain; rinse with cold water until cool. Set aside. In large skillet, over medium heat, melt butter. Add garlic, chili powder, cumin and oregano; cook 1 minute. Remove from heat. Stir in bread cubes until coated. On eight (8-inch) skewers, alternately arrange peppers and bread cubes. Place on rack in broiler pan. Broil 4 inches from heat until bread is lightly toasted, about 2 minutes, turning once. Serve kebabs with salsa.

Makes 8 servings.

Jalapeño Corn Breads

Salad oil
1 package (12 ounces) cornbread-muffin mix
⅔ cup milk
1 large egg
1 can (12 ounces) Mexican-style corn, drained
2 tablespoons finely chopped pickled jalapeño peppers
1 can (6.5 ounces) nacho cheese sauce with green chiles

1. Preheat oven to 425°F. With salad oil, generously grease 2 cast-iron cornstick pans. Place in oven; heat 15 minutes.

2. Meanwhile, in large bowl, combine muffin mix, milk and egg. Stir in corn and jalapeños. Spoon batter into hot cornstick molds, dividing evenly. Bake until golden, about 10 minutes.

3. Meanwhile, heat sauce as package label directs. Remove cornsticks from pans; serve with sauce.

Makes 10 to 14 cornsticks.

Onion Tiles

1 tablespoon yellow cornmeal
2 tablespoons olive oil
1 medium onion, thinly sliced
1 small clove garlic, crushed
1½ teaspoons chili powder
1 package (10 ounces) refrigerated pizza dough
½ cup (2 ounces) shredded Monterey Jack cheese
2 tablespoons chopped green chiles
¼ teaspoon cracked black pepper

1. Preheat oven to 425°F. Grease 13-by-9-by-2-inch baking pan. Sprinkle with cornmeal; set aside.

2. In small saucepan, heat oil over medium heat. Add onion and garlic; cook, stirring until tender, about 5 minutes. Add chili powder; cook, stirring, 1 minute.

3. Unroll dough; arrange in prepared pan to cover bottom and extend slightly up sides. With fingertips, press deep indentations in dough at 1-inch intervals. Sprinkle dough with cheese; scatter onion mixture on top. Sprinkle with chiles and pepper. Drizzle oil remaining in saucepan over surface. Bake until golden, about 15 minutes. To serve, cut into strips.

Makes 8 servings.

Quesadillas

12 flour tortillas
¾ pound Monterey Jack cheese, shredded
1 tablespoon ground cumin
3 cans (4-ounce size) chopped green chiles
¾ cup pitted black olives
1 medium red onion, chopped
¼ cup salad oil

1. Lay out 6 tortillas. In bowl, combine next five ingredients, and distribute evenly over each tortilla. Cover each with another tortilla.

2. Heat oil in a large skillet over medium-high heat. Fry tortillas, one at a time, until bottom is crisp. With a wide pancake turner, turn, and fry other side until crisp. Remove from heat, and drain on paper towels. Cut into 8 wedges. Repeat with remaining quesadillas. Serve with sour cream, if desired.

Makes 48 wedges.

■ You may want to apply an egg-white coating to the rim of a punch bowl and glaze with coarse salt. The Margarita-inspired presentation will enhance the arrival of the popular Tex-Mex appetizers quesadillas.

Lite Eating: Stir-Fries With a Delicious Difference

Clockwise from left: Chicken-Grapefruit Stir-Fry, Stir-Fried Chilied Shrimp, Gingered Pork lo Mein.

Chicken-Grapefruit Stir-Fry

1 pound boneless chicken
  breasts, skinned
½ pound spinach
1 green pepper
1 red pepper
1 large pink grapefruit
1 tablespoon cornstarch
¼ teaspoon crushed
  red-pepper flakes
3 tablespoons light soy sauce
2 tablespoons salad oil
2 green onions, chopped
½ teaspoon salt
¼ cup chicken broth
1 tablespoon dry-roasted
  cashews

1. Cut chicken into strips; set aside. Remove and discard stems from spinach; wash and pat dry leaves. Set aside. Cut peppers into 1½-inch strips; set aside. Peel, seed and section grapefruit; set aside.

2. In medium bowl, mix chicken with cornstarch, red-pepper flakes and soy sauce. In wok or large skillet, heat oil over medium-high heat. Add chicken mixture; stir-fry 3 minutes. Add peppers, green onions and salt; stir-fry 1 minute. Add broth; simmer, covered, until chicken is cooked and vegetables are tender-crisp, about 3 minutes. Add spinach; stir-fry until wilted, about 1 minute. Add grapefruit; toss to coat. Garnish with cashews.

Makes 4 servings, 321 calories each.

Gingered Pork lo Mein

1 package (8 ounces) spaghetti
1 pound pork tenderloin
½ pound mushrooms
3 green onions
2 medium cloves garlic
1 medium carrot
2 tablespoons salad oil
1 tablespoon dark sesame oil
1 tablespoon grated pared
  ginger root
¼ pound snow peas, trimmed
¼ teaspoon salt
⅓ cup bottled stir-fry sauce

1. Cook spaghetti as package label directs; drain. Set aside. Meanwhile, cut pork crosswise and mushrooms lengthwise into ⅛-inch slices; set aside. Cut green onions into 2-inch lengths; set aside. Crush garlic. Set aside. Pare carrot; cut into 2¼-by-¼-inch strips. Set aside.

2. In wok or large skillet, heat oils over medium-high heat until hot. Add pork and ginger; stir-fry 3 minutes. Add mushrooms, green onions, garlic, carrot, snow peas and salt. Stir-fry until vegetables are tender-crisp, about 2 minutes. Add spaghetti and stir-fry sauce; bring to boiling, stirring, until sauce is slightly thickened.

Makes 6 servings, 366 calories each.

Stir-Fried Chilied Shrimp

2 tablespoons salad oil
1 hot green or red chile
  pepper, seeded and chopped
1 large orange pepper, seeded
  and julienned
1 small onion, sliced
1 medium clove garlic, crushed
½ teaspoon salt
1 pound large shrimp, peeled
  and deveined, tails intact
3 tablespoons chopped cilantro
  (fresh coriander) leaves
1 teaspoon grated lime peel
¼ cup fresh lime juice
2 cups hot cooked white rice

1. In wok or large skillet, heat oil over medium-high heat. Add peppers, onion, garlic and salt; stir-fry until vegetables are tender-crisp, about 4 minutes.

2. Add shrimp; stir-fry until cooked, about 2 minutes. Add cilantro, lime peel and lime juice; heat through. Serve with rice.

Makes 4 servings, 255 calories each.

Micro-Way: Heart-Smart Cooking—Low in Cholesterol

Crusted Stuffed Turkey Breast

Stuffing
¼ pound mushrooms, finely chopped
1 medium onion, finely chopped
2 medium cloves garlic, crushed
1 package (10 ounces) frozen chopped spinach, thawed and squeezed dry
1½ cups cooked white or favorite rice
1 cup shredded carrot
½ teaspoon dried thyme leaves, crushed
¼ teaspoon pepper
⅛ teaspoon ground nutmeg
1 large egg white, slightly beaten

6-pound turkey breast, boned and skinned
¼ cup cholesterol-free mayonnaise
1 cup cornflake crumbs

1. Make stuffing: In glass bowl, combine mushrooms, onion and garlic. Cover; cook on HIGH 4 minutes, stirring once. Stir in remaining stuffing ingredients.
2. Place turkey breast, smooth side down, on work surface. Make horizontal cuts in thicker parts. With meat mallet, pound turkey to 14-by-9-inch rectangle. Cover with stuffing mixture to within 1 inch of edges; fold short sides over. Roll up, jelly-roll fashion; tie with kitchen string. Brush with mayonnaise; roll in crumbs.
3. Place turkey roll, seam side down, in microwave-safe baking dish. Cover with paper towel; cook on HIGH 10 minutes. Cover ends of roll with aluminum foil and then paper towel. Cook on MEDIUM 35 minutes, or until internal temperature registers 170°F on meat thermometer, rotating dish after 15 minutes. Let stand 5 minutes. Remove string before slicing.
Makes 8 to 10 servings.

Veal Marsala Stew

1 large onion, chopped
1 large clove garlic, crushed
1 tablespoon olive oil
2-pound boneless veal shoulder, cut into 1-inch cubes
¼ cup unsifted all-purpose flour
⅛ teaspoon pepper
1 can (14½ ounces) tomatoes
½ cup Marsala wine
3 carrots, diced
½ pound mushrooms, quartered
1 teaspoon Italian seasoning
1 envelope low-sodium chicken-flavored bouillon granules
½ package (10-ounce size) frozen peas

In microwave-safe casserole, combine onion, garlic and oil. Cover; vent. Cook on HIGH 3 minutes, stirring once. In bowl, toss veal with flour; add to onion mixture. Cover; cook on HIGH 10 minutes, stirring once. Stir in all remaining ingredients except peas. Cover; cook on HIGH 8 minutes. Stir; cover. Cook on MEDIUM 40 minutes, stirring occasionally. Stir in peas; cook on HIGH 5 minutes.
Makes 6 servings.

Polynesian Fish Packets

4 large or 8 small romaine lettuce leaves
1½ pounds red-snapper fillets, skinned and cut into 4 pieces about 1-inch-thick each
1 tablespoon lemon juice
Dash pepper
4 green onions, chopped
1 celery stalk, sliced
1 medium red pepper, sliced
¼ cup sliced water chestnuts
1 can (8 ounces) pineapple chunks
2 tablespoons cornstarch
1 tablespoon sugar
½ teaspoon salt
¼ teaspoon ground ginger
½ cup orange juice
1 tablespoon cider vinegar
½ teaspoon lemon-and-herb seasoning

1. Place lettuce in 10-inch round microwave-safe baking dish. Cover with plastic wrap; cook on HIGH 1 minute. Let stand 1 minute. Place leaves on work surface; in center of each leaf, place a piece of fish. Sprinkle each with lemon juice, dividing evenly, and pepper. Wrap lettuce leaves around fish pieces; secure with wooden picks. Set aside.

2. In same dish, place next 4 ingredients; cover. Cook on HIGH 3 minutes, stirring once. Place fish packets, seam side up, on vegetables around edge of dish. Cover; cook on HIGH 5 minutes. Turn packets over; cook, covered, until fish feels firm, about 2 minutes.

3. Transfer packets to serving platter; keep warm. Drain pineapple juice into glass measure; stir in cornstarch until blended. Add to vegetable mixture with pineapple chunks, sugar and remaining ingredients.

Clockwise from left: Crusted Stuffed Turkey Breast, Veal Marsala Stew, Polynesian Fish Packets.

Cook on HIGH 3 minutes, stirring occasionally, until sauce boils and is clear and thickened. Pour sauce mixture around packets.

Makes 4 servings.

April

Variety abounds in our annual collection of chicken recipes. Listed below, the titles include updated American favorites, as well as chicken with a foreign accent. They are all pictured, beginning with the rich chowder, scones and majestic roasted chicken shown here.

Chicken and Barley Chowder

Seeded Buckwheat Scones

Herb-Roasted Chicken

Fruited Mexican Chicken   Chicken Brochettes

Family-Favorite Potpie

Cordon Bleu Roulade

Chicken-Liver Pasta Pie

Braised Chicken With Vegetables

Drumsticks Scampi

Curried Chicken Wings   Fried Ravioli

Szechwan Chicken in a Nest

Chinese Chicken Legs

All-New Chicken Cookbook

Show off your culinary creativity with these tasteful variations on a chicken theme.

Chicken and Barley Chowder

(pictured, page 63)

2 tablespoons caraway seeds
1 tablespoon peppercorns
4 pounds chicken parts
2 celery stalks
6 parsley sprigs
4 quarts water
1 tablespoon salt
½ cup uncooked pearl barley
½ pound thickly sliced bacon
2 large carrots
3 medium leeks
1 small head cabbage
1 package (10 ounces) frozen peas
1 large Granny Smith apple, shredded
1 cup heavy cream
¼ teaspoon freshly ground pepper
Seeded Buckwheat Scones (recipe follows)

1. Put caraway seeds and peppercorns on triple-thick, 6-inch-square cheesecloth; tie up with string. In 6-quart Dutch oven, combine spice bag, chicken, celery, parsley and water. Bring to boiling. Skim off foam. Add salt; simmer, uncovered, 1½ hours. With slotted spoon, remove meat to bowl. Set aside.

2. Strain broth; discard solids. Skim off fat. Bring to boiling; add barley. Simmer 30 minutes.

3. Cut bacon crosswise into thin strips; set aside. Pare and slice carrots; set aside. Split and rinse leeks; cut off and discard green portion. Slice white portion; set aside. Shred cabbage coarsely; set aside.

4. In skillet, sauté bacon. Line dish with paper towels; with slotted spoon, remove bacon to dish. Pour off all but 2 tablespoons drippings; heat over medium-high heat. Add carrots and leeks; sauté 3 minutes. Add cabbage, one-third at a time; sauté until softened. Add sautéed vegetables to broth; stir in peas, apple and half the bacon. Bring to boiling; simmer 20 minutes, or until vegetables and barley are tender.

5. Shred meat into bite-size pieces; set aside. In saucepan, over medium heat, simmer cream until reduced by half. Add meat and cream to soup; heat. Stir in pepper. Pour into tureen; top with reserved bacon. Serve with scones.

Makes about 12 servings.

Seeded Buckwheat Scones

(pictured, page 63)

2¾ cups unsifted all-purpose flour
½ cup unsifted buckwheat flour
1 tablespoon baking powder
2 teaspoons sugar
1½ teaspoons salt
¾ teaspoon baking soda
½ cup shortening
¼ cup dried currants
1½ cups buttermilk
1 large egg, beaten
1 teaspoon caraway seeds
1 teaspoon sesame seeds

1. Preheat oven to 450°F. Lightly grease large baking sheet; set aside.

2. In large bowl, combine flours, baking powder, sugar, salt and baking soda. Add shortening; with pastry blender or two knives, cut in shortening until mixture resembles coarse crumbs. Add currants and buttermilk; with fork, stir just until dry ingredients are moistened.

3. Turn dough out onto lightly floured surface; knead 10 to 12 times. Pat into a 9-inch round. With

---

Page 63: Chicken and Barley Chowder, Seeded Buckwheat Scones, Herb-Roasted Chicken.

Pages 64 and 65: (Clockwise from top left) Fruited Mexican Chicken, Family-Favorite Potpie, Cordon Bleu Roulade, Chicken Brochettes.

Pages 66 and 67: (Clockwise from top left) Chicken-Liver Pasta Pie, Curried Chicken Wings, Fried Ravioli, Szechwan Chicken in a Nest, Drumsticks Scampi, Braised Chicken With Vegetables.

floured knife, cut dough into 12 wedges. Lightly brush tops with beaten egg, being careful egg does not drip onto cut edges. While egg is wet, sprinkle tops with seeds. Place 1 inch apart on baking sheet. Bake until golden brown, about 15 minutes. Serve warm.

Makes 12 servings.

Herb-Roasted Chicken

(pictured, page 63)

Herb butter
½ cup butter or margarine
2 tablespoons lemon juice
3 tablespoons snipped chives
1 teaspoon dried tarragon
    leaves, crushed

Stuffing
¼ cup butter or margarine
1 large celery stalk, chopped
1 small onion, chopped
1½ cups chicken broth
½ cup dry white wine
1 cup uncooked long-grain rice
¼ teaspoon ground nutmeg
1 cup chopped mixed dried
    fruit
½ cup chopped pecans
½ cup raisins

6½-pound roasting chicken
1 pound parsnips, pared and
    cut into ½-inch pieces
1 pint brussels sprouts, halved
3 leeks, cleaned and sliced

1. Make herb butter: In small saucepan, melt butter; stir in lemon juice, chives and tarragon. Set aside.
2. Make stuffing: In medium saucepan, melt butter. Add celery and onion; sauté 3 minutes. Add broth and wine. Bring to boiling; stir in rice and nutmeg. Cover; simmer mixture 20 minutes, or until liquid

is absorbed. Stir in dried fruit, pecans and raisins; set aside to cool.
3. Preheat oven to 350°F. Lightly spoon stuffing into neck and body cavities. Bring neck skin over stuffing; secure with poultry pins. Close body cavity with poultry pins; lace with string. Tie legs together; pin wings to breast. Place extra stuffing in greased baking dish; cover, and bake last 30 minutes chicken is in oven. Insert meat thermometer into thickest portion of thigh, away from bone. In large roasting pan, combine parsnips, brussels sprouts and leeks. Place chicken on top; baste with some reserved herb butter. Cover with aluminum foil; roast 1½ hours, basting occasionally. Remove foil; roast chicken ½ hour longer, or until golden and meat thermometer registers 170°F. Serve roasted vegetables with chicken and stuffing.

Makes 6 to 8 servings.

Fruited Mexican Chicken

(pictured, page 64)

3 medium red peppers
1½ teaspoons salt
¼ teaspoon pepper
3½-pound broiler-fryer, cut
    into 8 pieces
¼ cup safflower or salad oil
1 large onion, sliced and
    separated into rings
2 large cloves garlic, minced
1 can (28 ounces) peeled plum
    tomatoes, drained
1 package (12 ounces) pitted
    prunes
2 (3-inch) cinnamon sticks
3 cups hot cooked couscous
¼ cup lightly toasted pine nuts
¼ cup chopped cilantro (fresh
    coriander) leaves

1. Roast peppers: Place peppers in broiler pan; broil 6 inches from heat until blackened on all sides, using tongs to turn peppers. Place peppers in plastic bag; tie bag to close. Let peppers steam in bag at least 15 minutes; let stand until cool enough to handle. Remove skin, ribs and seeds; slice into ¾-inch-wide strips. Set aside.
2. In small cup, mix salt and pepper. Rub chicken pieces on all sides with salt mixture, dividing evenly. In 3-quart Dutch oven, heat oil over medium-high heat until hot. Add half the chicken; cook a few minutes on all sides, until golden. Remove to a platter; cook remaining chicken. Remove to platter. Pour off all but 2 tablespoons drippings from Dutch oven. To drippings, add onion and garlic; sauté 2 minutes. Return chicken to Dutch oven; add tomatoes. Simmer, covered, 10 minutes; stir occasionally. Stir in prunes and cinnamon sticks. Cook, covered, until chicken is almost tender, about 20 minutes; stir occasionally. Stir in reserved peppers. Simmer, covered, 5 minutes, or until chicken is done. Remove cinnamon sticks.
3. In medium bowl, combine couscous, pine nuts and cilantro. Spoon onto serving platter; spoon chicken mixture on top.

Makes 4 to 6 servings.

■ You cooked up a storm—but forgot to line your roasting pan with aluminum foil. What to do? Here's a helpful hint: Add water and a few drops of liquid detergent to your pan and place it in a warm oven or over low heat for several minutes; rinse thoroughly. Soon your roasting pan is squeaky clean.

Family-Favorite Potpie

(pictured, page 65)

Pastry
1 cup unsifted all-purpose flour
1 teaspoon dried thyme leaves, crushed
¾ teaspoon salt
¼ cup shortening
1 tablespoon cold butter
1½ to 2 tablespoons ice water

Filling
½ cup butter or margarine
2 tablespoons salad oil
10 ounces shiitake mushrooms, sliced
4 medium leeks, white part only, thinly sliced
3 large carrots, pared and thinly sliced
1 package (10 ounces) frozen peas
2 pounds boneless chicken thighs and breasts, skinned and cut into 1-inch pieces
¼ cup unsifted all-purpose flour
3 cups chicken broth
1 cup heavy cream
4 green onions, sliced
¼ cup chopped parsley
½ teaspoon dried thyme leaves, crushed
½ teaspoon salt
¼ teaspoon pepper

1 large egg
1 tablespoon water

1. Make pastry: In food processor, combine flour, thyme and salt. Add shortening and butter; using pulsing motion, process ingredients until mixture resembles coarse crumbs. With machine running, add water, 1 tablespoon at a time, processing just until dough begins to hold together. Remove dough from bowl; shape into a disk. Wrap in plastic wrap. Refrigerate dough 30 minutes or up to 2 days.
2. Make filling: In large skillet, over medium-high heat, melt 3 tablespoons butter in 1 tablespoon oil. Add mushrooms, and cook until browned, stirring occasionally. With slotted spoon, remove to large bowl. In same skillet, over medium heat, melt 2 tablespoons butter. Add leeks and carrots; sauté until tender-crisp, stirring occasionally. With slotted spoon, remove leeks and carrots and add to bowl with mushrooms; stir in peas. In same skillet, over medium-high heat, melt remaining butter in 1 tablespoon oil. Add chicken; sauté until browned. With slotted spoon, remove chicken and add to bowl with vegetables.
3. To drippings in skillet, add flour, stirring until smooth. Cook until bubbly. Gradually add chicken broth and heavy cream, whisking until smooth. Bring to boiling, stirring; cook until thickened, about 5 minutes. Pour into bowl with chicken. Add green onions, parsley, thyme, salt and pepper. Pour mixture into a shallow 2½-quart casserole. Set aside.
4. Preheat oven to 400°F. In small cup, with fork, beat egg with water until blended. Set aside.
5. On lightly floured surface, roll out dough to ¼-inch-thick round. Cut out a round 1 inch smaller than inside of casserole; crimp edges. Transfer to top of chicken mixture. With pastry brush, brush top of pastry round with egg mixture. Cut chicken shapes from remaining pastry. Place pastry chickens on top of pastry round; brush with egg mixture. Bake 50 minutes, or until crust is golden brown.
Makes 6 servings.

■ Cast-iron skillets are wonderful for cooking because they distribute heat evenly, but rusting can be a problem. To prevent this, wash the skillet in warm, soapy water, dry it with paper towels and place it on a low-heat burner or in a warm oven for a few minutes until completely dry.

Cordon Bleu Roulade

(pictured, page 65)

Salad oil
2 celery stalks, cut into 2-inch pieces
1 small onion, quartered
1½ pounds boneless chicken breasts, skinned and cubed
1½ cups uncooked quick-cooking rolled oats
1 jar (15 ounces) spaghetti sauce
1 large egg
⅓ cup grated Parmesan cheese
1 teaspoon poultry seasoning
1 teaspoon dried rosemary leaves
½ teaspoon salt
⅛ teaspoon pepper
¼ pound thinly sliced Virginia ham
½ pound thinly sliced provolone cheese
1 small green pepper
1 small red pepper
1 small yellow pepper

1. Preheat oven to 350°F. Grease a large sheet of aluminum foil with oil; set aside.
2. In food processor, process celery and onion until finely chopped. Add chicken; process until finely chopped. Add oats, ½ cup spaghetti sauce, the egg, Parmesan cheese, poultry seasoning, rosemary, salt and pepper. Process until blended.
3. Transfer chicken mixture to prepared aluminum foil. With spatula, spread to a 16-by-9-inch rectangle. Arrange ham slices on top, leaving a 1-inch border on all sides. Reserve 2 slices cheese; arrange remainder over ham. Slice peppers into ¼-inch-wide slices; arrange over all.
4. Starting with one long side of rectangle, roll up, jelly-roll fashion, using foil to lift mixture. Seal ends; place, seam side down, in roasting pan. Bake 40 minutes.
5. Meanwhile, heat remaining spaghetti sauce until hot. Just before serving roulade, arrange reserved

cheese slices on top; cover with spaghetti sauce.

Makes 6 to 8 servings.

Chicken Brochettes
(pictured, page 64)

½ cup olive oil
1 small green pepper, cut into 1½-inch pieces
1 tablespoon ground coriander
1 teaspoon dried thyme leaves, crushed
1 teaspoon salt
1 large clove garlic, minced
1 pound boneless chicken breasts, skinned and cut into 1-inch-wide strips
½ pound jumbo shrimp, peeled and deveined, with tails intact
12 large cherry tomatoes
2 large onions, quartered lengthwise
12 bay leaves (see *Note*)
1 cup boiling water

Lemon-Pepper Sauce
1 teaspoon salt
¼ teaspoon cracked pepper
¼ cup fresh lemon juice, strained
½ teaspoon Dijon-style mustard
½ cup olive oil

1 package (4 ounces) chicken-flavored rice mix with pasta and almonds

1. In 3-quart saucepan, heat oil over medium-high heat. Add green pepper; sauté 1 minute. Remove pan from heat; cool pepper in pan to room temperature. Stir in coriander, thyme, salt and garlic. Add chicken, shrimp, tomatoes and onions. Toss gently until coated. Transfer mixture to large bowl. Cover; refrigerate at least 2 hours or overnight.

2. Meanwhile, place bay leaves in small bowl. Add boiling water. Let soak 2 hours or overnight.

3. Make lemon-pepper sauce: In jar with tight-fitting lid, combine salt, cracked pepper, lemon juice and mustard. Shake to blend. Add oil; shake to blend. Set aside.

4. Prepare rice mix as package label directs. Meanwhile, on each of four 14-inch skewers, alternately arrange chicken, shrimp, green pepper, onions, tomatoes and bay leaves, threading chicken strips around shrimp and vegetables. Reserve marinade. Broil brochettes 6 inches from heat, turning once and basting with reserved marinade, until chicken is cooked, about 8 minutes. Serve brochettes with prepared rice and the sauce.

Makes 4 servings.

Note: Do not eat bay leaves.

Chicken-Liver Pasta Pie
(pictured, page 66)

2 large eggs
¼ cup grated Parmesan cheese
2 tablespoons salad oil
10 cooked lasagna noodles
¼ cup butter or margarine
1 pound chicken livers, halved
1 package (9 ounces) frozen artichoke hearts, thawed
½ pound medium mushrooms, quartered
1 medium onion, sliced
1 medium red pepper, chopped
2 medium cloves garlic, crushed
½ teaspoon dried marjoram leaves, crushed
¼ teaspoon dried thyme leaves, crushed
1 teaspoon salt
¼ teaspoon pepper
½ pound escarole, washed and cut into ½-inch-wide strips
¼ cup unsifted all-purpose flour
¼ cup dry vermouth
¾ cup milk
1 cup (4 ounces) shredded mozzarella cheese

1. In large bowl, whisk eggs with Parmesan cheese and oil until blended. Add noodles; toss to coat. Arrange noodles, spoke fashion, in 9-inch pie plate, allowing noodles to extend over edge of plate. Set aside.

2. Preheat oven to 350°F. In large skillet, over medium-high heat, melt 2 tablespoons butter. Add chicken livers; sauté 5 minutes. Remove livers to small bowl; clean skillet. In same skillet, over medium-high heat, melt remaining butter. Add artichoke hearts, mushrooms, onion, red pepper, garlic, marjoram, thyme, salt and pepper; sauté 3 minutes. Stir in escarole. Cook, covered, 3 minutes, or until escarole wilts.

3. In small glass measure, blend flour with vermouth; stir in milk until smooth. Stir flour mixture into mixture in skillet. Bring to boiling, stirring constantly; cook 1 minute or until thickened, about 1 minute. Remove skillet from heat. Stir in chicken livers and mozzarella. Spoon mixture into prepared pie plate, mounding slightly. Bring ends of noodles up and over filling. Bake 30 minutes, until noodles are golden and filling is bubbly. Let stand 10 minutes before cutting.

Makes 8 servings.

■ Here's a way to get a head start on meals. When cooked chicken is needed for salads, casseroles or other dishes, try poaching the chicken in the microwave: Place skinless pieces in a microwave-safe baking dish and sprinkle chicken with two tablespoons broth or water per piece. Cover baking dish with microwave-safe plastic wrap, and cook four to eight minutes per pound on HIGH, or until juices run clear. Rearrange chicken once or twice during cooking; let stand, covered, for three minutes. In addition to being a real time-saver, this method yields wonderfully succulent chicken.

All-New Chicken Cookbook

Curried Chicken Wings

(pictured, page 67)

**16 large chicken wings (about
  3½ pounds)**
1 tablespoon ground cumin
1 teaspoon salt
1 teaspoon sugar
2 teaspoons soy sauce
1 teaspoon lime juice

Curried Peanut Sauce
1 large red pepper
**1 tablespoon peanut or salad
  oil**
2 tablespoons minced onion
2 tablespoons curry powder
¼ teaspoon ground red pepper
**1½ cups coconut milk (see
  Note)**
**½ cup chunky-style peanut
  butter**
1 tablespoon sugar
**½ teaspoon crushed
  red-pepper flakes**
1 tablespoon lime juice

Salad oil
**2 tablespoons minced cilantro
  (fresh coriander) leaves**
Cucumber spears

1. Remove and discard wing tips. Separate remaining wing sections at joint; trim off excess skin. In medium bowl, combine cumin, salt, sugar, soy sauce and lime juice, stirring to form a paste. Add wings; toss to coat evenly. Set aside.

2. Make peanut sauce: Place pepper on oven rack 6 inches from heat. Broil until blackened on all sides, turning pepper with tongs. With tongs, remove pepper to sink; rinse under cold water until cool enough to handle. Remove blackened skin and stem, the ribs and seeds. Coarsely chop pepper; set aside. In small skillet, heat oil over medium heat until hot. Add onion; sauté until softened, about 1 minute. Add curry powder and ground red pepper; cook 1 minute. Stir in chopped pepper. Set aside. In medium saucepan,

heat coconut milk to boiling. Stir in onion mixture, peanut butter and sugar. Simmer 5 minutes. (Sauce will have curdled appearance.) Pour mixture into blender; process until smooth. Return sauce to saucepan; stir in pepper flakes and lime juice. Heat to simmering; keep warm.

3. In deep-fat fryer, heat 2 inches oil to 375°F. Line baking sheet with paper towels; set aside. Cook chicken wings, one-fourth at a time, until deep golden brown, about 4 minutes. With slotted spoon, transfer wings to prepared sheet to drain.

4. Stir cilantro into sauce; use as dipping sauce for wings and cucumber spears.

Makes 8 to 10 appetizer servings.
Note: Available in Spanish grocery stores. If unavailable, in medium saucepan, heat 4 ounces flaked or shredded coconut with 1½ cups milk until boiling, stirring constantly. Remove from heat; cool to room temperature. Pour into bowl through double-thickness cheesecloth in fine sieve; with back of spoon, press out as much liquid as possible. Discard solids.

Fried Ravioli

(pictured, page 67)

**¾ pound shredded cooked
  boneless chicken**
**1 package (10 ounces) frozen
  chopped spinach, thawed and
  squeezed dry**
**8 ounces shredded mozzarella
  cheese**
3 green onions, chopped
**⅓ cup chopped sun-dried
  tomatoes in oil, drained**
**1 tablespoon salt-free herb
  blend**
¼ teaspoon salt
⅛ teaspoon ground red pepper
1 large egg
1 tablespoon water
14 egg-roll wrappers
Salad oil

1. In medium bowl, combine chicken, spinach, mozzarella, green onions, tomatoes, herb blend, salt and ground red pepper. Set aside.

2. In small cup, with fork, beat egg with water until blended. Set cup aside.

3. On clean surface, place 1 egg-roll wrapper. With small pastry brush, brush some egg mixture around edges of wrapper and across and down center to make a cross marking 4 squares on wrapper. Spoon 1 heaping tablespoon chicken mixture in center of each square; flatten slightly. Place another wrapper on top; seal, pressing wrappers together at egg mixture. Using a pastry wheel with zigzag edges, cut through wrappers along cross marks to make 4 ravioli. Repeat with remaining wrappers and chicken and egg mixtures. Place on baking sheet; wrap with plastic wrap. Ravioli can be prepared to this point and refrigerated up to 24 hours.

4. Preheat oven to 325°F. Line large baking sheet with brown paper or paper towels; set aside. In large skillet, heat ¾ inch oil until hot. Fry ravioli, 3 at a time, until golden on both sides, about 3 minutes, turning once. Remove with slotted spoon to drain on prepared baking sheet. Keep warm in oven while frying remaining ravioli. If desired, serve with hot tomato sauce.

Makes 6 to 8 appetizer servings.

■ Liven up your cooking with the taste of fresh herbs. Fresh ginger, for instance, is more popular—and more available—than ever. It's wonderful on fish and chicken dishes. Buy ginger in the produce section of your supermarket, refrigerate in a paper bag and use within a week. If you need to store the ginger longer, freeze it in a plastic bag; or pare the ginger, and store it in a jar of dry sherry in the refrigerator.

Braised Chicken With Vegetables

(pictured, page 66)

1 can (10¾ ounces) condensed chicken broth
1 cup dry white wine or vermouth
1 tablespoon dillseeds
1 teaspoon dried thyme leaves
3½- to 4-pound broiler-fryer, quartered
1 teaspoon salt
¼ cup salad oil
4 medium red potatoes, halved (1 pound)
1 pound carrots, pared and cut crosswise in half
1 package (16 ounces) frozen whole small onions
1½-pound head cabbage, quartered through core

Horseradish Sauce
3 tablespoons butter or margarine
3 tablespoons all-purpose flour
1 cup milk
¼ teaspoon salt
⅛ teaspoon ground red pepper
⅛ teaspoon coarsely ground black pepper
½ cup drained prepared white horseradish

1. In 12-quart stockpot, combine broth and wine. Put dillseeds and thyme in triple-thick, square cheesecloth; tie with kitchen string. Add to broth mixture. Set aside.

2. Sprinkle chicken with ½ teaspoon salt, dividing evenly. In large skillet, heat oil over medium heat until hot. Add meat, cook until browned. Place in broth mixture; add potatoes, carrots and onions. Bring to boiling; simmer, covered, 15 minutes. Add cabbage and ½ teaspoon salt. Cover; simmer until vegetables are tender-crisp, about 45 minutes. Stir occasionally.

3. Meanwhile, make horseradish sauce: In medium saucepan, over low heat, melt butter. Stir in flour and cook, stirring until bubbling.

Gradually stir in milk until smooth. Remove about 1 cup broth mixture from stockpot; pass through fine sieve into small glass measure. Spoon off fat. Stir ¾ cup defatted broth into sauce mixture until blended; return remaining broth to stockpot. Over medium-high heat, cook sauce mixture, stirring constantly, until boiling. Simmer until thickened, about 1 minute. Stir in salt, ground red pepper, ground black pepper and horseradish.

4. With slotted spoon, remove chicken and vegetables to large platter. Remove and discard herb packet. Pass sauce separately.

Makes 4 servings.

Szechwan Chicken In a Nest

(pictured, page 67)

3-pound broiler-fryer

Marinade
1 teaspoon Szechwan peppercorns
½ cup hoisin sauce
3 tablespoons dark sesame oil
4 teaspoons soy sauce
1 tablespoon grated ginger root
1 medium clove garlic, minced
3 tablespoons water

1 cup jasmine tea leaves
2 tablespoons firmly packed brown sugar
Salad oil
1 package (2 ounces) cellophane noodles (see *Note*)
Green-onion brushes

1. With kitchen string, tie chicken legs together. With poultry pins, secure wings to body. Place in plastic bag; set aside.

2. Make marinade: In small skillet, heat peppercorns over medium heat until hot. Place in mortar; crush with pestle. (Or place in heavy plastic bag; use rolling pin, mallet or

bottom of saucepan to crush.) Place in 1-cup glass measure. Add remaining marinade ingredients; mix well. Pour marinade over chicken in bag. Tie bag to close; squeeze bag to distribute marinade over chicken. Refrigerate 12 hours or overnight, turning chicken occasionally to distribute marinade.

3. Place wire rack in large stockpot with 1½ inches water. Drain chicken, reserving marinade; place chicken in glass pie plate. Place plate on rack. Bring water to boiling. Cover; steam 45 minutes, or until the chicken is cooked. Cool; transfer to clean plate. Pat dry.

4. With aluminum foil, line wok or Dutch oven, extending edges of foil over sides of pan. Place tea leaves in bottom of wok; sprinkle with sugar. Place rack over tea and sugar; place chicken on rack. Cover with large sheet of foil; join foil ends with foil lining wok, sealing ends tightly to form a packet. Cover wok; heat over medium heat to burn tea and brown sugar. Smoke chicken to desired degree of flavor, about 20 minutes.

5. Turn off heat under wok; let chicken stand 10 minutes without opening foil packet. Carefully open foil, averting face from opening to avoid inhaling smoke. Transfer chicken to serving platter; serve hot or cold.

6. To fry noodles to accompany hot chicken, in clean wok or in Dutch oven, heat 2 inches salad oil to 360°F. Place noodles in hot oil, turning them over as they expand and become white. With tongs or chopsticks, remove noodles, breaking apart and returning any uncooked portion to oil. Drain on paper towels; place around chicken on serving platter. Garnish with green-onion brushes.

7. In small saucepan, heat marinade to boiling. Pass separately.

Makes 4 servings.

Note: Available in Oriental grocery stores.

Drumsticks Scampi
(pictured, page 66)

¼ cup butter or margarine
2 medium onions, quartered
1 green pepper, cut into 2-inch
  pieces
⅓ cup chopped Italian parsley
4 medium cloves garlic,
  crushed
½ teaspoon dried basil leaves,
  crushed
1 teaspoon salt
⅛ teaspoon pepper
2 tablespoons lemon juice
8 chicken drumsticks (about
  2½ pounds)
2 tablespoons grated Parmesan
  cheese
4 cups bite-size pieces of
  rinsed assorted greens
¼ cup thinly sliced sun-dried
  tomatoes in oil, drained
2 tablespoons balsamic vinegar

1. Preheat oven to 400°F. Place butter in roasting pan; heat in oven until butter melts. Remove pan from oven; stir in onions, pepper, parsley, garlic, basil, salt, pepper and lemon juice until mixed. Arrange drumsticks in pan around vegetable mixture; sprinkle drumsticks with Parmesan cheese. Bake 30 minutes, or until chicken and vegetables are tender, stirring occasionally.

2. In large bowl, toss greens with tomatoes and vinegar; arrange on serving platter. Top with drumsticks and vegetable mixture.

Makes 4 servings.

Chinese Chicken Legs
(pictured, below)

¾ cup uncooked long-grain
  rice
¾ pound snow peas
1 large red pepper
5 tablespoons salad oil
2 green onions, chopped
1 tablespoon chopped ginger
  root
3 tablespoons dry sherry
1 large egg
¼ teaspoon garlic powder
6 whole chicken legs (about 3
  pounds)
3 tablespoons honey
¼ cup soy sauce
1-pound head Chinese cabbage
2 medium carrots, julienned
1 teaspoon salt
1 can (15 ounces) straw
  mushrooms

1. Cook rice as package label directs. Meanwhile, trim snow peas; chop enough to measure 1 cup. Reserve remainder. Cut pepper into ½-inch-wide strips; chop enough strips to measure 2 tablespoons. Reserve remainder.

2. In medium saucepan, heat 2 tablespoons oil over medium heat. Add chopped snow peas and red pepper, the green onions and ginger root; sauté until tender-crisp, about 5 minutes. Remove skillet from heat; cool slightly. Stir in cooked rice, the sherry, egg and garlic powder.

3. Preheat oven to 400°F. With fingers, carefully loosen skin on each chicken leg to form a pocket. Spoon some stuffing into each pocket, dividing evenly. Place chicken legs in roasting pan. In cup, combine honey with 2 tablespoons soy sauce until blended. Brush chicken with honey mixture, dividing evenly. Bake 50 minutes, or until chicken is tender and golden, basting occasionally with remaining honey mixture.

4. Meanwhile, cut off and discard core from cabbage; cut leaves crosswise into 2-inch pieces. In large skillet or wok, heat 3 tablespoons oil over high heat until hot. Add cabbage, carrots, reserved snow peas and red pepper, remaining soy sauce and the salt. Stir-fry until vegetables are tender-crisp, about 5 minutes. Add mushrooms; heat through. Place cabbage mixture on serving dish; top with chicken legs.

Makes 6 servings.

■ To store purchased chicken, remove plastic wrap; rewrap in waxed or butcher's paper to allow meat to breathe.

Chinese Chicken Legs.

Quick & Easy: Good Breakfasts On the Go

Eye-opener Nog

1 large ripe banana, sliced
1½ cups milk
1 container (8 ounces)
vanilla-flavored yogurt
2 tablespoons light pancake
syrup
1 cup frozen whole and hulled
strawberries

In blender container, blend banana, milk, yogurt and syrup until smooth. With blender running, add frozen berries, one at a time; blend until smooth. Pour into 4 tall glasses, dividing evenly. If desired, garnish each glass with a banana slice and a fresh whole, unhulled strawberry.

Makes 4 servings.

Clockwise from top: Fruit-Topped Waffles, Eye-opener Nog, Dilly Smoked-Salmon Frittata, Brie Shirred Eggs.

Fruit-Topped Waffles

1 package (10 ounces) frozen
   whole-grain waffles (8)
2 tablespoons cornstarch
1½ cups cranberry-apple juice
1 tablespoon butter or
   margarine
2 small Granny Smith apples,
   cored and sliced
⅓ cup raisins
3 tablespoons sugar
¼ teaspoon ground cinnamon
¼ teaspoon vanilla extract
Cooked bacon

1. Heat waffles as package label
directs. Meanwhile, in small cup,
blend cornstarch with ¼ cup juice;
set aside.

2. In 10-inch skillet, melt butter.
Add apples; sauté 3 minutes. Add
raisins, sugar, cinnamon, remaining
juice and the vanilla. Bring to boiling; stir in cornstarch mixture.
Cook, stirring until thickened.
Spoon over waffles; serve waffles
with bacon.

Makes 4 servings.

Dilly Smoked-Salmon Frittata

6 large eggs
1 cup sour cream
¼ cup unsifted all-purpose
   flour
¼ pound smoked salmon, cut
   into ¼-inch-wide strips
1 cup (4 ounces) shredded
   Swedish fontina cheese
3 green onions, chopped
2 tablespoons snipped fresh
   dill
1 tablespoon butter or
   margarine
Additional sour cream
Dill sprig

1. Preheat oven to 375°F. In medium bowl, whisk eggs, sour cream
and flour until blended. Stir in
salmon, cheese, green onions and
fresh dill.

2. In 10-inch skillet with oven-
safe handle, over medium heat, melt
butter. When butter sizzles, add egg
mixture. Bake 20 minutes, until set.
Garnish with additional sour cream
and dill sprig.

Makes 6 to 8 servings.

Brie Shirred Eggs

Nonstick cooking spray
¼ pound Brie cheese, diced
¼ pound boiled ham, diced
2 green onions, minced
4 large eggs
¼ cup heavy cream
Pepper

1. Preheat oven to 400°F. With
cooking spray, grease four 6-ounce
custard cups; place cheese, ham and
onions in cups, dividing evenly.
Break 1 egg into each cup; drizzle 1
tablespoon heavy cream into each.
Sprinkle with pepper.

2. Place custard cups in large
roasting pan; place pan on oven
rack. Fill pan with enough hot water
to come up 1 inch on sides of custard cups. Bake 18 minutes, or until
eggs are set to the desired degree of
doneness. Serve eggs from cups.

Makes 4 servings.

Baked Hash au Gratin

2 tablespoons butter or
   margarine
2 tablespoons salad oil
1 cup coarsely chopped
   onion
1 cup coarsely chopped
   green pepper
¼ teaspoon dried thyme
   leaves
¼ teaspoon pepper
4 cups chopped cooked potato
2 cans (15½-ounce size)
   corned-beef hash
¾ cup beef broth
1 cup grated sharp Cheddar
   cheese

1. Preheat oven to 375°F. Grease
2-quart oval baking dish.

2. Heat butter and oil in medium
skillet; sauté onion and green pepper, stirring, until tender, about 5
minutes. Add thyme and pepper;
mix well.

3. In large bowl, combine onion
mixture, potato, hash and beef
broth; mix well.

4. Turn into baking dish. Spread
evenly, mounding slightly in center.
Bake, uncovered, 30 minutes, or
until browned.

5. Remove from oven. Sprinkle
with grated cheese in crisscross pattern. Return to oven. Bake 5 minutes, or just until cheese is melted.
Serve hot.

Makes 6 servings.

How to Brew a Perfect Cup of Coffee

■ Start with the right blend for
your brewing equipment—a
coarse grind for a percolator, a
fine one for a drip pot.

■ Use fresh, cold water. (Hot tap
water tastes flat and stale.)

■ Measure one to two level tablespoons of coffee for each six-
ounce cup.

■ When brewing is over, remove
the grounds to prevent the coffee
from having a bitter taste.

■ Serve coffee immediately—it
stays fresh for only a half hour.

■ Never reheat coffee—that will
spoil its taste. Instead, the coffee
should be kept warm in a thermal
carafe.

Lite Eating: Oat-bran Entrées—Savory and Slimming

Sesame-Oat Flounder

Nonstick cooking spray
1 cup oat bran
2 tablespoons sesame seeds
1 teaspoon dried thyme
  leaves
¼ teaspoon ground white
  pepper
1 large egg
1 tablespoon lemon juice
6 flounder fillets (4 ounces
  each)

Roasted Red-Pepper
  Mayonnaise
1 jar (7 ounces) roasted red
  peppers, drained
⅓ cup reduced-cholesterol
  mayonnaise
1 tablespoon lemon juice

1. Preheat oven to 425°F. Grease baking sheet with cooking spray. On waxed paper, mix oat bran, sesame seeds, thyme and white pepper. In pie plate, beat egg with lemon juice. Dip each fillet into egg mixture and then oat-bran mixture to coat both sides. Place on baking sheet.

2. Spray tops of fillets with cooking spray. Bake 8 minutes, until fish is cooked and golden.

3. Make mayonnaise: In food processor, blend mayonnaise ingredients until smooth. Serve with fish.

Makes 6 servings, 192 calories each; makes ¾ cup mayonnaise, 26 calories per tablespoon.

Clockwise from top: Mosaic Stuffed Cabbage, Sesame-Oat Flounder, Vegetable Burgers.

Mosaic Stuffed Cabbage

1 tablespoon salad oil
1 large onion, chopped
1 cup diced carrots
¼ cup chopped green
    pepper
¼ cup chopped red
    pepper
1 package (12 ounces)
    frozen hash-brown
    potatoes
1 pound extra-lean ham,
    ground or finely chopped
2 large eggs
½ cup oat bran
2 tablespoons minced
    parsley
½ teaspoon salt
¼ teaspoon pepper
5-pound head green cabbage

1. In large nonstick skillet, heat oil over medium heat. Add onion, carrots and peppers; sauté 5 minutes, until tender. Stir in potatoes; cook 8 minutes, until golden. Transfer to bowl; stir in ham, eggs, oat bran, parsley, salt and pepper.

2. Remove cabbage core, leaving 2½-inch-wide opening. With melon-baller, hollow out cabbage from core end, leaving ½-inch-thick shell of leaves.

3. Place wire rack in 8-quart Dutch oven with ½ inch water. Place cabbage on rack; bring water to boiling. Cover; steam 5 minutes. Line dish with paper towels. Remove cabbage from pan; place on dish. Cool 5 minutes. Stuff cabbage with ham mixture. With small piece of aluminum foil, cover opening; secure to cabbage with kitchen string. Place cabbage, foil side down, on rack in Dutch oven with ½ inch water. Steam, covered, 45 minutes, or until cabbage is tender. Using string lift cabbage onto prepared pie dish. Let stand 15 minutes. Remove string and foil; cut into wedges.

Makes 8 servings, 184 calories each.

Vegetable Burgers

1 package (10 ounces) frozen
    cut green beans
1 package (10 ounces) frozen
    chopped spinach
1 tablespoon reduced-calorie
    margarine
1 onion, finely chopped
1 large clove garlic, crushed
4 ounces feta cheese,
    crumbled
1 large egg
¾ cup fine dry bread
    crumbs
½ cup oat bran
½ teaspoon salt
⅛ teaspoon pepper
Nonstick cooking spray

Tomato Dressing
2 tomatoes, seeded and
    chopped
1 small yellow pepper,
    chopped
1 small cucumber, pared,
    seeded and chopped
2 tablespoons red-wine
    vinegar
¼ teaspoon dried basil
    leaves
¼ teaspoon salt
⅛ teaspoon pepper

1. Preheat oven to 350°F. Cook green beans and spinach as package labels direct. Drain; squeeze dry. Place in food processor; set aside. In large skillet, over medium heat, melt margarine. Add onion and garlic; sauté 5 minutes, or until tender. Add to spinach mixture with cheese and egg. Puree. Transfer to bowl. Stir in bread crumbs, bran, salt and pepper. Let stand 10 minutes.

2. Grease baking sheet with cooking spray. Form spinach mixture into oval patties ½ inch thick. Place on prepared baking sheet. Bake 15 minutes, or until firm and lightly browned.

3. Meanwhile, make dressing: Combine dressing ingredients. Stir until blended. Serve burgers with dressing.

Makes 8 servings, 161 calories each; makes 2 cups dressing, 14 calories per tablespoon.

Tips for Using Oat Bran

■ Stir into cooked cereal or sprinkle on top of cold cereal.

■ Stir some oat bran into your crumb or pastry crusts.

■ Oat bran may be used as a thickener in soups and stews.

■ Sprinkle some oat bran between the layers of your lasagna to soak up extra liquid.

■ Enhance your meatloaf: for every 1 cup bread crumbs, use ½ cup crumbs and ½ cup oat bran.

■ Heat 2 tablespoons reduced-calorie margarine in skillet; add ⅓ cup oat bran and ⅓ cup bread crumbs; sauté until golden. Use as topping for vegetables.

■ Here's a yogurt-cucumber sauce to serve with any oat bran entrée: Place 1 small cucumber, pared, seeded and finely chopped, in medium strainer; sprinkle with ½ teaspoon salt. Let stand 15 minutes; press with back of spoon, and let drain. In medium bowl, combine 1 container (8-ounce size) low-fat plain yogurt, 1 tablespoon of chopped chives or green-onion tops, 1 medium clove of garlic, crushed, and dash of freshly ground pepper; stir in cucumber. Cover with plastic wrap; refrigerate until ready to serve.

Micro-Way: Super Soups, Hot or Cold

Russian Borscht

2 cans (about 14 ounces each)
   beef broth
1½ pounds medium beets
½ teaspoon salt
⅛ teaspoon pepper
1 pound beef chuck, cut into
   ½-inch cubes
1 can (1 pound) whole tomatoes
¼ pound cabbage, thinly
   shredded
1 large carrot, pared and
   julienned
1 medium onion, chopped
2 tablespoons brown sugar
2 cloves garlic, crushed
¼ cup tomato paste
¼ cup cider vinegar
1 cup sour cream
¼ cup fresh snipped dill

1. Add water to beef broth to make 4 cups. In 3-quart glass bowl, combine broth and beets. Cover; vent. Cook on HIGH 20 minutes, or until beets are tender. Remove beets from broth; cool. With paring knife, trim and julienne beets.

2. To broth, add salt and next 10 ingredients. Cover; vent. Cook on HIGH 20 minutes, stirring once. Add beets. Cover; vent. Heat on HIGH 1 minute. Serve hot or cold; garnish with sour cream and dill.

Makes 6 to 8 servings.

■ Store your leftover soup in microwave-safe, single-serving containers. Just reheat—and eat! (Stir several times while cooking to distribute heat evenly.)

Clockwise from left: Pea and Fennel Soup, Brandied Peach Soup, Russian Borscht.

Pea and Fennel Soup

6 slices bacon
½ cup chopped onion
½ small fennel bulb, chopped
   (about ½ cup)
½ teaspoon salt
¼ teaspoon ground white
   pepper
1 cup dry white wine
2 cans (about 14 ounces each)
   chicken broth
1 package (10 ounces) frozen
   peas

1. In 3-quart glass bowl, cook bacon until crisp; remove and crumble. Set aside. Add onion and fennel to bacon drippings. Cover with plastic wrap; vent. Cook on HIGH 5 minutes, stirring once. Add salt, white pepper and wine. Add water to chicken broth to make 4 cups; stir into onion mixture. Cover; vent. Cook on HIGH until boiling, about 6 minutes. Add peas. Cover; vent. Cook on HIGH 8 minutes.

2. With slotted spoon, remove vegetables to food processor or blender. Puree; pour into broth. Cook on HIGH until heated through. Soup may be served hot or cold. Sprinkle with reserved bacon. If desired, garnish with dill.

Makes 8 servings.

Brandied Peach Soup

1 can (29 ounces) peach halves
½ teaspoon ground cinnamon
⅛ teaspoon ground white pepper
1 cup dry or sweet white wine
2 tablespoons cornstarch
½ cup water
½ cup sour cream
1 tablespoon brandy
1 tablespoon lemon juice

1. Drain peaches; reserve 1 cup syrup. Puree peaches in blender or food processor. In 3-quart glass bowl, mix reserved syrup, the peach puree, cinnamon, white pepper and wine. Cover with plastic wrap; vent. Cook on HIGH 4 minutes.

2. In small cup, blend cornstarch with water; whisk into peach mixture. Cover; cook on HIGH until boiling, about 4 minutes, stirring mixture once.

3. In small bowl, whisk sour cream, brandy and lemon juice; whisk into peach mixture. Soup may be served hot or cold. Pour into tureen; if desired, garnish soup with sliced peaches.

Makes 4 servings.

May

Starting here are elegant entrées that are easy to prepare in just minutes. As appealing to the eye as to the palate, all of these main-meal dishes are pictured. Two to try—lamb chops coated with crunchy nuts and beef stroganoff with zucchini and peppers.

Pecan Lamb Chops   Fruited Rice Pilaf

Beef Dijon Stroganoff   Shrimp Scampi Salad

Grilled Citrus Swordfish

Raisin Pork Cutlets

Veal Scallops Romano With Panzanella

Chicken Puttanesca

Zucchini-Noodle Pancake   Ginger Beef

Broiled Salmon With Salsa

Fruited Smoked Pork Chops

20-Minute Cookbook

Simple entrées become sophisticated "fast" foods with quick, new twists on old favorites.

Pecan Lamb Chops

(pictured, page 81)

1 large egg white
1 tablespoon Dijon mustard
⅓ cup finely chopped pecans
¼ cup fine dry bread crumbs
1 small clove garlic, crushed
2 tablespoons salad oil
4 (4 ounces each) loin lamb
  chops, 1 inch thick and
  trimmed
Fruited Rice Pilaf (recipe
  follows)
Hot sugar snap peas, cooked
  with julienned orange peel

1. In shallow bowl, with fork, lightly beat egg white. Add mustard; beat until blended. Set aside. On sheet of waxed paper, combine

---

Page 81: Pecan Lamb Chops, Fruited Rice Pilaf, Beef Dijon Stroganoff.

Pages 82 and 83: (Clockwise from top) Shrimp Scampi Salad, Grilled Citrus Swordfish, Raisin Pork Cutlets, Veal Scallops Romano With Panzanella. (Inset) Fruited Smoked Pork Chops.

Pages 84 and 85: (Clockwise from left) Chicken Puttanesca, Zucchini-Noodle Pancake, Ginger Beef, Broiled Salmon With Salsa.

pecans, bread crumbs and garlic; set mixture aside.

2. In large skillet, heat oil over medium-low heat. Dip each lamb chop in egg-white mixture to coat both sides; drain off excess. Dip in pecan mixture to coat both sides; shake off excess. Place in skillet. Cook until well browned and of desired degree of doneness, about 7 minutes on each side. Serve chops with Fruited Rice Pilaf and sugar snap peas.

Makes 4 servings.

Fruited Rice Pilaf

(pictured, page 81)

1 package (about 4 ounces)
  boil-in-bag rice
1 tablespoon finely chopped
  dried apricots
1 tablespoon butter or
  margarine
1 tablespoon currants
1 tablespoon chopped
  parsley
1 tablespoon golden
  raisins
⅛ teaspoon turmeric

Cook rice as package label directs. In bowl, toss hot rice with remaining ingredients.

Makes 4 servings.

Beef Dijon Stroganoff

(pictured, page 81)

1-pound sirloin steak, slightly
  frozen
2 tablespoons salad oil
1 large onion, cut into wedges
1 small red pepper, cut into
  strips
1 medium zucchini, cut into
  ¼-inch-thick slices
½ teaspoon dried tarragon
  leaves, crushed
1 jar (6 ounces) whole
  mushrooms, drained
½ cup beef broth
2 tablespoons Dijon mustard
1 cup sour cream
Hot cooked spaghetti squash

1. Cut steak across the grain into thin slices. In 12-inch skillet, heat oil over high heat. Add steak; sauté 1 minute. With slotted spoon, remove steak strips; set aside.

2. To drippings in skillet, add onion and pepper; over medium heat, sauté 3 minutes. Add zucchini; sauté 1 minute. Increase heat to medium-high; add tarragon, mushrooms, broth and mustard to skillet. Stir until blended. Reduce heat to low; stir in sour cream. Heat through 1 minute; do not simmer. Serve with spaghetti squash.

Makes 4 to 6 servings.

■ To determine the number of servings per pound of meat, remember: Boneless cuts yield three to four servings per pound; cuts with bone yield two to three servings per pound; cuts with a lot of bone yield one to one and a half servings per pound.

Grilled Citrus Swordfish

(pictured, pages 82 and 83)

Sauce
2 tablespoons salad oil
1 medium onion, chopped
1 small red pepper, chopped
1 jalapeño pepper, seeded and minced
1 tablespoon sugar
1 teaspoon grated lime peel
¾ teaspoon salt
½ teaspoon grated ginger root
¾ cup orange juice
¼ cup lime juice
1 teaspoon cornstarch
1 tablespoon water
1 small orange, peeled and cut into ¾-inch pieces
1 tablespoon minced cilantro (fresh coriander) leaves

4 (8 ounces each) swordfish steaks, ¾ inch thick
Salt
Pepper

1. Make sauce: In medium saucepan, heat oil over medium heat. Add onion, red pepper and jalapeño pepper; sauté 3 minutes, or until vegetables are tender-crisp. Add sugar, lime peel, salt, ginger, orange juice and lime juice; bring to boiling. Simmer, covered, 6 minutes to blend flavors. In custard cup, blend cornstarch with water; stir into sauce with orange pieces and cilantro. Bring to boiling, stirring constantly; cook 1 minute longer or until thickened. Keep warm.

2. Place swordfish steaks on rack in broiler pan; lightly sprinkle each with some salt and pepper. Broil 6 inches from heat, 5 minutes. Turn steaks; broil 4 minutes longer, or until fish is just cooked. Place on platter; top with sauce.

Makes 4 servings.

Raisin Pork Cutlets

(pictured, page 83)

1 large egg
Water
⅓ cup unsifted all-purpose flour
½ teaspoon salt
1 pound pork loin cutlets, ⅛ inch thick
2 tablespoons butter or margarine
⅓ cup raisins
1 chicken-flavored bouillon cube or 1 envelope chicken-flavored bouillon granules
1 tablespoon brown sugar
1 teaspoon julienned lemon peel
½ cup dry vermouth
1 tablespoon lemon juice
1 tablespoon minced parsley

1. In pie plate, with fork, beat egg with 1 tablespoon water until blended. Set aside. On waxed paper, mix flour with salt. Dip 1 cutlet into egg mixture until coated on both sides; drain off excess. Dip in flour mixture until coated on both sides; shake off excess. Place on plate. Repeat with remaining cutlets and egg and flour mixtures.

2. In 12-inch skillet, over medium heat, melt butter. Add cutlets; sauté until cooked through, about 2 minutes on each side. Place on heated serving platter; cover loosely with sheet of aluminum foil.

3. In same skillet, bring ½ cup water, raisins and all remaining ingredients except parsley to boiling, stirring. Simmer, stirring constantly, until liquid in pan is reduced to about ¾ cup. Stir in parsley. Pour sauce over cutlets. If desired, serve with spinach fettuccine and steamed acorn-squash rings.

Makes 4 servings.

Veal Scallops Romano With Panzanella

(pictured, page 82)

2 tablespoons salad oil
8 veal scallops (1 pound)
2 cups sliced mushrooms
1 small zucchini, sliced
½ package (10-ounce size) frozen baby lima beans
1 can (8 ounces) tomato sauce
1 teaspoon grated lemon peel
½ teaspoon salt
¼ teaspoon freshly ground pepper
Shredded Parmesan cheese
Panzanella (recipe follows)

1. In large skillet, heat oil over medium-high heat. Add only enough scallops to pan to fit without crowding; cook on both sides. Remove to heated platter. Repeat with remaining scallops.

2. Add mushrooms and zucchini to skillet; sauté 2 minutes, until tender-crisp. Add lima beans and tomato sauce; bring to boiling. Simmer 1 minute. Stir in lemon peel, salt and pepper. Spoon mixture over scallops; sprinkle with cheese. Serve with Panzanella.

Makes 4 servings.

Panzanella

(pictured, page 82)

4 cups (¾-inch) cubes stale French bread
1½ cups diced tomato
¼ cup toasted pine nuts
¼ cup chopped red onion
1 tablespoon minced parsley
⅓ cup bottled oil-and-vinegar dressing

In large bowl, mix all ingredients. Cover; set aside at room temperature until ready to serve.

Makes 4 servings.

Shrimp Scampi Salad
(pictured, page 82)

8 cups assorted salad greens
1 jar (7 ounces) roasted red peppers, drained and coarsely chopped
2 jars (6-ounce size) marinated artichoke hearts, drained with marinade reserved
1 pound deveined shelled medium shrimp
2 small cloves garlic, crushed
2 tablespoons lemon juice
2 teaspoons Dijon mustard
¼ teaspoon salt
½ teaspoon pepper
2 cups garlic-and-cheese-flavored croutons

1. In large bowl, arrange salad greens. Sprinkle with peppers and artichokes; set aside.
2. In large skillet, heat 6 tablespoons reserved artichoke marinade over medium-high heat. Add shrimp; sauté until pink and just cooked, about 4½ minutes. With slotted spoon, place shrimp on salad greens.
3. To drippings in pan, add garlic, lemon juice and mustard; bring to boiling, stirring. If necessary, boil to reduce liquid to ½ cup. Stir in salt and pepper; pour over greens. Toss to coat. Sprinkle with croutons.
Makes 4 to 6 servings.

Chicken Puttanesca
(pictured, page 84)

2 whole boneless chicken breasts
2 tablespoons salad oil
1 small red onion, thinly sliced
1 can (14½ ounces) Italian-style stewed tomatoes
1 package (10 ounces) frozen Italian green beans
½ cup sliced black olives
2 tablespoons capers
1 tablespoon pesto sauce
1 large clove garlic, crushed
¼ teaspoon crushed red-pepper flakes
Hot cooked pasta

1. Cut chicken into ¾-inch cubes. In large skillet, heat oil over medium heat. Add chicken; sauté until cooked through, about 4 minutes. With slotted spoon, remove chicken to bowl.
2. To drippings in pan, add onion; sauté 1 minute. Add tomatoes; bring to boiling. Stir in next six ingredients. Cover; simmer 2 minutes, or until beans are hot. Stir in chicken; heat through. Serve with pasta.
Makes 4 servings.

Zucchini-Noodle Pancake
(pictured, pages 84 and 85)

1¼ pounds zucchini, coarsely shredded (about 3 cups)
1 cup cooked spaghetti
1 cup (4 ounces) shredded Swiss cheese
¼ cup unsifted all-purpose flour
4 large eggs, lightly beaten
1 small onion, grated
1 teaspoon salt
⅛ teaspoon pepper
1 tablespoon butter or margarine
1 tablespoon salad oil

Tomato Sauce
2 tablespoons salad oil
2 medium cloves garlic, crushed
3 medium tomatoes, chopped
1 green onion, minced
2 tablespoons minced Italian parsley
½ teaspoon dried basil leaves, crushed
½ teaspoon salt
⅛ teaspoon pepper
1 tablespoon red-wine vinegar

2 tablespoons toasted pine nuts

1. In large bowl, combine zucchini with spaghetti, cheese, flour, eggs, onion, salt and pepper. Set mixture aside.

2. In 10-inch nonstick skillet, over medium heat, melt butter in oil. Add zucchini mixture; with spatula, firmly press mixture over bottom and sides of skillet. Cook 6 minutes, or until underside is golden, shaking pan occasionally to keep pancake moving freely.
3. Meanwhile, make sauce: In medium saucepan, heat oil over medium heat. Add garlic; sauté 2 minutes. Stir in tomatoes, green onion, parsley, basil, salt, pepper and vinegar; heat through. Keep warm.
4. When pancake is cooked on bottom, cover skillet handle with aluminum foil. Broil pancake 5 inches from heat, 5 minutes, or until top of pancake is cooked and golden. Sprinkle with pine nuts. Spoon some sauce over pancake; pass remainder. Serve pancake from skillet.
Makes 4 servings.

Ginger Beef
(pictured, page 85)

1 tablespoon cornstarch
3 tablespoons soy sauce
2 tablespoons dry sherry
2 tablespoons bottled chili sauce
1 pound boneless top round beef, ¾ inch thick and slightly frozen
4 tablespoons salad oil
½ pound asparagus, cut into 1-inch pieces
2 celery stalks, cut into 2-inch diagonal pieces
1 large onion, cut crosswise into ¼-inch-thick slices and separated into rings
1 package (10 ounces) frozen baby carrots, thawed
2 tablespoons water
1 teaspoon grated ginger root
1 can (15 ounces) baby corn, drained

1. In small glass measure, mix cornstarch, soy sauce, sherry and

chili sauce until blended. Set mixture aside. Cut beef across the grain into thin slices. Set aside.

2. In wok or 12-inch skillet, heat 2 tablespoons oil over medium-high heat. Add asparagus, celery, onion and carrots; stir-fry 1 minute. Add water; stir-fry 1 minute, or until vegetables are tender-crisp. Remove vegetables to large bowl, and keep warm.

3. In same wok, heat remaining 2 tablespoons oil over medium-high heat. Add ginger; stir-fry 30 seconds, until fragrant. Add beef; stir-fry until cooked through, about 2 minutes. Stir cornstarch mixture to recombine; stir into beef mixture. Stir-fry until sauce thickens. Add asparagus mixture and corn; stir-fry until heated through, about 1 minute. If desired, serve with hot cooked rice.

Makes 4 to 6 servings.

Broiled Salmon With Salsa

(pictured, page 84)

Salad oil
4 (4 to 5 ounces each) fillets
  salmon, skinned
¼ teaspoon ground cumin

Salsa
1 cup coarsely chopped tomato
½ cup diced avocado
½ cup diced papaya
2 tablespoons finely chopped
  red onion
1 tablespoon minced cilantro
  (fresh coriander) leaves
Dash ground red pepper
1 tablespoon lime juice
¼ teaspoon salt
¼ teaspoon pepper
1 tablespoon salad oil

Warm flour tortillas
Sour cream

1. With oil, grease broiler pan. Place salmon fillets in broiler pan. In custard cup, combine cumin and 1 tablespoon oil; brush fillets with oil mixture.

2. In medium bowl, mix salsa ingredients. Set aside.

3. Broil fillets 5 inches from heat, 5 minutes, or just until fillets are cooked. Transfer to warm serving platter; top with salsa. Serve with tortillas and sour cream.

Makes 4 servings.

Fruited Smoked Pork Chops

(pictured, page 83)

2 tablespoons butter or
  margarine
1 medium red cooking apple,
  quartered, cored and sliced
1 large pear, quartered, cored
  and sliced
1 small lime, thinly sliced
1 tablespoon brown sugar
¼ teaspoon salt
6 fully cooked smoked pork
  chops

Couscous With Corn
1½ cups water
1 chicken-flavored bouillon
  cube or 1 envelope
  chicken-flavored bouillon
  granules
¾ teaspoon ground cumin
½ teaspoon salt
3 tablespoons tomato
  paste
2 tablespoons butter or
  margarine
1 cup uncooked couscous
1 can (7 ounces) whole-kernel
  corn, drained

1. In large skillet, over medium heat, melt butter. Add apple, pear and lime; sauté 2 minutes. Stir in brown sugar and salt; cook until bubbly. Remove pan from heat; cover. Keep warm while cooking pork chops.

2. Place pork chops in broiler pan. Broil 6 inches from heat, 10 minutes, turning chops over after 5 minutes.

3. Meanwhile, make couscous: In medium saucepan, over high heat, bring water, bouillon, cumin, salt, tomato paste and butter to boiling. Stir in couscous and corn. Remove pan from heat. Cover; let stand until liquid is absorbed, about 5 minutes. Stir with fork.

4. Place pork chops on warm serving platter; top with fruit mixture. Serve with couscous and, if desired, cooked asparagus.

Makes 6 servings.

■ Confronted with creating a meal in less than 30 minutes? Plan ahead with one of these:

—Confetti Rice: Combine 3 cups cooked rice with 1 cup cubed baked ham, ¼ cup each sliced green onion, sliced celery and chopped red pepper. Stir in ¾ cup mayonnaise and 2 teaspoons each seasoned salt and dried parsley flakes. Chill. Serve an ice cream-scoopful of rice on a fruit-salad plate.

—Buttered Garlic Noodles With Tuna: Combine ¼ cup melted butter or margarine, ½ teaspoon each garlic powder and spiced salt and one 6½-ounce can of tuna, drained. Toss with 8-ounce package of noodles, cooked and drained. Garnish with ¼ cup shredded Cheddar cheese.

—Soup and Sandwiches: Make sandwiches ahead and freeze them. For best results, use day-old bread and spread with butter or margarine to keep sandwiches from becoming soggy. Use meat, poultry, fish, cheese or peanut butter; avoid fresh vegetables, jam, hard-boiled eggs, and salad dressing or mayonnaise. Cured meats will undergo flavor changes during long-term freezing, so prepare and freeze this type only a day ahead.

Elegant Eats: High-Style Toast

Croissant French Toast

2 teaspoons sugar
⅛ teaspoon ground cinnamon
2 large eggs, beaten
¼ cup milk
½ teaspoon vanilla extract
2 croissants
1 tablespoon butter or
margarine

1. In a pie plate, mix sugar and cinnamon; whisk in eggs, milk and vanilla.

2. Cut croissants in half horizontally; place in egg mixture. Let soak a few minutes.

3. In skillet, melt butter over medium-high heat. Add croissants; brown on both sides. Serve immediately; if desired, sprinkle with confectioners' sugar and garnish with fresh strawberries.

Makes 2 servings.

■ Serve a quick Sunday-style breakfast. Gently simmer prunes or dried pears in cranapple juice with a cinnamon stick for about 5 minutes. Add two oranges, peeled and sectioned; cover and cool. Use as a topping on waffles or pancakes.

Croissant French Toast.

Quick & Easy: Sensational Sandwiches That Make a Meal

Clockwise from top left: Chicken and Brie Round, Fried Bologna Roll, Mediterranean Grill.

Chicken and Brie Round

Dressing
½ cup whole-grain Dijon
   mustard
½ cup sour cream
3 tablespoons honey

2 packages (9-ounce size)
   breaded chicken-breast fillets
2 tablespoons salad oil
2 large onions, sliced
1 (12-inch) warm loaf
   sourdough bread, sliced into
   thirds horizontally
½ bunch watercress
½ pound Brie cheese, cut into
   ¼-inch-wide slices

1. Preheat oven to 450°F. In bowl, blend dressing ingredients; set aside. Place chicken fillets on baking sheet; bake 10 minutes, turning once. Meanwhile, heat oil in large skillet over medium heat. Add onions; sauté until golden brown, 10 minutes.

2. On each of bottom two-thirds of bread, layer, in order and dividing evenly, watercress, Brie, chicken, onions and ¼ cup dressing. Stack prepared layers, placing top third bread slice over all. Pass remaining dressing.

Makes 4 to 6 servings.

Fried Bologna Roll

6 hard rolls, split
½ cup prepared sandwich
   spread with pickles
6 ounces bologna, thinly
   sliced
2 tablespoons butter or
   margarine
8 large eggs
½ teaspoon salt
¼ teaspoon pepper
2 tablespoons water
4 ounces Swiss cheese, thinly
   sliced
6 leaves green-leaf lettuce

1. Preheat oven to 300°F. Spread cut sides of each roll with sandwich spread, dividing evenly. Place on baking sheet, cut side up. Heat in oven until warm. Quarter bologna slices; in medium skillet, over medium heat, fry bologna until lightly browned and curled. Place on bottom halves of rolls, dividing evenly. Keep bologna rolls warm in oven.

2. In same skillet, melt butter. In bowl, with fork, beat eggs with salt, pepper and water until blended. Place egg mixture in skillet; cook, stirring occasionally, until eggs are to the desired degree of doneness. Place eggs on bologna on rolls, dividing evenly; top with cheese, lettuce and top halves of rolls.

Makes 6 servings.

Mediterranean Grill

¼ cup mayonnaise
¼ cup grated Parmesan cheese
8 (½-inch-thick) slices Italian
   bread
6 ounces Italian fontina cheese,
   thinly sliced
1 medium tomato, thinly sliced
4 large leaves arugula
½ red onion, thinly sliced
¼ cup pesto
3 tablespoons butter or
   margarine, melted

1. In bowl, blend mayonnaise with Parmesan; spread over one side of each bread slice, dividing evenly. On prepared side of each of 4 bread slices, layer, in order and dividing evenly, half the fontina, all the tomato slices, the arugula, onion, pesto, remaining fontina and remaining bread, prepared side down. Brush top of each with some of half the butter.

2. In large skillet, over medium-low heat, grill sandwiches, buttered side down, until golden brown. Brush top of each with some of the remaining butter; turn sandwiches over. Cook until golden brown and cheese melts.

Makes 4 servings.

Lite Eating: Mother's Day Delights

Lemon Shortbread With Fruit Mélange

Shortbread
¾ cup unsifted all-purpose
  flour
⅓ cup confectioners' sugar
½ teaspoon baking powder
¼ cup low-calorie margarine
2 teaspoons grated lemon peel
1½ teaspoons skim milk
½ teaspoon vanilla extract
Nonstick cooking spray
2 ounces chocolate candy
  melting wafers, melted

Fruit Mélange
1 cup blueberries
2 kiwifruit, pared and sliced
1 navel orange, sectioned
1 Granny Smith apple, cored
½ honeydew melon, rind
  removed
½ pineapple, pared

1. Make shortbread: In food processor, process flour, sugar, baking powder, margarine and lemon peel until crumbly. Add milk and vanilla; process just until dough forms. Press into a disk. Cover; chill 1 hour.

2. Preheat oven to 350°F. With cooking spray, grease 2 baking sheets. On floured surface, roll dough to ⅛-inch thickness; using 1½-inch heart-shape cutter, cut out

Clockwise from left: Raspberry Cloud Cake, Lemon Shortbread With Fruit Mélange, Strawberry Crêpe Gâteau.

dough. Place hearts on baking sheets. Bake until golden, about 5 minutes. Cool on wire rack. Dip one side of each cookie in chocolate. Let stand until chocolate hardens.

3. Make fruit mélange: Place berries and kiwifruit in bowl. Over bowl, halve orange sections; add to fruit. Cut apple, melon and pineapple into chunks; stir into fruit. Serve with shortbread.

Makes about 48 cookies, 21 calories each; makes 10 servings mélange, 53 calories each.

Raspberry Cloud Cake

9-inch angel-food cake

Frosting
4 teaspoons unflavored gelatine
½ cup water
¼ cup sugar
⅔ cup light corn syrup
2 teaspoons vanilla extract
Red food color

1½ cups raspberries
Mint sprigs

1. Cut cake horizontally in half. Place bottom half on serving plate.

2. Make frosting: In top of double boiler, soak gelatine in water 5 minutes. Over hot water, dissolve gelatine and sugar. Pour into large bowl of electric mixer. Add corn syrup and vanilla. At high speed, beat until fluffy; with food color, tint pale pink.

3. In bowl, mix half the frosting with 1 cup berries; spread over cake

on plate. Cover with top of cake. Spread with frosting. Garnish with remaining berries and mint.

Makes 16 servings, 65 calories each.

Strawberry Crêpe Gâteau

2 cups low-fat vanilla yogurt
1 pint strawberries, sliced
4 envelopes artificial sweetener

Crêpes
¾ cup unsifted all-purpose
  flour
1 teaspoon baking powder
½ teaspoon salt
¾ cup skim milk
½ cup egg substitute
¼ cup water
½ teaspoon vanilla extract

1. Line sieve with cheesecloth; set over bowl. Place yogurt in sieve; refrigerate 1 hour. In bowl, toss strawberries with sweetener. Cover; refrigerate.

2. Make crêpes: On waxed paper, mix flour, baking powder and salt. In blender, mix milk, egg substitute, water and vanilla. Add flour mixture; blend until smooth. Heat 6-inch nonstick skillet over medium-high heat. For each crêpe, pour in ¼ cup batter; swirl to coat bottom of pan. Cook until browned on bottom; lightly brown on other side. Cool. On plate, layer crêpes with yogurt and strawberries.

Makes 6 servings, 128 calories each.

Micro-Way: Frozen Vegetables Served With a Flourish

Glazed Vegetables

1 package (20 ounces) frozen
  baby carrots
1 package (10 ounces) frozen
  pearl onions
1 package (8 ounces) frozen
  sugar snap peas, thawed and
  drained
½ cup light-brown sugar
4 teaspoons unsweetened cocoa
  powder
2 teaspoons cornstarch
½ cup frozen orange-pineapple
  juice concentrate, thawed
¼ cup butter or margarine

In glass bowl, cook carrots and
onions, covered, on HIGH 12 minutes, stirring once. Drain. Add peas.
In another glass bowl, mix sugar,
cocoa and cornstarch. Stir in juice.
Add butter. Cook on HIGH 5 minutes, stirring twice, until thickened.
Add to vegetables; heat on HIGH 3
minutes.

Makes 6 to 8 servings.

Creamy Green Beans

4 slices bacon
1 small onion, chopped
2 packages (9-ounce size)
  frozen cut green beans
1 can (10¾ ounces) condensed
  creamy chicken-mushroom
  soup, undiluted
½ cup plain yogurt
1 teaspoon dried chervil leaves

On microwave-safe broiling rack,
cook bacon on HIGH 5 minutes;
crumble. In 1 tablespoon drippings
in 2-quart glass casserole, cook
onion on HIGH 1½ minutes. Add
green beans. Cover; cook on HIGH
12 minutes, stirring once. Mix remaining ingredients; add to green
beans; cook on HIGH 2 minutes.
Top with bacon.

Makes 6 to 8 servings.

Cheesy Broccoli Bake

1 package (1 pound) frozen
  broccoli, carrot, water
  chestnut and red-pepper
  combination
1 tablespoon butter or
  margarine
1 tablespoon all-purpose
  flour
½ teaspoon dried tarragon
  leaves
½ teaspoon salt
⅛ teaspoon pepper
⅔ cup milk
4 ounces cream cheese,
  cubed
1 cup flavored croutons

In glass bowl, mix vegetables and
¼ cup water. Cover; cook on HIGH
12 minutes, stirring once. Drain. In
2-quart glass casserole, melt butter
on HIGH 30 seconds; blend in flour,
tarragon, salt, pepper and milk.
Cook, uncovered, 3 minutes or until
thickened, stirring once; stir in
cheese until melted. Add vegetables.
Cook on HIGH 3 minutes; stir. Top
with croutons.

Makes 4 to 6 servings.

Corn Pudding Pie

3 green peppers, quartered
½ cup yellow cornmeal
1 tablespoon sugar
½ teaspoon salt
⅛ teaspoon pepper
2 cups milk
1 package (10 ounces) frozen
  corn, thawed
½ cup frozen chopped red and
  green peppers, thawed
4 green onions, chopped
½ teaspoon baking powder
4 large eggs, beaten
½ cup butter, melted

Arrange peppers around sides of
9-inch glass pie plate. Cover; cook
on HIGH 6 minutes, rotating dish
once. In glass bowl, mix cornmeal,
sugar, salt, pepper and milk. Cover;
cook on HIGH 6 minutes, until
thickened, stirring once. Add remaining ingredients; cook 6 minutes, stirring once. Pour over
peppers. Cook on MEDIUM 10 minutes, rotating dish twice; cook on
HIGH 5 minutes, rotating dish once.
Let stand 5 minutes. If desired, serve
with salsa.

Makes 6 to 8 servings.

*Clockwise from left: Corn
Pudding Pie, Glazed Vegetables,
Creamy Green Beans, Cheesy
Broccoli Bake.*

June

Summertime and the dining is easy—and alfresco.
Pair Lamb Chops à la Rosemary with
All-American Potato Salad; then top the meal off
with Strawberry-Rhubarb Sorbet. Add these
recipes and others pictured and listed below to
your outdoor menus.

Lamb Chops à la Rosemary

All-American Potato Salad

Strawberry-Rhubarb Sorbet

Zesty Grilled Apricot Brisket

Grilled Squash Aioli   Tortilla Rolls

Spiced Raspberry Shortcake

Outdoor Eating Cookbook

Go beyond backyard burgers and franks and enjoy grilled brisket of beef or tortillas with a colorful trio of fillings.

All-American Potato Salad

(pictured, page 97)

3 pounds new red potatoes, scrubbed

Dressing
1 tablespoon sugar
¾ cup mayonnaise
2 tablespoons light cream
1 tablespoon cider vinegar
2 teaspoons Dijon-style mustard
1 teaspoon salt
⅛ teaspoon pepper

1 celery stalk, thinly sliced
1 small onion, minced
1 small red pepper, cut into ¼-inch-thick strips

1. Cut potatoes in half; in 3 quarts boiling, salted water in Dutch oven, cook potatoes 12 minutes, or until easily pierced with a fork. Drain; place in large bowl of ice and water.

Page 97: Lamb Chops à la Rosemary, All-American Potato Salad, Strawberry-Rhubarb Sorbet.

Pages 98 and 99: (Clockwise from top) Zesty Grilled Apricot Brisket, Grilled Squash Aioli, Spiced Raspberry Shortcake, Tortilla Rolls.

When cool, place in colander; set aside until well drained.

2. In large bowl, combine dressing ingredients. Add potatoes, celery, onion and red pepper; toss gently to coat. Cover with plastic wrap; refrigerate at least 1 hour to blend ingredients.

Makes 8 servings.

Strawberry-Rhubarb Sorbet

(pictured, page 97)

½ cup sugar
½ cup water
5 cups chopped fresh rhubarb
1 pint strawberries
¾ cup unsweetened pink grapefruit juice
2 tablespoons framboise

1. In medium saucepan, bring sugar and water to boiling. Add rhubarb; return to boiling. Reduce heat; cover and simmer 5 minutes, or until rhubarb is soft.

2. Stem strawberries and place in food processor. Add undrained rhubarb and process until pureed. Add grapefruit juice and framboise; process mixture to combine.

3. Pour into 13-by-9-by-2-inch pan. Chill until cold. Freeze until edges are firm; stir. Freeze until solid. Cut into 1-inch pieces. Process in food processor until smooth

and creamy, but still frozen, in batches if necessary. (Do not over-process.) Serve immediately or place in containers and freeze until serving. If frozen, let soften slightly before serving.

Makes 8 to 10 servings.

Lamb Chops à la Rosemary

(pictured, page 97)

Marinade
⅓ cup parsley sprigs
3 medium cloves garlic, peeled
2 anchovy fillets
2 tablespoons rosemary leaves
¾ teaspoon dried thyme leaves
½ teaspoon freshly ground pepper
¼ cup olive oil
2 tablespoons red wine
1 teaspoon Dijon-style mustard
½ teaspoon salt

8 loin lamb chops, 1¼ inches thick (about 7 ounces each), with fat trimmed
2 large red peppers
4 Belgian endive
2 medium zucchini
8 fresh rosemary sprigs
About ½ cup olive oil
½ teaspoon salt
⅛ teaspoon pepper
1 teaspoon lemon juice
1 teaspoon balsamic vinegar

1. Make marinade: In food processor, puree marinade ingredients. On platter, rub marinade over lamb chops. Cover with plastic wrap; refrigerate 1½ hours.

2. Prepare outdoor grill for barbecue. When coals are very hot, using DIRECT METHOD (see page 103), roast peppers 5 inches from heat until blackened on all sides. With tongs, place peppers in heavy plastic bag; tie end of bag. Let peppers stand until cool; peel, seed and quarter.

3. Meanwhile, cut each endive in half lengthwise; cut zucchini crosswise into ½-inch-thick slices. Set vegetables aside.

4. Wrap tail of each chop around outside of chop; wrap a rosemary sprig around outside of each chop. Tie with kitchen string.

5. Grill chops about 4 minutes each side, or until of desired doneness. Grill endive about 2 minutes each side and zucchini about 1 minute each side, or until tender-crisp, brushing vegetables with some oil while grilling. Place lamb chops and vegetables on a warm platter; keep meat and vegetables warm.

6. In food processor, puree red peppers with 3 tablespoons oil, salt, pepper, lemon juice and vinegar. Serve with chops and vegetables.

Makes 4 to 6 servings.

■ For really smoky flavor, barbecue with wood chips. Oak complements most kinds of food. Alder's delicate flavor enhances fish and chicken dishes; mesquite imparts a robust taste.

■ In general, smaller, thicker pieces of meat require longer cooking per pound on a grill than large pieces.

Zesty Grilled Apricot Brisket

(pictured, page 99)

4-pound beef brisket
1 medium onion, quartered
10 whole cloves

Sauce
1 can (1 pound) apricot halves
½ teaspoon curry powder
1 teaspoon salt
¼ teaspoon pepper
1 jar (12 ounces) apricot preserves
2 tablespoons prepared mustard
1 tablespoon cornstarch
⅓ cup sweet vermouth
2 green onions, minced

1. In 8-quart Dutch oven, place brisket, onion, cloves and enough water to cover. Bring to boiling; simmer, covered, 2½ hours, or until tender. Drain brisket; discard onion and cloves. (*Note:* Brisket can be prepared up to this point a day in advance of grilling and refrigerated until grilling time.)

2. Prepare outdoor grill for barbecue. Meanwhile, make sauce: Coarsely chop 7 apricot halves; set aside. Reserve remaining apricot halves. In small saucepan, combine curry powder, salt, pepper, preserves and mustard. In custard cup, mix cornstarch with vermouth; stir into curry mixture. Bring to boiling, stirring constantly; simmer 1 minute, or until clear and thickened. Set mixture aside.

3. Using DIRECT METHOD (see page 103), grill brisket 6 inches from heat, 30 minutes, or until lightly browned, turning occasionally and basting frequently with sauce. During last 5 minutes of cooking, grill reserved apricot halves on both sides until heated

through. Place brisket on serving platter; garnish with apricot halves and, if desired, mâche (lamb's lettuce). Stir chopped apricots and green onions into remaining sauce; heat through. Serve with brisket.

Makes 6 to 8 servings.

Tortilla Rolls

(pictured, page 98)

24 (8-inch) flour tortillas
Guacamole Filling (recipe below)
2 cups shredded lettuce
1 cup prepared salsa
Seafood Medley Filling (recipe on next page)
Bacon and Gazpacho Filling (recipe on next page)
1½ cups (6 ounces) shredded Monterey Jack cheese

On each flour tortilla, spread ⅓ cup of one filling. Sprinkle each portion of Guacamole Filling with ¼ cup shredded lettuce; top with 2 tablespoons salsa. Sprinkle each portion of Bacon and Gazpacho Filling with 3 tablespoons cheese. Roll up tortilla to enclose filling; serve immediately.

Makes 8 servings of each filling.

Guacamole Filling

3 ripe avocados, pared and coarsely mashed
1 small onion, chopped
2 cloves garlic, crushed
½ cup chopped roasted red pepper
1 teaspoon seasoned salt
½ teaspoon seasoned pepper
2 tablespoons lemon juice

In medium bowl, combine all ingredients. Serve within ½ hour.

Makes 2½ cups.

Seafood Medley Filling

½ pound surimi (fish and crab or lobster blend)
½ cup mayonnaise or whipped salad dressing
1 tablespoon lemon juice
1 cup chopped celery
½ cup chopped green pepper
½ cup chopped red pepper
¼ cup snipped fresh dill
¼ cup chopped green onion
2 large hard-cooked eggs, chopped

In medium bowl, mix surimi with mayonnaise and lemon juice until blended. Stir in remaining ingredients. Cover, and refrigerate until serving.
Makes 4 cups.

Bacon and Gazpacho Filling

1 package (1¼ ounces) taco-seasoning mix
¼ cup water
½ pound bacon, cooked until crisp and crumbled
2 medium tomatoes, chopped
1 medium cucumber, chopped
1 small onion, chopped
1 can (4 ounces) chopped green chiles, drained

In medium bowl, combine seasoning mix with water until blended. Add remaining ingredients; stir until blended. Cover; refrigerate until serving.
Makes 3 cups.

■ When cooking on the outdoor grill, keep this in mind: Foods set over the coals in shallow containers will cook faster than those in deep containers. Always remember to stir food in containers often to distribute the heat.

■ Trim meats well to avoid the flare-ups from dripping fat.

Grilled Squash Aioli

(pictured, page 99)

2 medium yellow squash (1 pound)
2 medium zucchini (1 pound)
1 bottle (8 ounces) Italian salad dressing

Aioli
4 anchovy fillets, drained and minced
2 tablespoons sun-dried tomatoes, minced
1 large clove garlic, crushed
½ cup butter, melted
¼ cup olive oil
2 tablespoons lemon juice
1 teaspoon Dijon-style mustard
Dash hot-red-pepper sauce

1 loaf French bread, cut diagonally into ¼-inch-wide slices (about 32)

1. Cut each squash and zucchini in half crosswise; cut each half lengthwise into ¼-inch-thick slices. In large bowl, toss squash and zucchini slices with Italian dressing; marinate vegetables at room temperature 1 hour.
2. Meanwhile, in small bowl, combine aioli ingredients. With small pastry brush, spread some aioli onto one side of each bread slice, dividing evenly; reserve remaining aioli. Set aside prepared bread.
3. Prepare outdoor grill for barbecue. On grill rack, place wire cooling rack so that wires cross at right angles. Place half of each squash, zucchini and bread slices, buttered side down, on grill. Using DIRECT METHOD (see page 103), grill squash, zucchini and bread until squash is tender-crisp and bread is toasted, about 2 minutes, turning once. Place bread, buttered side up, on serving platter; top each bread slice with a grilled slice of squash and zucchini. Repeat with remaining squash, zucchini and bread. Serve with reserved aioli.
Makes 8 to 10 servings.

Spiced Raspberry Shortcake

(pictured, pages 98 and 99)

2 large navel oranges
1 pint raspberries
2 tablespoons sugar
1 tablespoon Grand Marnier or other orange-flavored liqueur

Shortcake
1¾ cups unsifted all-purpose flour
3 tablespoons light-brown sugar
2 teaspoons baking powder
1½ teaspoons five-spice powder (see *Note*)
½ teaspoon baking soda
¼ teaspoon salt
6 tablespoons cold butter
½ cup toasted slivered almonds
¾ cup buttermilk

1 cup heavy cream
½ cup crème fraîche
2 tablespoons confectioners' sugar
2 tablespoons crystallized ginger, minced

1. Remove and discard peel from oranges. Divide into sections; cut sections into 1-inch pieces. Place in medium bowl; add raspberries, sugar and liqueur. Toss to combine; set aside.
2. Preheat oven to 425°F. Grease large baking sheet; set aside. In medium bowl, mix flour with sugar, baking powder, spice powder, baking soda and salt. Cut butter into ¼-inch cubes; add to flour mixture. With pastry blender or 2 knives, cut butter into flour mixture until mixture resembles coarse crumbs. Stir in almonds. With fork, stir in buttermilk just until mixture forms a dough. On lightly floured surface, knead dough twice; pat into a 10-by-4-by-1-inch rectangle. Cut crosswise into 8 equal strips. Place strips on baking sheet. Bake 12 minutes, or

until golden brown. Remove to wire rack to cool.

3. In small bowl of electric mixer, at medium-high speed, beat cream with crème fraîche until thickened. Add sugar; at high speed, beat until stiff peaks form when beaters are raised. Fold in ginger.

4. Split shortcakes in half horizontally. Spread cut side of each bottom half with some cream; top with some fruit mixture, dividing evenly. Cover each with shortcake top; spread each with some whipped-cream mixture. Top with remaining fruit mixture, dividing evenly. Serve dessert immediately.

Makes 8 servings.

Note: Available in Oriental food stores.

Beef Gyro With Grilled Vegetables

Marinade
¾ teaspoon salt
¼ teaspoon pepper
2 tablespoons chopped parsley
1 large clove garlic, crushed
½ cup olive oil
¼ cup lemon juice

2-pound eye-of-round roast
1 pound small new red potatoes
1 pound leeks, trimmed and washed
2 Japanese eggplants
4 Italian plum tomatoes
8 large pita breads
2 packages (5-ounce size) garlic-and-herb-flavored cheese, well chilled
1 head Boston lettuce, washed and patted dry

1. Prepare outdoor grill for barbecue. In small bowl, combine marinade ingredients. Place eye roast on grill 5 inches from heat; brush on all sides with marinade. Using INDIRECT METHOD (see box, right),

cook eye roast, with grill covered, 20 minutes, turning and basting roast after 10 minutes.

2. Meanwhile, with lemon zester, remove a strip from each potato. In 2 inches boiling, salted water in 5-quart Dutch oven, cook potatoes and leeks, covered, 10 minutes. Drain; place potatoes on grill. Brush with marinade; cook 5 minutes. Cut eggplants crosswise into 3-inch lengths. Place leeks and eggplant on grill with eye roast and potatoes. Turn eye roast and potatoes; brush all with marinade. Cook 4 minutes. Turn all ingredients on grill. Cut tomatoes in half lengthwise. Place tomatoes, cut side up, on grill; brush all ingredients on the grill with marinade. Cook tomatoes until hot, about 2 minutes. Cook beef until internal temperature is 140°F for medium-rare, about 35 minutes.

3. While vegetables are cooking, cut pitas in half horizontally. Wrap pitas in aluminum foil; heat on grill until warm.

4. Slice each cheese horizontally into 4 rounds. Thinly slice eye roast; place several slices into each pita with some lettuce and a slice of cheese. Serve sandwiches with grilled vegetables.

Makes 8 servings.

Hummus bi Tahini With Fresh Grilled Vegetables

1 can (15 to 19 ounces) chickpeas (garbanzos)
1 large clove garlic
3 tablespoons tahini (sesame paste)
2 tablespoons lemon juice
½ teaspoon salt
Paprika
Grilled Vegetables (recipe follows)

Drain chickpeas, reserving liquid; set aside. In blender finely chop

garlic and tahini. Add 3 tablespoons chickpea liquid, the lemon juice and salt. Puree until smooth. Add chickpeas; blend until smooth. Put in serving bowl; top with paprika. Use as dip for Grilled Vegetables.

Makes about 2 cups.

Grilled Vegetables

1 medium zucchini
1 medium yellow squash
1 small eggplant
1 green pepper
1 red pepper
Salad oil

Cut zucchini, squash and eggplant into ½-inch-thick slices. Cut peppers into 1-inch-wide lengthwise strips. Brush vegetables on one side with oil; place, oiled side down, in barbecue basket in single layer. Grill just until brown.

Makes 8 servings.

Barbecue Basics

■ DIRECT METHOD (ideal for searing chops, steaks and burgers): Place food over the hottest part of the fire.

■ INDIRECT METHOD (great for grilling ribs, roasts, vegetables and fish): Cover the grill or wrap foods in foil; then place food on grill, away from heat source. (If using a charcoal-type barbecue, arrange briquettes on one side, and cook on the other.)

■ TO USE WOOD CHIPS: With a charcoal-type grill, wait until coals are red-hot and covered with white ash; then spread presoaked chips evenly over the coals. With a gas grill, preheat for at least 10 minutes on high; then sprinkle on wet chips. Start to cook food on grill when the chips begin to smoke.

Quick & Easy: Say "Cheese" For Great Eating

Summer Vegetable Quiche

1 tablespoon butter or
   margarine
1 small onion, chopped
1 small yellow squash
   (4 ounces), sliced
9-inch frozen deep-dish pie
   crust, thawed
1 cup (4 ounces) shredded
   Gruyère or Swiss cheese
4 large eggs
½ teaspoon salt
¼ teaspoon pepper
1 cup half-and-half
2 tablespoons pesto sauce
1 Italian plum tomato, sliced

1. Preheat oven to 375°F. In large skillet, melt butter. Add onion and squash; sauté until tender-crisp, 5 minutes. Set aside.

2. Flute edges of pie crust; place pie plate on baking sheet. Sprinkle cheese over bottom of crust; spoon onion and squash over cheese. Set pie aside.

3. In medium bowl, whisk eggs with salt, pepper, half-and-half and pesto just until mixed, not frothy. Pour mixture into prepared pie crust; arrange tomato slices on top. Bake quiche on lower rack of oven 50 minutes, or until custard is puffy and set in center. Cool on wire rack 10 minutes before serving.

Makes 6 servings.

Sausage-Penne Bake

½ pound hot Italian sausage
2 large eggs
1 cup ricotta cheese
½ teaspoon salt
2 cups (8 ounces) shredded
   smoked mozzarella cheese
½ cup sliced olives
½ cup grated Parmesan cheese
¼ cup chopped parsley
1 teaspoon crushed red-pepper
   flakes
1½ packages (8-ounce size)
   penne pasta, cooked

1. Preheat oven to 400°F. Grease 2-quart baking dish; set aside.

2. Remove sausage from casing. In medium skillet, crumble sausage. Over medium-high heat, sauté sausage until browned; with slotted spoon, remove sausage and drain on paper-towel-lined plate.

3. In large bowl, whisk eggs with ricotta; stir in sausage, salt and remaining ingredients. Spoon into prepared dish. Bake 15 minutes, or until mixture is bubbly and top is lightly browned.

Makes 6 servings.

■ Keep some cheese snacks on hand: Cube 10 ounces Cheddar cheese, 3 ounces cream cheese and ¼ cup butter; place in glass bowl. Soften in microwave on HIGH 5 minutes; mix well. Add 1 teaspoon dried onion flakes; roll into balls. Coat with sesame seeds; store in refrigerator.

Baked Goat-Cheese Salad

8 cups mixed salad greens
1 small red onion, thinly sliced
⅓ cup toasted chopped walnuts
¾ pound goat cheese
½ cup bottled red-wine
   vinaigrette dressing
¼ teaspoon freshly ground
   pepper
1 tablespoon red-wine vinegar
Assorted crackers and
   breadsticks

1. Preheat oven to 350°F. Lightly grease small baking sheet; set aside.

2. In large salad bowl, toss salad greens with onion; set aside. Place nuts on sheet of waxed paper; roll goat cheese in nuts to cover completely. Place cheese on prepared baking sheet; drizzle with 2 tablespoons dressing. Bake 5 minutes, or until heated through.

3. Meanwhile, in small saucepan, combine pepper with remaining dressing and the vinegar; heat over medium heat until hot. Pour dressing over greens mixture; toss. Place cheese in center of salad; serve with crackers and breadsticks.

Makes 6 servings.

Clockwise from top left: Baked Goat-Cheese Salad, Summer Vegetable Quiche, Sausage-Penne Bake.

Lite Eating: Cool Salads for Hot Summer Days

Bean Sprout Toss

Dressing
2 teaspoons sugar
1 tablespoon low-sodium soy sauce
2 teaspoons lemon juice
1 teaspoon grated ginger root
1 teaspoon dark sesame oil
1 tablespoon salad oil

1 bunch watercress
1 cup bean sprouts, rinsed and drained
½ small head iceberg lettuce, torn into pieces
½ medium red pepper, diced
1 tablespoon sesame seeds

1. In small bowl, mix dressing ingredients. Set aside.

2. Remove and discard any roots and coarse stems from watercress. In large bowl, combine watercress with remaining ingredients. Add dressing; toss until coated.

Makes 5 servings, 69 calories each.

Wiltproof Salad

1 pound green beans, trimmed
1 package (9 ounces) frozen artichoke hearts, thawed
1 cup thinly sliced carrots
1 small zucchini, thinly sliced
¼ cup minced parsley
⅓ cup reduced-calorie Italian dressing
1 tablespoon white-wine vinegar
3 tablespoons crumbled feta cheese
¼ teaspoon freshly ground pepper

1. In medium saucepan, in 2 quarts boiling, salted water, cook green beans 2 minutes. Add artichokes; cook 2 minutes, or until green beans are tender-crisp. Drain in colander; rinse with cold water until cool.

2. In large bowl, combine vegetables and parsley. Add dressing and vinegar; toss to coat. Cover; refrigerate overnight. Place salad on platter; sprinkle with cheese and ground pepper.

Makes 6 servings, 94 calories each.

■ Add salad dressings to leafy greens just before serving them so that they won't wilt. And do as the French do: Mix the dressing in the bottom of the salad bowl, cross the serving spoon and fork over it and set the washed and crisped greens on top. Place damp paper towels over the greens; cover with plastic wrap. To serve, toss the salad for perfectly dressed, crisp greens.

Eggplant-Tomato Cups

2 medium eggplants
   (1½ pounds)
4 Italian plum tomatoes, cut
   into ¾-inch pieces
1 medium onion, halved
   lengthwise, thinly sliced
1 medium green pepper, cut
   into strips
1 teaspoon dried oregano
   leaves, crushed
½ teaspoon salt
2 tablespoons olive oil
2 tablespoons red-wine vinegar
6 radicchio leaves

1. Preheat oven to 350°F. Place eggplants in roasting pan; bake 40 minutes, or until tender. Let eggplants stand in large bowl of ice and water until cool.

2. Meanwhile, in large bowl, combine tomatoes, onion, green pepper, oregano, salt, oil and vinegar; toss until mixed. Set aside.

3. When eggplant is cool enough to handle, peel off skin. Cut eggplant into 1-inch pieces; stir into tomato mixture.

4. Place radicchio-leaf "cups" on serving dish; fill each with eggplant mixture, dividing evenly.

Makes 6 servings, 94 calories each.

■ Use extra salad to make this interesting soup the next day: Puree the salad, dressing and all, and add chicken or vegetable broth; chill well. Serve with a dab of yogurt and a sprinkling of chives.

Clockwise from top right: Bean Sprout Toss, Wiltproof Salad, Eggplant-Tomato Cups.

July

Give your backyard cookouts a flavor boost with
deliciously different barbecue fare, such as
fruit-glazed Cornish hens, spinach-filled roulades
and corn on the cob with dill butter. These
dishes and other outdoor specialties
are listed below.

Raspberry-Grilled Cornish Hens

Pinwheels Florentine   Grilled Corn With Dill Butter

Stuffed Grilled Sea Bass   Border Burgers

Sweet-and-Sour Pork Loin   Polynesian Pork Burger

Texas Tummy Dogs   Dilly Citrus Salmon

Stuffed Tomatoes Monterey

Basil-Grilled Bread

Sausage-and-Pepper Kebabs

Confetti Potatoes

Summer Barbecue Cookbook

Savor the flavors of summer with barbecue delights.

Raspberry-Grilled Cornish Hens
(pictured, page 109)

2 Cornish hens (1½ pounds each)
1 pint raspberries
3 large cloves garlic, crushed
2 teaspoons grated lemon peel
¼ teaspoon pepper
½ cup raspberry vinegar
⅓ cup olive oil
¼ teaspoon salt
2 tablespoons honey
1 tablespoon chopped mint
Mint sprigs

1. Split hens; remove and discard backbone. Set hens aside.

Page 109: Raspberry-Grilled Cornish Hens, Pinwheels Florentine, Grilled Corn With Dill Butter.

Pages 110 and 111: (Clockwise from top left) Stuffed Grilled Sea Bass, Border Burgers, Sweet-and-Sour Pork Loin, Polynesian Pork Burger, Texas Tummy Dogs.

Pages 112 and 113: (Clockwise from top right) Dilly Citrus Salmon, Stuffed Tomatoes Monterey, Basil-Grilled Bread, Sausage-and-Pepper Kebabs, Confetti Potatoes.

2. In food processor or blender, puree half the berries. Pass through sieve placed over small bowl; discard seeds. To the puree, add garlic, lemon peel, pepper, raspberry vinegar and oil. Whisk until blended. Set aside 3 tablespoons marinade for sauce; place remaining marinade in large plastic food-storage bag. Add hens to bag. Seal bag; place on dish. Refrigerate 4 to 6 hours, turning hens occasionally to coat.

3. Prepare outdoor grill for barbecue. Drain hens, reserving marinade for basting. Place hens, skin side down, on grill. Using INDIRECT METHOD (see page 103), grill hens 6 inches from medium-hot coals with grill covered, turning and basting frequently, 40 minutes, or until juices run clear when thigh is pierced. Place hens on platter; cover loosely with aluminum foil.

4. In small saucepan, combine reserved 3 tablespoons raspberry marinade with salt and honey. Simmer 1 minute. Remove from heat; gently stir in remaining raspberries and the chopped mint. Garnish hens with mint sprigs; serve with sauce.

Makes 4 servings.

■ The more "crowded" your grill is, the longer your cooking time will be.

Pinwheels Florentine
(pictured, page 109)

Filling
1 package (10 ounces) frozen chopped spinach, thawed and squeezed dry
½ cup butter or margarine, softened
¾ cup chopped parsley
½ cup chopped onion
½ cup chopped Italian plum tomatoes
2 large cloves garlic, crushed
1 tablespoon dark sesame oil
1 tablespoon coarse Dijon-style mustard
½ teaspoon salt
¼ teaspoon pepper

1½ pounds round steak, thinly sliced (about 8 slices)

Marinade
¼ cup soy sauce
1 tablespoon dark sesame oil
2 tablespoons red-wine vinegar

1. In medium bowl, mix filling ingredients. On large sheet of aluminum foil, place 4 steak slices with long edges overlapping slightly; spread half of filling mixture over steak to within ½ inch of edges. Starting from one long side of steak rectangle, using foil to lift steaks, roll up steaks and filling, jelly-roll fashion. Using kitchen string, tie roll at 1-inch intervals. Place roll in glass

baking dish. Repeat with remaining steaks and filling mixture.

2. In small glass measure, mix marinade ingredients; pour marinade over steak rolls. Cover with plastic wrap; let stand at room temperature 1 hour.

3. Prepare outdoor grill for barbecue. Drain steak rolls, reserving marinade. Using DIRECT METHOD (see page 103), grill steak rolls over low coals with grill covered, 20 minutes. Turn rolls; brush with some reserved marinade. Grill 20 minutes longer, basting occasionally with reserved marinade, for medium-rare. Let rolls stand 10 minutes before slicing. Remove string; slice each roll crosswise at 1-inch intervals.

Makes about 8 servings.

Grilled Corn With Dill Butter
(pictured, page 109)

8 ears fresh corn in husks
½ cup butter, at room temperature
1 roasted red pepper, chopped
2 tablespoons snipped fresh dill
½ teaspoon salt
⅛ teaspoon pepper

1. Prepare outdoor grill for barbecue. Peel husks from corn (but do not break them off ears) to within 2 inches of stem. Remove silk; pull husks back up over ears. Soak corn in cold water 20 minutes.

2. Place butter in food processor; process until smooth. Add red pepper; process until smooth. Add dill, salt and pepper; process until blended. Place butter mixture in serving dish.

3. Remove corn from water; shake to remove excess water. Pull husks up over corn; secure with long strip of husk tied at the top of each ear. Using DIRECT METHOD (see page 103), grill corn over hot coals about 20 minutes, turning every 5 minutes, until a kernel pulls away from ear cleanly and easily. Serve with prepared butter.

Makes 8 servings.

Polynesian Pork Burger
(pictured, page 110)

Filling
1 can (8 ounces) pineapple tidbits
1 tablespoon salad oil
1 small red pepper, thinly sliced
1 medium onion, thinly sliced
2 green onions, thinly sliced
¼ cup macadamia nuts, chopped
2 tablespoons chopped water chestnuts

1¼ pounds ground pork
¾ pound ground sirloin
1 tablespoon soy sauce

Glaze
¼ teaspoon ground ginger
¼ cup apricot preserves
¼ cup ketchup

1. Make filling: Drain pineapple, reserving 1 tablespoon juice. Set aside. In medium skillet, heat oil over medium heat until hot; add red pepper and onion. Sauté until onion is tender and slightly browned, about 8 minutes. In medium bowl, combine ¼ cup pineapple, the red-pepper mixture, green onions, macadamia nuts and water chestnuts. Set mixture aside.

2. Prepare outdoor grill for barbecue. In large bowl, combine pork and beef. Add soy sauce; mix lightly. Divide mixture in half; on each of two sheets of waxed paper, shape half the mixture into a 9-inch patty. Top one patty with red-pepper mixture, spreading mixture to within ½ inch of edges. Holding edge of waxed paper on second patty, invert second patty over filling. Remove waxed paper; press patties together at edges. Refrigerate until ready to grill; remove waxed paper before grilling.

3. Make glaze: In small saucepan, combine ginger, preserves, ketchup and reserved pineapple juice. Over low heat, cook until preserves melt. Keep warm.

4. Using DIRECT METHOD (see page 103), cook burger with grill covered, 6 inches from medium-hot coals, 9 minutes. To turn, slide a baking sheet without sides under burger; top with another baking sheet without sides. Invert baking sheets and burger; slide burger onto grill. Cook, basting occasionally with glaze, 9 minutes, or until cooked. Slide burger onto baking sheet; transfer to platter.

5. Stir remaining pineapple into glaze; reheat. Spoon glaze over burger. To serve, cut burger into wedges.

Makes 6 to 8 servings.

■ Here's the way to frost-proof plastic-wrapped frozen foods: Before you seal the plastic bag, insert a drinking straw, holding the bag's opening snugly around the straw, and gently suck as much air as possible out of the bag. Then, remove the straw, and quickly seal the bag—an easy airtight container.

Summer Barbecue Cookbook

Sweet-and-Sour Pork Loin

(pictured, page 111)

Sauce
1 tablespoon salad oil
2 tablespoons minced onion
½ cup sugar
2 tablespoons cornstarch
¾ cup red-wine vinegar
½ cup water
⅓ cup ketchup
¼ cup soy sauce

3-pound boneless pork loin

2½ pounds small new red
   potatoes
1 medium red onion
2 tablespoons olive oil
½ teaspoon garlic powder
½ teaspoon salt
¼ teaspoon pepper

1. Prepare outdoor grill for barbecue. Make sauce: In medium saucepan, heat oil over medium heat. Add onion; sauté until softened, about 2 minutes. Stir in remaining sauce ingredients. Bring to boiling; cook, stirring, 1 minute, or until mixture is clear and thickened. Remove pan from heat; set aside.

2. Using INDIRECT METHOD (see page 103), grill pork 6 inches from medium-low coals with grill covered, 1½ hours, or until meat thermometer inserted in center of roast registers 170°F. Turn meat occasionally and brush with sauce during last 30 minutes of cooking time; use disposable aluminum-foil drip pan under grill rack directly under pork roast.

3. Meanwhile, halve potatoes; cut onion into wedges. Place vegetables in a single layer on double thickness of heavy-duty foil large enough to fold over vegetables. Sprinkle vegetables with olive oil, garlic powder, salt and pepper. Seal edges of foil together over vegetables. Place foil packet on grill rack next to pork. Cook 30 minutes, or until vegetables are tender, turning foil packet occasionally. Serve vegetables with pork; pass sauce.

Makes 6 servings.

Border Burgers

(pictured, page 111)

2 pounds ground sirloin
¾ cup (3 ounces) shredded
   Cheddar cheese
¾ cup (3 ounces) shredded
   Monterey Jack cheese
1 can (4 ounces) chopped mild
   green chiles
1 teaspoon ground cumin
¼ teaspoon pepper
¼ teaspoon salt
1 can (15 ounces) pinto beans
   in chili sauce
6 hard rolls, split
Lettuce leaves, washed and
   patted dry
1 small red onion, chopped
1 ripe avocado, pared, sliced

1. Prepare outdoor grill for barbecue. In large bowl, combine sirloin, ¼ cup Cheddar cheese, ¼ cup Monterey Jack cheese, the chiles, cumin, pepper and salt. Shape mixture into 6 (4-by-½-inch) patties, dividing evenly. Set aside.

2. Drain beans, reserving 2 tablespoons liquid. Place beans and reserved liquid in small saucepan. Heat until hot; keep warm.

3. Using DIRECT METHOD (see page 103), grill burgers 4 inches over hot coals, 6 minutes each side for medium-rare. Grill rolls, cut side down, until toasted, about 1 minute. Place one lettuce leaf on each roll; top each with one burger. Top burgers with beans, remaining cheeses, the onion and avocado, dividing evenly.

Makes 6 servings.

Texas Tummy Dogs

(pictured, page 110)

8 thick slices bacon
8 all-beef frankfurters
4 ounces Monterey Jack cheese
¼ cup butter or margarine,
   melted
¼ cup Dijon-style mustard
8 hot dog rolls
1 small onion, thinly sliced
   crosswise
1 can (4 ounces) chopped mild
   green chiles, drained

1. Prepare outdoor grill for barbecue. In large skillet, over medium heat, sauté bacon 3 minutes, or until halfway cooked. Set aside.

2. Split frankfurters lengthwise, cutting halfway through along center of each. Cut cheese into 8 long strips; place a strip of cheese into slit in each frankfurter. Wrap a bacon slice around each prepared frankfurter; secure with wooden picks.

3. Using DIRECT METHOD (see page 103), grill frankfurters, with cheese side to one side, 6 inches from medium-low coals until hot, about 5 minutes.

4. Meanwhile, in small bowl, blend melted butter with mustard. Cut hot dog rolls in half lengthwise almost completely through. Brush some of the mixture over cut side of each roll; reserve remainder.

5. Turn each frankfurter to cook other side; grill 3 minutes, or until cheese melts. Place rolls, cut side down, next to frankfurters; grill until lightly toasted. Remove wooden picks from frankfurters; place each frankfurter on a roll.

6. Separate onion slices into rings. Serve onions and chiles with frankfurters. Pass remaining butter-mustard sauce.

Makes 8 servings.

■ To wrap food to grill, place in center of aluminum-foil sheet large enough so that you can bring foil edges together and fold them over several times before reaching the surface of food. Join side edges, folding over several times for an airtight package.

Stuffed Grilled Sea Bass

(pictured, page 110)

Stuffing
¼ pound pancetta, diced
½ pound mushrooms, sliced
1 medium onion, chopped
½ small head bok choy
 (6 ounces)
1 small red pepper, julienned
1 small yellow pepper,
 julienned
¼ teaspoon freshly ground
 pepper
¼ teaspoon salt
¼ cup fresh lemon juice
2 tablespoons soy sauce

2- to 3-pound sea bass, dressed
 and scaled with head and tail
 intact
Salad oil
Lemon wedges

1. Make stuffing: In large skillet, over medium heat, sauté pancetta until browned. Add mushrooms and onion; sauté 5 minutes, or until tender. Stir in bok choy and peppers. Cover; steam 4 minutes, or until vegetables are tender. Stir in ground pepper, salt, 3 tablespoons lemon juice and soy sauce; set aside.

2. Prepare outdoor grill for barbecue. Rinse fish under cold water; pat dry. With small sharp knife, without cutting skin, cut fish cavity to extend toward tail. Sprinkle inside cavity with remaining 1 tablespoon lemon juice; fill with stuffing mixture. (Place any remaining mixture in disposable aluminum-foil pan; cover tightly with sheet of aluminum foil. Cook alongside fish during last 20 minutes of cooking.) With poultry pins and kitchen string, close fish cavity.

3. With oil, grease hinged fish-grilling rack; brush fish with oil. Place fish in rack. Using INDIRECT METHOD (see page 103), cook fish with grill covered, 30 minutes. Turn fish in rack; cook, covered, 20 minutes longer, or until fish is cooked

and stuffing is hot. If desired, garnish with lemon-peel twist. Serve immediately with extra stuffing; pass lemon wedges.

Makes 4 servings.

Stuffed Tomatoes Monterey

(pictured, page 113)

3 small zucchini
Salad oil
¾ cup uncooked small
 bow-tie pasta
1½ cups (6 ounces)
 shredded Monterey Jack
 cheese
¼ cup chopped fresh
 basil leaves
¼ teaspoon pepper
¼ teaspoon salt
6 large tomatoes

1. Preheat grill for outdoor barbecue. Thinly slice zucchini lengthwise; brush one side of each slice of zucchini with salad oil. Using DIRECT METHOD (see page 103), cook zucchini, oiled side down, with grill covered, 2 minutes, or until lightly grilled. Brush zucchini with oil; turn zucchini over and lightly grill other side. Transfer zucchini to cutting board; coarsely chop. Set zucchini aside.

2. In 2-quart saucepan, bring 1½ quarts salted water to boiling. Add pasta; cook 8 minutes, or until al dente. Drain. In medium bowl, combine pasta, zucchini, cheese, basil, pepper and salt. Set aside.

3. Cut off blossom end of tomatoes. With spoon, remove and discard seeds and pulp from centers of tomatoes. Fill tomatoes with pasta-zucchini mixture, dividing evenly. Using INDIRECT METHOD (see page 103), cook stuffed tomatoes with grill covered, 30 minutes, or until cheese melts and tomatoes are heated through.

Makes 6 servings.

Dilly Citrus Salmon

(pictured, page 113)

Dill Butter
¼ cup unsalted butter,
 softened
1 tablespoon snipped fresh
 dill
½ teaspoon lemon juice
½ teaspoon prepared mustard
⅛ teaspoon hot-red-pepper
 sauce

2-pound salmon fillet, about
 1½ inches thick at thickest
 part
1 tablespoon olive oil
1 bunch fresh dill, rinsed and
 dried
1 small lemon, thinly sliced
1 small lime, thinly sliced
1 small onion, thinly sliced
Pepper
Salt

1. Make dill butter: In small bowl, mix ingredients until blended. Spoon butter mixture into pastry bag fitted with rosette tip; pipe butter rosettes onto sheet of waxed paper. Refrigerate rosettes until serving.

2. Prepare outdoor grill for barbecue. Rinse salmon with cold water; pat dry with paper towels. Arrange grill rack 6 inches from coals; brush rack and both sides of salmon with oil. Place dill on grill; top with salmon, skin side down. Arrange lemon, lime and onion slices over salmon. Using DIRECT METHOD (see page 103), cook fish with grill covered, 25 minutes, or just until fish is cooked and meat thermometer inserted in thickest portion of fish registers 120°F. (Do not turn fish.)

3. With wide spatula, transfer fish to platter. Sprinkle lightly with pepper and salt; serve with dill butter rosettes.

Makes 4 servings.

Summer Barbecue Cookbook

Confetti Potatoes
(pictured, page 112)

4 large baking potatoes, baked and cooled
¼ teaspoon pepper
¼ teaspoon salt
1 cup sour cream
½ pound bacon, cooked until crisp and crumbled
1 cup (4 ounces) shredded Cheddar cheese
3 green onions, chopped
1 can (4 ounces) chopped pimiento, drained

1. Prepare outdoor grill for barbecue. Make an *X* in one rounded side of each potato; peel back skin from cut. With spoon, remove insides to large bowl, leaving a ¼-inch-thick shell.

2. To cooked potatoes in bowl, add pepper, salt and sour cream. With potato masher, beat mixture until smooth. Stir in remaining ingredients. Spoon mixture into potato shells, piling mixture slightly.

3. Using INDIRECT METHOD (see page 103), cook potatoes with grill covered, 45 minutes, or until cheese melts and potatoes are heated through. Serve immediately.
Makes 4 servings.

Basil-Grilled Bread
(pictured, page 113)

1 medium clove garlic
½ cup unsalted butter or margarine
2 tablespoons sun-dried tomatoes
1 cup (4 ounces) shredded Provolone cheese
¼ cup chopped fresh basil leaves
1 loaf (1 pound) Italian bread

1. Prepare outdoor grill for barbecue. In food processor, mince garlic. Add butter and tomatoes; process until smooth. Transfer to bowl; stir in cheese and basil.

2. With serrated knife, slice bread diagonally almost all the way through 12 times, at 1½-inch intervals. Spread 1 rounded tablespoonful butter mixture between sections, using half of butter mixture. Turn loaf so that ends are reversed; slice loaf diagonally almost all the way through 12 times, making diamond patterns of 1½-inch sections of bread. Spread with remaining butter mixture.

3. Wrap bread with heavy-duty aluminum foil. Place loaf, top side up, 5 to 6 inches from medium coals. Using INDIRECT METHOD (see page 103), heat bread with grill covered, 8 minutes, or until loaf is heated through.
Makes 6 servings.

Luscious Barbecue Ribs

5 pounds spare ribs

Sauce
2 tablespoons butter or margarine
1 small onion, minced
⅓ cup firmly packed light-brown sugar
2 tablespoons dry mustard
1 large clove garlic, crushed
¼ teaspoon pepper
½ teaspoon salt
¾ cup ketchup
½ cup cider vinegar
2 tablespoons lemon juice
1 tablespoon Worcestershire sauce
4 drops hot-red-pepper sauce

1½ teaspoons paprika
½ teaspoon chili powder
½ teaspoon pepper
¼ teaspoon ground cumin
¼ teaspoon ground red pepper
¼ teaspoon salt

1. In 6-quart Dutch oven, cover ribs with water. Bring to boiling. Cover; simmer 45 minutes, or until ribs are tender.

2. Meanwhile, make sauce: In small saucepan, over medium heat, melt butter. Add onion; sauté 3 minutes, or until soft. Stir in remaining sauce ingredients until blended. Bring to boiling; simmer, stirring occasionally, 25 minutes.

3. Prepare outdoor grill for barbecue. Drain ribs; place on jelly-roll pan. In small bowl, mix remaining ingredients. Sprinkle mixture over both sides of ribs, rubbing in mixture to coat evenly. Using DIRECT METHOD (see page 103), cook ribs 6 inches from medium-hot coals 5 minutes, or until ribs begin to brown. Brush ribs with some sauce; cook ribs on other side 5 minutes, or until browned and heated through. Cut ribs into 2-rib pieces; serve with remaining sauce.
Makes 4 servings.

Sausage-and-Pepper Kebabs
(pictured, page 112)

Marinade
½ teaspoon salt
1 cup bottled smoke-flavored barbecue sauce
⅓ cup salad oil
¼ cup water
3 tablespoons cider vinegar
Dash hot-red-pepper sauce

1 pound bratwurst
1 pound kielbasa
1 pound knackwurst
1 large green pepper
1 large orange pepper
1 large red pepper
1 large yellow pepper
2 bunches green onions

1. In medium bowl, mix marinade ingredients. Set aside.

2. In 4 cups boiling water in medium saucepan, cook bratwurst 5 minutes. Drain; cool slightly.

3. Cut all sausages into 1½-inch lengths. Set aside. Halve peppers; remove and discard stems and seeds. Quarter each pepper half lengthwise; cut each piece crosswise. Set aside. Trim onions; cut into 3-inch lengths.

4. On each of 10 (12-inch) metal skewers, using photograph as a guide, arrange sausages, peppers and green onions. Place kebabs in large baking dish; pour marinade over kebabs. Cover with plastic wrap; refrigerate several hours or overnight.

5. Prepare outdoor grill for barbecue. Drain kebabs, reserving marinade. Using DIRECT METHOD (see page 103), cook kebabs with grill covered, 10 minutes over low coals. With potholders, turn kebabs; brush with reserved marinade. Cook with grill covered, 8 minutes longer, or until peppers are tender-crisp.

Makes 10 servings.

Mesquite-Smoked Bluefish

3 handfuls mesquite chunks
Salad oil
½ cup mayonnaise
1½ tablespoons rosemary
    leaves
½ teaspoon salt
⅛ teaspoon pepper
2 tablespoons lemon juice
5 fillets (8 ounces each)
    bluefish
1 large onion, cut into ¼-inch
    thick slices
5 strips bacon
5 sprigs rosemary

1. Prepare grill for outdoor barbecue. Wrap mesquite in double thickness of aluminum foil to form a packet; punch 5 or 6 large holes in top of packet. Place packet on hot coals. With oil, grease inside of hinged wire grill rack.

2. In small bowl, whisk mayonnaise with rosemary, salt, pepper and lemon juice until blended. Lightly brush both sides of fillets and onion slices with all but 3 tablespoons mixture. Place fillets, skin side up, in single layer on grill rack; top each with onion, bacon and rosemary sprigs, dividing evenly.

3. Bring both sides of grill rack together to enclose fish; place hinged rack on grill rack set 4 inches from coals. Cover grill; cook fish 6 minutes, or until fish is cooked only on side nearest coals. Turn fish in hinged rack; cover grill. Cook fish 6 minutes longer, or until done. Remove fish to serving platter; drizzle with reserved mayonnaise mixture.

Makes 5 servings.

Lime-Grilled Flank Steak

Marinade
½ cup lime juice
¼ cup salad oil
2 medium cloves garlic,
    crushed
2 teaspoons grated ginger root
¼ teaspoon pepper
2 tablespoons honey
2 tablespoons dry sherry
2 teaspoons soy sauce

2-pound flank steak
2 mangoes, firm but ripe
2 tablespoons salad oil
1 red pepper, coarsely chopped
1 lime, thinly sliced
1 tablespoon chopped cilantro
    (fresh coriander) leaves
⅛ teaspoon salt
8 large green onions

1. In medium bowl, combine marinade ingredients. Reserve 1 tablespoon mixture; place remainder in glass baking dish. Add steak; turn to coat. Cover with plastic wrap; marinate in refrigerator 4 to 6 hours, turning steak occasionally.

2. Prepare grill for outdoor barbecue. Pare mangoes. Cut one lengthwise into quarters; coarsely chop remaining mangoes. In large skillet, heat 1 tablespoon oil over medium heat until hot. Add red pepper; sauté until tender-crisp, about 3 minutes. Add chopped mangoes, the lime, cilantro, salt and reserved marinade. Heat, stirring, until hot, about 2 minutes. Set aside.

3. Drain steak, reserving marinade; place on grill 4 inches from hot coals. Cook 10 minutes, basting occasionally with reserved marinade. Turn meat; cook 10 minutes on other side for medium-rare, basting occasionally with marinade.

4. Meanwhile, trim green onions; brush with remaining oil. Place on grill with steak during last 4 minutes of cooking time, turning green onions after 2 minutes. Place mango slices on grill during last 2 minutes of grilling steak and onions, turning slices after 1 minute.

5. To serve, reheat pepper-mango mixture. Transfer steak, green onions and mango slices to cutting board; thinly slice steak across the grain on the diagonal. Serve with pepper-mango mixture, the green onions and mango slices.

Makes 4 to 8 servings.

Great Grilling Tips

■ Arrange standard briquettes in a pyramid, and ignite with starter. Allow 25 to 30 minutes for charcoal to heat. When briquettes are ash-gray by daylight or glowing red by night, they're ready for you to begin cooking.

■ Reduce the temperature by raising the grid, spreading the charcoal out and, in a covered cooker, closing the vents halfway.

■ Raise the temperature by lowering the grid, bringing briquettes closer together and opening the vents.

Quick & Easy: Picnic Salad Pack-alongs

Tricolor Tortellini Salad

2 packages (10-ounce size) tricolor tortellini

Dressing
¼ cup fresh basil leaves
2 green onions, cut into 2-inch lengths
2 tablespoons parsley sprigs
1 tablespoon snipped fresh dill
½ teaspoon salt
¼ teaspoon pepper
½ cup olive oil
¼ cup champagne vinegar

2 medium tomatoes, chopped
8 ounces feta cheese
½ cup sliced black olives

1. Cook tortellini as package label directs. Drain; set aside to cool.

2. Meanwhile, make dressing: In food processor, chop basil, onions, parsley and dill; add salt and pepper. In small glass measure, combine oil and vinegar; with motor running, pour in oil-vinegar mixture. Process dressing until ingredients are blended.

3. In large bowl, toss tortellini with dressing, tomatoes, cheese and olives. Cover with plastic wrap; refrigerate until serving time. If desired, serve in bowl lined with lettuce leaves.

Makes 8 servings.

Hawaiian Turkey Salad

1 package (1 pound) frozen broccoli, cauliflower and red-pepper combination
⅛ teaspoon pepper
⅓ cup mayonnaise or whipped salad dressing
⅓ cup sour cream
2 tablespoons cider vinegar
⅓ cup bottled chutney, chopped
2 cups seedless green and red grapes
1 package (1 pound) cooked boneless turkey breast, cut into ½-inch cubes
1 can (8 ounces) pineapple chunks, drained
½ cup chopped toasted macadamia nuts

1. Cook vegetable combination as package label directs. Drain; rinse with cold water. Set aside.

2. In large bowl, mix pepper, mayonnaise, sour cream and vinegar until blended. Add chutney, vegetables and remaining ingredients; toss until coated. If desired, serve in bowl lined with lettuce leaves.

Makes 6 to 8 servings.

Clockwise from top left: Hawaiian Turkey Salad, Tricolor Tortellini Salad, Gazpacho Salad.

Quick & Easy

Gazpacho Salad

Dressing
1 large clove garlic, crushed
1 can (6 ounces) vegetable
juice
¼ cup olive oil
2 tablespoons red-wine vinegar
⅛ to ¼ teaspoon hot-red-
pepper sauce

4 ripe tomatoes, cut into
wedges
1½ cups seasoned croutons
1 can (6 ounces) extra-large
pitted black olives, drained
1 large green pepper, cut into
large dice
1 medium cucumber, scored
and thinly sliced crosswise
1 small red onion, cut into
wedges

1. In small bowl, whisk dressing ingredients until blended. Set aside.

2. In shallow serving dish, using photograph as a guide, arrange remaining ingredients. Pass dressing separately.

Makes 6 to 8 servings.

■ Fruit salads are good first courses, side dishes and desserts. Because most fruits are sweet enough without extra sugar added, they are ideal to serve to dieting guests. For more sweetness, though, honey, syrup and preserves can be added. And a small amount of fruit-flavored liqueur, rum, brandy or a simple sugar syrup infused with flavor from vanilla beans adds a sophisticated touch to a mélange of favorite seasonal fruits.

Lite Eating: Bread Winners—Great for The Grill

Green-Onion Tortillas

6 flour tortillas, halved
2 small red peppers, quartered and seeded
2 cans (4-ounce size) chopped mild green chiles, drained
3 tablespoons chopped cilantro
½ teaspoon salt
⅛ teaspoon pepper
⅓ cup fresh lime juice
2 tablespoons olive oil
24 large green onions
½ teaspoon coarse (kosher) salt

1. Prepare outdoor grill for barbecue. Wrap tortillas in sheet of heavy-duty aluminum foil; using INDIRECT METHOD (see page 103), heat until warm. Meanwhile, using DIRECT METHOD (see page 103), roast peppers, skin side down, until blackened. Transfer to plastic bag; seal. Let peppers cool; remove skins.

2. Chop peppers; in bowl, toss peppers with chiles, cilantro, salt, pepper, 3 tablespoons lime juice and 1 tablespoon oil.

3. Brush onions with remaining 1 tablespoon oil; using DIRECT METHOD, grill 2 minutes on each side. Remove to platter; sprinkle with coarse salt and remaining 2⅓ tablespoons lime juice. Wrap each tortilla half around 2 onions; arrange on platter. Spoon pepper mixture over tortillas.

Makes 12 servings, 109 calories each.

Mini Greek Pizzas

1 large eggplant, trimmed
Salt
1 large tomato, seeded and diced
1 jar (4 ounces) marinated mushrooms
10 black olives, sliced
2 tablespoons chopped parsley
½ teaspoon dried oregano leaves
½ teaspoon freshly ground pepper
¼ teaspoon salt
6 small pita breads
Salad oil
½ small red onion, sliced
6 ounces goat cheese, crumbled

1. Slice eggplant crosswise into 24 slices; sprinkle each slice lightly on both sides with salt. Place on paper towels to drain.

2. Place tomato in bowl; add liquid from mushrooms. Chop mushrooms; add to tomato with olives, parsley, oregano, pepper and salt.

3. Prepare outdoor grill for barbecue. Halve pitas to make 12 rounds; using DIRECT METHOD (see page 103), toast on cut side.

4. With paper towels, pat eggplant slices dry. Brush grill rack with oil; using DIRECT METHOD, grill slices 1 minute on each side. Place 2 slices on each pita half. Spoon tomato mixture on each; top with onion, then cheese. Transfer pizzas to grill. Heat through with grill covered, about 2 minutes.

Makes 12 servings, 114 calories each.

Gingerbread-Fruit Kebabs

1 package (14 ounces) gingerbread mix
⅓ cup bottled chutney
1 can (6 ounces) pineapple juice
1 small pineapple, pared and cored
3 large kiwifruit, pared
24 whole unhulled strawberries

1. Prepare gingerbread according to package directions; cool. Cut into 36 equal pieces.

2. Prepare outdoor grill for barbecue. Chop chutney; mix with pineapple juice.

3. Quarter pineapple lengthwise; cut each quarter crosswise into 8 pieces. Quarter kiwifruit lengthwise. On 12 skewers, arrange fruit and gingerbread. Brush with some chutney. Using DIRECT METHOD (see page 103), heat 3 minutes on each side, or until toasted. Pass chutney.

Makes 12 servings, 212 calories each.

Clockwise from top left: Green-Onion Tortillas, Mini Greek Pizzas, Gingerbread-Fruit Kebabs.

August

One of the singular pleasures of summer dining is enjoying fresh-picked vegetables in a variety of tempting dishes. The colorful salad shown here is served with a tangy vinaigrette and crisp bread. Others too, listed below and pictured, capture the best of the season.

Cobb Salad   Dill Chapatis

Vegetables Vinaigrette   No-Noodle Lasagna

Carrot Muffins Macadamia

Mediterranean Mahimahi

Potato-Mussel Salad   Sausage Pronto

BLT Soup   Walnut Bread

Cheesy Veggie Fondue

Fresh-from-the-Garden Cookbook

Enjoy the versatility of vegetables in everything from soup and bread to entrées and side dishes.

Cobb Salad
(pictured, page 125)

1 head Bibb lettuce, washed
and crisped
1 head romaine lettuce, washed
and crisped
¼ pound bacon, cooked and
crumbled
1 pound boneless chicken
breasts, cooked and diced
(2 cups)
½ small bunch watercress
1 medium avocado, diced
½ cup sliced radishes
4 hard-cooked large eggs,
quartered lengthwise
1½ cups cooked peas
2 medium tomatoes, diced
2 ounces blue cheese,
crumbled

Page 125: (From front) Cobb Salad, Dill Chapatis.

Pages 126 and 127: (Counterclockwise from top) Vegetables Vinaigrette, No-Noodle Lasagna, Carrot Muffins Macadamia, Mediterranean Mahimahi.

Pages 128 and 129: (Clockwise from top left) Potato-Mussel Salad, Sausage Pronto, BLT Soup, Walnut Bread, Cheesy Veggie Fondue.

Special Vinaigrette
½ teaspoon salt
⅛ teaspoon pepper
1 teaspoon sugar
1 teaspoon dry mustard
1 medium clove garlic
⅓ cup red-wine vinegar
2 tablespoons balsamic vinegar
½ teaspoon Worcestershire
sauce
1 cup olive oil

Dill Chapatis (recipe follows)

1. On large platter, arrange lettuce leaves. Using photograph as a guide, arrange bacon, chicken, watercress, avocado, radishes, eggs, peas, tomatoes and cheese over lettuce. Cover with plastic wrap; refrigerate until serving.

2. Make special vinaigrette: In blender, mix all vinaigrette ingredients except oil. With blender running, gradually add oil in a thin stream until dressing is blended and slightly thickened. Pour into sauceboat; set aside.

3. Just before serving, drizzle ½ cup dressing over salad; toss lightly. Pass remaining dressing. Serve with Dill Chapatis.

Makes 6 to 8 servings.

Dill Chapatis
(pictured, page 125)

¼ cup butter or margarine,
melted
2 tablespoons snipped fresh
dill
1 cup unsifted all-purpose flour
½ teaspoon salt
⅓ to ½ cup water

1. In small bowl, mix butter and dill. Set aside.

2. In medium bowl, mix flour with salt. Gradually stir in water until soft dough forms. Turn dough out onto lightly floured surface; knead until dough is very pliable. Cover with damp kitchen towel; let stand 20 minutes.

3. Grease small skillet; set aside. For each chapati, break off a walnut-size piece of dough; flatten between fingers, and dip into flour. On lightly floured surface, roll dough into thin round. Heat skillet over medium heat until hot; cook chapati until lightly browned on each side, about 2 minutes in all. Remove from pan; brush with some dill butter. Repeat with remaining dough and dill butter, greasing skillet as necessary.

Makes about 15 chapatis.

■ **Blanch fresh vegetables** quickly and easily in your microwave. Rinse and place them in a flat microwave-safe dish; cook until tender-crisp. This enhances color and locks in nutrients.

No-Noodle Lasagna

(pictured, page 126)

2 large green peppers
2 large red peppers
Salad oil
1-pound eggplant
3 zucchini, trimmed
½ teaspoon pepper
½ teaspoon salt
1 jar (15 ounces) marinara
    sauce
4 flat anchovy fillets
1 clove garlic, crushed
⅓ cup olive oil
1 container (15 ounces)
    part-skim ricotta cheese
1 package (8 ounces)
    mozzarella cheese, shredded

1. Halve, core and seed peppers. Place, skin side up, on baking sheet; brush lightly with salad oil. Broil 3 to 4 inches from heat until blackened, about 10 minutes. With tongs, transfer peppers to plastic bag; close bag tightly. Let stand 10 minutes.

2. Meanwhile, pare eggplant; cut crosswise into ¼-inch-thick slices. Spread in a single layer on clean baking sheet. Set aside. Cut zucchini lengthwise into ¼-inch-thick slices. Arrange in a single layer on another baking sheet. Brush eggplant and zucchini lightly with salad oil; sprinkle with pepper and salt, dividing evenly. Broil vegetables until browned on both sides, about 4 minutes in all. Set aside.

3. Preheat oven to 375°F. Remove skin from peppers; cut each half lengthwise into 3 slices. Set peppers aside.

4. In bottom of 12-by-8-by-2-inch baking dish, spread ¼ cup marinara sauce. Top with eggplant, overlapping slices slightly. In small bowl, mash anchovies with garlic and olive oil to form a paste; spread ⅓ of mixture over eggplant. Spread half

the ricotta on top; sprinkle with ⅓ of mozzarella. Spread ¼ cup sauce on top; arrange peppers evenly over sauce. Dot with half of remaining anchovy mixture and the remaining ricotta; sprinkle with half of remaining mozzarella. Spread ¼ cup sauce on top; arrange zucchini, overlapping slightly, over all. Dot with remaining anchovy mixture. Cover with remaining sauce; sprinkle with remaining mozzarella. Bake 15 minutes, until hot and bubbly.

Makes 6 to 8 servings.

Carrot Muffins Macadamia

(pictured, page 126)

2 cups milk
2 teaspoons cider vinegar
1½ cups shreds-of-wheat bran
    cereal
1 cup boiling water
1 cup firmly packed
    light-brown sugar
¼ cup molasses
½ cup salad oil
3 large eggs, at room
    temperature
2¼ cups unsifted all-purpose
    flour
3½ teaspoons baking soda
1 teaspoon salt
1½ cups wheat bran flakes
    cereal
1⅓ cups shredded carrots
1 package (7 ounces) chopped
    dates
1 jar (3½ ounces) macadamia
    nuts, chopped

1. In glass measure, mix milk with vinegar. Let stand 30 minutes, until soured.

2. After 20 minutes, in small bowl, mix shreds-of-wheat cereal with water. Let mixture stand 10 minutes.

3. After 10 minutes, in large bowl of electric mixer, at medium speed, mix sugar with molasses and oil. Beat in eggs, one at a time. Stir in sour milk and soaked cereal.

4. On sheet of waxed paper, mix flour with baking soda and salt. Beat flour mixture into sugar mixture just until blended. Stir in wheat bran flakes cereal, carrots, dates and nuts. Let stand 1 hour, or cover and refrigerate up to 1 day before baking.

5. To bake muffins, preheat oven to 400°F. Line 32 (2½-inch) muffin cups with paper liners. With ice cream scoop or spoon, pour batter into prepared cups, dividing evenly. Bake 25 minutes, or until wooden pick inserted in center of muffin comes out clean (chilled batter will take a few minutes longer to cook). Remove muffins from pans; cool on wire rack.

Makes 32 muffins.

■ A favorite European appetizer is a dip composed of blanched, diced vegetables and bound with a deliciously seasoned mayonnaise. Low-calorie, cholesterol-free mayonnaise makes this combination enjoyable for heart-healthy Americans. Simply mix 1 cup of each: blanched, diced carrots, green beans, peas, red pepper, potatoes and turnips with ½ cup mayonnaise, 2 tablespoons lemon juice and 2 teaspoons prepared mustard to make a loose coating. Season with 2 tablespoons each chopped fresh herbs and chopped green onion, and ½ teaspoon each salt and freshly ground pepper. Use thin slices of French bread or assorted Scandinavian crisp breads as "dippers." Makes about 8 appetizer servings.

Fresh-from-the-Garden Cookbook

Mediterranean Mahimahi

(pictured, pages 126 and 127)

¼ cup olive oil
1 large onion, cut into ¼-inch wedges
2 large cloves garlic, crushed
1 pound fresh spinach, trimmed and washed
2 tablespoons chopped fresh basil leaves
4 medium tomatoes, cut into wedges
½ cup pitted olives, halved
2 tablespoons lemon juice
4 celery stalks
Salad oil
2 pounds (½-inch-thick) mahimahi fillets (about 4)
½ teaspoon lemon pepper
Lemon wedges

1. Prepare grill for outdoor barbecue. In large skillet, heat olive oil over medium-high heat until hot. Add onion and garlic; sauté 3 minutes. Stir in spinach and basil. Cover; over low heat, cook 5 minutes, stirring occasionally. Stir in tomatoes, olives and lemon juice; cook 2 minutes longer. Cover; set aside.

2. Brush celery stalks with salad oil. Using DIRECT METHOD (see page 103), cook celery over medium coals, 5 minutes, or until browned. With tongs, turn stalks; cook 5 minutes longer. Remove to cutting board. Cut stalks diagonally into ¼-inch-thick slices; stir into spinach mixture. Cover; set aside.

3. Arrange grill rack 6 inches from coals; brush rack and both sides of fish with salad oil. Place fish, skin side down, on grill. Sprinkle fish with lemon pepper. Cook fish, with grill covered, 15 minutes, or until cooked and meat thermometer inserted in thickest portion of fish registers 120°F. (Do not turn fish.)

4. Heat spinach mixture until hot; place on heated platter. Place mahimahi on top; serve with lemon wedges.

Makes 4 servings.

Vegetables Vinaigrette

(pictured, pages 126 and 127)

½ pound green beans, trimmed
½ pound wax beans, trimmed
½ pound sugar snap peas, trimmed
½ pound baby pattypan squash
½ bunch broccoli, cut into flowerets
¾ teaspoon pepper
¾ teaspoon salt
2 tablespoons minced shallots
1 clove garlic, minced
1 cup olive oil
¼ cup cider vinegar
2 tablespoons balsamic vinegar
½ cup sliced radishes
1 pint cherry tomatoes, cut into halves
½ pint yellow pear tomatoes
1 bunch chives, snipped

1. In large saucepan, on steamer placed over 1 inch of boiling water, cook green beans until tender-crisp. (Do not overcook.) Remove beans from pan; rinse with cold water until cool. Set aside. Repeat with wax beans, peas, squash and broccoli, cooking each vegetable separately.

2. In large bowl, combine pepper, salt, shallots, garlic, oil and vinegars. Whisk until dressing is blended and thickened. Add cooked vegetables, the radishes and tomatoes; toss until coated. Marinate in refrigerator several hours, stirring occasionally. Just before serving, arrange on platter; sprinkle with chives.

Makes 6 to 8 servings.

■ Everyone loves broccoli flowerets, but what to do with the stems? The answer: Serve them, too! First peel with a sharp knife. Cut about ⅛ inch into the stem, and discard the outside. Then cut the stem into three bite-size strips and serve along with other vegetables and dip.

Sausage Pronto

(pictured, page 129)

1½ pounds sweet Italian sausage
2 tablespoons salad oil
1 pound small zucchini, cut diagonally into ½-inch-thick slices
½ pound mushrooms, quartered
1 medium onion, cut into ¼-inch wedges
1 medium red pepper, cut into ½-inch-thick slices
2 large cloves garlic, crushed
1 pound plum tomatoes, coarsely chopped
¼ cup Marsala wine
¼ cup dry red wine
¼ teaspoon salt
⅛ teaspoon pepper
1 pound pasta, cooked

1. With a fork, prick sausage. In large skillet, heat oil over medium heat until hot. Add sausage; cook 15 minutes, turning occasionally, until browned on all sides. Remove to cutting board; cut diagonally into ½-inch-thick slices.

2. Return sausage to pan; over medium heat, cook 2 minutes longer. With slotted spoon, remove sausage to bowl; keep warm. To drippings in pan, over medium-high heat, add zucchini, mushrooms, onion, red pepper and garlic; sauté 3 minutes. Add tomatoes and wines, stirring to loosen browned bits. Stir in salt and pepper. Stir in sausage; serve dish with hot pasta.

Makes 8 servings.

■ Marinade in a minute: Try Italian salad dressing—bottled or homemade—when you don't have the ingredients on hand to make marinade. Just substitute the dressing in the same amount as your recipe calls for; it lends a delicious flavor to vegetables, fish and meats.

BLT Soup

(pictured, page 129)

1 package (1 pound) bacon
2 tablespoons olive oil
2 large carrots, sliced
2 large onions, sliced
2½ pounds plum tomatoes,
    seeded and chopped
3 cups chicken broth
½ teaspoon pepper
1 cup milk
1 cup shredded escarole

Walnut Bread (recipe follows)

1. Line baking sheet with paper towels; set aside. In large skillet, over medium-high heat, cook bacon until crisp. With tongs, remove bacon to baking sheet. Reserve 3 tablespoons drippings for walnut bread. Crumble bacon; set aside.

2. In 3-quart saucepan, heat oil over medium heat. Add carrots and onions; sauté 5 minutes. Stir in tomatoes and broth; heat to simmering. Cover; simmer 20 minutes.

3. Pour mixture into 2-quart, heat-safe glass measure. In batches, in food processor, puree mixture; pour into saucepan. Stir in pepper and milk; heat over medium-high heat. Sprinkle with escarole and bacon; pour into tureen or soup bowls. Serve with Walnut Bread.
   Makes 6 servings.

Walnut Bread

(pictured, page 129)

1 package (10 ounces)
    refrigerated pizza dough
3 tablespoons bacon fat (see
    BLT Soup, above)
1 can (4 ounces) chopped
    walnuts
½ teaspoon freshly cracked
    pepper

1. Preheat oven to 425°F. Grease 10-inch nonstick skillet. Pat pizza dough into skillet to line, folding over corners. Brush top of dough with bacon fat; sprinkle with nuts,

and press into dough. Sprinkle with pepper.

2. Bake 15 minutes, or until crust is golden brown. Serve warm with BLT Soup.
   Makes 6 servings.

Potato-Mussel Salad

(pictured, pages 128 and 129)

Dressing
¾ teaspoon salt
⅛ teaspoon pepper
2 teaspoons chopped fresh
    basil leaves
2 teaspoons grated lemon peel
¾ cup olive oil
⅓ cup white-wine vinegar
4 teaspoons Dijon mustard

2 pounds medium new
    potatoes, scrubbed
½ pound snow peas, cut in
    half diagonally
3 cups dry white wine
2 dozen mussels, scrubbed
4 green onions, trimmed and
    sliced
½ pint red cherry tomatoes
½ pint yellow cherry tomatoes

1. In jar with tight-fitting lid, combine dressing ingredients; shake until blended. Set aside.

2. In 5-quart saucepan, in 3 quarts boiling, salted water, cook potatoes, covered, 20 minutes, or until tender. With slotted spoon, remove potatoes to colander to drain and cool. To boiling water in which potatoes were cooked, add peas; cook 1 minute. Remove to sieve; rinse with cold water. Set aside.

3. In large skillet, heat wine to boiling. Add mussels; cover. Steam 3 minutes, or until mussels open. With slotted spoon, remove mussels to bowl. Remove mussels from shell; place in small bowl. Add ¼ cup dressing; toss to coat. Set aside.

4. Quarter potatoes; place in medium bowl with green onions. Toss with ½ cup dressing; set aside.

5. On large platter, arrange peas, potatoes, tomatoes and mussels. Drizzle with remaining dressing.
   Makes 4 servings.

Cheesy Veggie Fondue

(pictured, page 128)

2 cups (8 ounces) shredded
    medium-sharp Cheddar
    cheese
2 cups (8 ounces) shredded
    Swiss cheese
2 tablespoons all-purpose flour
1¼ cups dry white wine
2 green onions, chopped
1 bunch chives, snipped

Dipping Vegetables
Broccoli flowerets
Baby carrots, trimmed and pared
Cauliflower flowerets
**Green onions, trimmed and cut
    into 3-inch lengths**
Sugar snap peas
Red- and yellow-pepper strips
Radishes, trimmed
Cherry tomatoes
Zucchini rounds

French bread, torn into chunks

1. In medium bowl, toss cheeses with flour until coated; set aside. In large heavy saucepan, over medium-high heat, bring wine to simmer. Whisk in ½ cup cheese mixture until cheeses melt and mixture is smooth. Continue adding cheese mixture, ½ cup at a time, whisking until the mixture is smooth. Whisk in green onions and half of the chives.

2. Pour mixture into fondue pot; set on large platter. Adjust heat under pot to keep fondue over low flame; whisk fondue and increase heat slightly to keep from separating. Sprinkle fondue with remaining chives. Place vegetables and bread on platter. To serve, with forks, dip vegetables and bread into fondue.
   Makes 4 to 6 servings.

Quick & Easy: Family-Favorite Grilled Chicken

Chicken Claudia

Marinade
1 head garlic
1 tablespoon grated lemon
  peel
1 tablespoon chopped
  rosemary leaves
¾ teaspoon freshly ground
  pepper
½ cup olive oil
¼ cup balsamic vinegar

6 chicken breast halves
¼ cup pitted and halved
  oil-cured olives
2 tablespoons sliced pimientos
1 tablespoon capers

1. Separate cloves from garlic
head; remove and discard skins.
Slice cloves; place in glass baking
dish with remaining marinade ingredients. Mix well. Add chicken; turn
to coat. Marinate in refrigerator one
hour or overnight, turning chicken
occasionally.

2. Prepare outdoor grill for barbecue. Drain chicken; place marinade in small saucepan. Using
DIRECT METHOD (see page 103),
cook chicken breasts 5 inches from
medium-hot coals, 15 minutes on
each side, basting occasionally with
reserved marinade.

3. Bring reserved marinade to
boiling; stir in remaining ingredients. Serve with chicken.
Makes 6 servings.

Ginger Chicken And Leeks

4 leeks, trimmed and
  halved lengthwise

Ginger Butter
¾ cup butter or
  margarine
1 tablespoon minced
  ginger root
1 tablespoon slivered
  lime peel
1 medium clove garlic,
  crushed
⅛ teaspoon ground white
  pepper
2 tablespoons lime juice
1 tablespoon honey

3½-pound chicken, cut
  into eighths

1. Prepare outdoor grill for barbecue. In large shallow saucepan, in
2 inches salted water, blanch leeks 5
minutes. Drain; set aside.

2. In small saucepan, combine
ginger butter ingredients. Heat until
butter melts. Brush chicken with
some butter mixture; place, skin
side up, on grill. Using DIRECT
METHOD (see page 103), cook
chicken 5 inches from medium-hot
coals, 15 minutes on each side, basting occasionally with ginger-butter
mixture.

3. Meanwhile, brush leeks with
ginger-butter mixture; grill with
chicken 10 minutes on each side.
Serve leeks with chicken.
Makes 4 to 6 servings.

Apri-Curry Chicken

Marinade
4 teaspoons curry
  powder
½ teaspoon salt
½ cup plain low-fat
  yogurt
⅓ cup apricot jam
2 tablespoons Dijon-style
  mustard

4 whole chicken legs
About ¼ cup toasted
  coconut

1. In glass baking dish, combine
marinade ingredients. Add chicken;
turn to coat. Marinate in refrigerator
1 to 5 hours.

2. Prepare outdoor grill for barbecue. Drain chicken, reserving
marinade. Using DIRECT METHOD
(see page 103), cook chicken 5
inches from medium-hot coals, 35
minutes, or until cooked, turning
occasionally and basting with marinade. Place on serving dish.

3. In small saucepan, heat remaining marinade to boiling. Pour some
marinade over chicken; sprinkle
with coconut. Serve remaining marinade with chicken.
Makes 4 servings.

*Clockwise from top: Chicken
Claudia, Ginger Chicken and
Leeks, Apri-Curry Chicken.*

■ For a flavor extravaganza, make
your own curry: In a heavy skillet,
combine 3 tablespoons coriander
seeds, 3 tablespoons dried red-
pepper flakes, 5 tablespoons mustard seeds and 1 tablespoon black
peppercorns. Cook mixture over
very low heat 15 minutes, stirring
occasionally. In blender or spice
grinder, combine roasted spices
with 3 tablespoons ground turmeric and 1 tablespoon each of
ground cinnamon, cloves and cardamom seeds. Process mixture
until it becomes a fine powder.
Store curry in airtight jar.

Lite Eating: Hamming It Up—Great Low-Calorie Dishes

Stuffed Artichokes

4 medium artichokes
¼ cup lemon juice
2 cups (7 ounces) chopped mushrooms
1 tablespoon water
¼ teaspoon salt
⅛ teaspoon pepper
1 cup (6 ounces) chopped extra-lean ham
2 tablespoons grated Parmesan cheese
1 tablespoon minced parsley
1 clove garlic, crushed
2 tablespoons dry white wine
1 tablespoon olive oil

1. With stainless-steel kitchen shears, trim ends of artichoke leaves ¾ inch from the top. Trim stem flush with base. With grapefruit spoon, remove and discard some center leaves and fuzzy choke. Brush ends of leaves with half the lemon juice, dividing evenly. In Dutch oven, on steamer placed over 1 inch boiling water, steam artichokes until knife tip easily pierces base, about 30 minutes. Remove from pan; drain and cool.

2. In skillet, over medium-high heat, sauté mushrooms with water 5 minutes. Remove pan from heat; stir in remaining lemon juice, the salt and remaining ingredients.

3. Open leaves slightly. Spoon mushroom mixture into center and open leaves, dividing evenly.

Makes 4 servings, 162 calories each.

Oriental Ham Steaks

4 slices (¼-inch-thick) extra-lean ham steak (1 pound)
¼ teaspoon ground ginger
2½ teaspoons soy sauce
2 teaspoons honey
1 red pepper, thinly sliced
1 cup sliced shiitake mushrooms
1 celery stalk, thinly sliced
½ cup frozen peas
½ cup sliced water chestnuts
2 green onions, thinly sliced
1 carrot, pared and shredded
⅛ teaspoon crushed red-pepper flakes
⅛ teaspoon salt
1 teaspoon dark sesame oil
1 tablespoon chopped peanuts

1. Place ham on broiler pan. In cup, mix ginger, ½ teaspoon soy sauce and the honey.

2. In nonstick skillet, over medium-high heat, sauté pepper and mushrooms 3 minutes. Add celery, peas and water chestnuts; cook 1 minute. Stir in green onions, carrot, pepper flakes, salt, oil and remaining soy sauce; keep warm.

3. Broil ham 4 inches from heat 3 minutes. Turn steaks; brush with ginger mixture. Broil 3 minutes. Sprinkle with nuts; serve with vegetable mixture.

Makes 4 servings, 261 calories each.

Ham and Cheesewiches

2 hoagie rolls
4 slices extra-lean ham (4 ounces)
3 slices low-fat provolone cheese (2 ounces)
1 roasted red pepper
1½ cups sliced mushrooms
1 small red onion, thinly sliced
2 cups bite-size pieces arugula
1 tablespoon minced basil leaves
⅛ teaspoon pepper
⅛ teaspoon salt
2 teaspoons red-wine vinegar
8 pitted black olives, sliced

1. Preheat oven to 350°F. Slice rolls in half horizontally, almost through. Remove and discard soft interior. Cut ham, cheese and pepper into ¼-inch-wide strips.

2. In nonstick skillet, over medium-high heat, lightly brown mushrooms. Add onion; sauté until moisture evaporates, about 1 minute. Remove from heat; stir in the red-pepper strips, arugula, basil, pepper, salt and vinegar.

3. Fill each roll with some vegetable mixture, ham, cheese and olives. Place on baking sheet; bake 10 minutes, until hot.

Makes 4 servings, 237 calories each.

Clockwise from bottom left: Stuffed Artichokes, Oriental Ham Steaks, Ham and Cheesewiches.

Micro-Way: Flavor To Relish All Year Long

Mango Medley Chutney

2 medium tomatoes, cut into
   ½-inch pieces
2 ripe mangoes, pared and
   chopped
1 small cantaloupe, pared,
   seeded, and cut into ½-inch
   pieces
1 cup raisins
½ cup firmly packed
   light-brown sugar
3 medium cloves garlic,
   crushed
1 tablespoon curry powder
1 tablespoon chopped
   crystallized ginger
1 tablespoon mustard seeds
¾ cup cider vingar
¼ cup lime juice
2 tablespoons cornstarch
3 tablespoons water

1. In 3-quart glass bowl, combine all ingredients except cornstarch and water. Cover with plastic wrap; cook on HIGH 10 minutes, stirring twice. Uncover; cook on HIGH 10 minutes, stirring occasionally.

2. In cup, blend cornstarch with water; stir into fruit mixture. Cook on HIGH 2 minutes, until mixture boils and thickens. Store in refrigerator, or place in sterilized jars and process as jar manufacturer directs.
   Makes 6 cups.

Clockwise from left: Corn-Pepper Relish, Zucchini-Pear Relish, Mango Medley Chutney.

Corn-Pepper Relish

4 cups fresh corn kernels
   (from about 4 large ears)
2 celery stalks, sliced
1 small onion, finely chopped
1 small green pepper, diced
1 small red pepper, diced
½ cup firmly packed
   light-brown sugar
¼ teaspoon celery seeds
¼ teaspoon crushed
   red-pepper flakes
¼ teaspoon turmeric
1 cup cider vinegar
1 tablespoon chopped cilantro
   (fresh coriander) leaves

In 3-quart glass bowl, combine all ingredients except cilantro. Cover with plastic wrap. Cook on HIGH 10 minutes, stirring twice. Uncover; cook on HIGH 10 minutes, stirring occasionally. Stir in cilantro. Store in refrigerator, or place in sterilized canning jars and process as jar manufacturer directs.
   Makes 4 cups.

Zucchini-Pear Relish

2 medium Bartlett pears
2 medium carrots, pared
1 pound zucchini, thinly sliced
1 medium onion, thinly sliced
1 medium red pepper, diced
½ cup sugar
1 tablespoon chopped
   crystallized ginger
1 teaspoon mustard seeds
¼ teaspoon crushed
   red-pepper flakes
1 cup distilled white vinegar

Core and cut pears into ½-inch pieces; place in 3-quart glass bowl. Using crinkle cutter, thinly slice carrots crosswise. Stir carrots and remaining ingredients into pears. Cover with plastic wrap; cook on HIGH 10 minutes, stirring twice. Uncover; cook on HIGH 5 minutes. Store in refrigerator, or place in sterilized canning jars and process as jar manufacturer directs.
   Makes 5 cups.

■ Sensitive noses, rejoice! Making relishes and chutney in the microwave will confine the dominating aroma of vinegar and strong spices to the oven.

■ Since small amounts of mixtures cook faster and more evenly in the microwave, it's easy to make a selection of preservables. A single bowl does the trick, and cleanup and getting ready for the next batch of goodies hardly takes a second thought.

■ Microwaving makes chutney-making worry-free since there is little chance for these sugary mixtures to scorch and stick. Use a deep, heat-safe bowl that's at least 4-cup capacity to allow for expansion as the mixture heats up. And since the bowl can get very hot, be sure to use pot holders to remove it from the microwave.

September

Pasta suits any course, from first to main dish. Our collection includes a pasta to meet every possibility: fettuccine, lasagna, ravioli, rotelle, spaghetti, ziti. Choose the recipes that are right for your menu from the dishes pictured and given on the next pages.

Fettuccine Peking   Lasagna Terrine

Shrimp and Penne Alfredo   Ziti Timbale

Chicken-Broccoli Lasagna Rolls

Pasta and Squash Frittata

Eggplant-Arugula Salad

Savory Spaghetti Pork Roast

Escarole Soup   Vermicelli Cheese Bake

Lemon Cream Ravioli   Sausage and Pasta Roulade

Plain & Fancy Pasta Cookbook

For a pasta with a party plus, try a twist on familiar shapes with lasagna rolls and a ziti-edged timbale.

Fettuccine Peking

(pictured, page 141)

2 green onions, chopped
1 tablespoon grated ginger root
⅓ cup soy sauce
1 tablespoon honey
2 teaspoons dark sesame oil
1 pound sliced cooked roast
  beef, cut into ½-inch-wide
  strips
1 package (8 ounces) tomato
  fettuccine
3 tablespoons salad oil
½ pound snow peas, trimmed
1 red pepper, seeded and
  cubed
2 medium cloves garlic,
  crushed
2 tablespoons toasted sesame
  seeds

Page 141: Fettuccine Peking, Lasagna Terrine.

Pages 142 and 143: (Clockwise from top left) Shrimp and Penne Alfredo, Ziti Timbale, Chicken-Broccoli Lasagna Rolls, Pasta and Squash Frittata, Eggplant-Arugula Salad.

Pages 144 and 145: (Clockwise from top left) Savory Spaghetti Pork Roast, Escarole Soup, Vermicelli Cheese Bake, Lemon Cream Ravioli, Sausage and Pasta Roulade.

1. In medium bowl, mix green onions, ginger, soy sauce, honey and sesame oil. Add beef; toss to coat. Set aside.

2. Cook fettuccine as package label directs; drain. Place in large bowl; toss with 1 tablespoon salad oil. Set aside.

3. In wok or large skillet, heat remaining 2 tablespoons salad oil over medium-high heat until hot. Add snow peas, red pepper and garlic; stir-fry until vegetables are tender-crisp, about 3 minutes. Add vegetable and beef mixtures to fettuccine; toss gently to mix well. Cover; refrigerate until serving (not longer than the day prepared), tossing occasionally. Before serving, sprinkle with sesame seeds.

Makes 6 servings.

■ Drain pasta immediately; don't rinse unless instructed by recipe.

■ For perfect pasta, pour a glass of cold water into the pot when the pasta reaches its desired consistency—this will instantly stop it from cooking. If the pasta's accompanying sauce is a little thin, don't worry. Before you drain the pasta, just add some of the starchy cooking water to the sauce—it will soak up extra liquid so that the sauce will have the proper consistency.

Lasagna Terrine

(pictured, page 141)

1 package (1 pound) curly
  lasagna noodles
¼ cup olive oil
1 medium onion, finely
  chopped
1 cup ricotta cheese
¼ pound mozzarella cheese,
  finely chopped
2 large eggs, beaten
½ teaspoon salt
¼ teaspoon pepper
½ pound sweet Italian sausage,
  casing removed
2 small carrots, pared and
  thinly sliced
1 package (10 ounces) frozen
  chopped spinach, thawed and
  squeezed dry
1 small eggplant (½ pound)
1½ cups sliced mushrooms
1 roasted red pepper, cubed
1 jar (6 ounces) marinated
  artichoke hearts, drained
½ cup sliced pitted black olives
1 medium yellow squash

Alfredo Sauce
3 tablespoons butter or
  margarine
3 tablespoons all-purpose flour
1 tablespoon tomato paste
2 cups hot milk
3 tablespoons grated Parmesan
  cheese
½ teaspoon salt
⅛ teaspoon pepper

1. Cook noodles as package label directs for al dente. Drain; rinse with cold water. Place enough noodles flat to cover baking sheet; cover with damp paper towels. Repeat with remaining noodles. Set aside.

2. In 10-inch skillet, heat 1 tablespoon oil over low heat. Add onion; sauté until soft, about 5 minutes. Place in medium bowl; stir in ricotta, mozzarella, eggs, salt and pepper. Place mixture in 3 medium bowls, dividing evenly.

3. In same skillet, over medium-high heat, brown sausage, breaking it up with a spoon. Stir in carrots and spinach; cook over medium heat, covered, until carrots are tender, about 6 minutes. Stir mixture into 1 bowl of ricotta mixture; set aside.

4. Cut eggplant into ½-inch cubes. In skillet used for sausage, heat 1 tablespoon oil over medium heat until hot. Add eggplant and mushrooms; sauté until tender, about 8 minutes. Remove from heat; stir in red pepper. Stir mixture into 1 bowl of ricotta mixture; set aside.

5. Coarsely chop artichokes and olives; add to third bowl of ricotta mixture. Cut squash into ⅜-inch cubes. In skillet used for eggplant, heat 1 tablespoon oil over medium-high heat until hot. Add squash; sauté until tender and moisture evaporates, about 4 minutes. Stir into ricotta mixture with artichokes.

6. Preheat oven to 350°F. With aluminum foil, line 9-by-5-by-3-inch loaf pan. With remaining oil, grease foil. Lay 6 noodles crosswise in pan, overlapping slightly. Lay 2 noodles in each end of inside of pan, arranging noodles so that long edges meet in the center. Spoon eggplant mixture evenly over noodles on bottom; cover with 2 noodles, cutting to fit. Spoon sausage mixture evenly over noodles; cover with 2 noodles, cutting to fit. Spoon artichoke mixture

evenly over noodles; cover with 2 noodles, cutting to fit. Fold noodles at ends of pan over all, pressing loaf firmly. Cover with foil. Bake 1 hour.

7. Meanwhile, make sauce: In small saucepan, over low heat, melt butter. Whisk in flour until blended; cook 1 minute, or until bubbly. Blend in tomato paste; cook 1 minute. Remove pan from heat; blend in milk. Bring to boiling, stirring until thickened; boil 1 minute. Stir in cheese, salt and pepper. Simmer 1 minute, whisking; keep warm. If desired, stir in cooked diced carrot and yellow squash.

8. Remove terrine from oven; let stand, uncovered, 10 minutes. Invert onto serving platter, leaving pan over terrine 10 minutes. Remove pan; remove foil. Serve terrine with sauce.

Makes 8 servings.

Shrimp and Penne Alfredo

(pictured, page 142)

½ **pound uncooked penne pasta**
2 **packages (1.6-ounce size) Alfredo sauce**
1½ **cups milk**
1 **teaspoon grated lemon peel**
2 **tablespoons butter or margarine**
½ **pound medium mushrooms, sliced**
1 **medium onion, chopped**
2 **large cloves garlic, crushed**
12 **ounces fresh spinach, rinsed well**
1 **pound large shrimp, shelled and deveined**
½ **pound shredded mozzarella cheese**
2 **tablespoons grated Parmesan cheese**

1. Preheat oven to 350°F. Cook pasta as package label directs. Drain; set aside.

2. Prepare sauce as package labels direct, using milk. Stir in lemon peel; set aside.

3. In large skillet, melt butter over medium-high heat. Add mushrooms, onion and garlic; sauté until onion is tender, about 3 minutes. Stir in spinach. Cover; cook until spinach is wilted, about 1 minute. Stir in shrimp. Cover; cook mixture 2 minutes.

4. Transfer mixture to large bowl; stir in pasta, sauce and mozzarella. Spoon into 2-quart baking dish; sprinkle with Parmesan. Bake 30 minutes.

Makes 4 to 6 servings.

Pasta Pointers

■ Fill pot with enough water for pasta to float freely—about 1 quart for every 2 ounces of pasta. To allow proper cooking and draining, limit pasta to 2 pounds per pot or colander.

■ Keep the water boiling vigorously as pasta cooks; stir frequently to prevent it from sticking together.

■ Cooking times vary with the size, shape and moisture content of pasta. Fresh varieties cook quickly—some in only a minute—while dried pasta may need from 4 to 15 minutes.

■ Undercook pasta that you will be using in recipes such as casseroles that will require further cooking.

Plain & Fancy Pasta Cookbook

Ziti Timbale
(pictured, page 143)

½ **pound uncooked ziti**
¼ **cup butter or margarine**
¼ **cup grated Parmesan cheese**
2 **tablespoons all-purpose flour**
1¼ **cups milk**
2 **large eggs, separated**
¾ **teaspoon salt**
1 **tablespoon olive oil**
1 **large clove garlic, crushed**
1 **medium onion, chopped**
1 **pound ground sirloin**
1 **large carrot, pared and shredded**
1 **bunch (4 ounces) arugula, coarsely chopped**
1 **can (14½ ounces) stewed tomatoes, drained**
¾ **teaspoon dried dillweed**
⅛ **teaspoon pepper**
4 **ounces mozzarella cheese, diced**

1. Cook ziti as package label directs for al dente. Drain; place in large bowl. Add 1 tablespoon butter; toss until coated. Add 1 tablespoon Parmesan; toss to coat. Set aside.

2. With 1 tablespoon butter, grease 2-quart soufflé dish. Preheat oven to 350°F.

3. In medium saucepan, over medium heat, melt remaining 2 tablespoons butter. Whisk in flour until blended; cook 1 minute, or until bubbly. Remove pan from heat; whisk in milk until blended. Bring to boiling, stirring until thickened; boil 1 minute. Remove from heat; let cool 5 minutes. In custard cup, blend egg yolks with a little of the hot sauce; stir mixture into remaining sauce in pan. Stir in remaining 3 tablespoons Parmesan and ¼ teaspoon salt. Set aside.

4. In 6-quart Dutch oven, heat oil over medium heat until hot. Add garlic and onion; sauté 2 minutes. Add sirloin; over medium-high heat, brown meat, breaking it up with a spoon. Add carrot, arugula and tomatoes; break up tomatoes with a spoon. Bring to boiling; over high heat, cook mixture, stirring occasionally, until excess moisture evaporates, about 3 minutes. Remove pan from heat; stir in dill, remaining ½ teaspoon salt and the pepper. Cool 15 minutes; stir in mozzarella and 3 tablespoons sauce.

5. Using photograph as a guide, arrange some of the ziti on end around side of prepared dish. Spoon 1½ cups sirloin mixture into dish; with back of spoon, press mixture against ziti, leaving center empty. Make a second circle of ziti, pressing noodles against sirloin mixture; spoon 1¼ cups sirloin mixture against second circle of ziti. Repeat with more ziti; spoon remaining sirloin mixture in center of dish, pressing down slightly.

6. In small bowl of electric mixer, at high speed, beat egg whites until stiff peaks form when beaters are raised. With rubber spatula, fold whites into sauce until no white streaks remain; pour over timbale. Top with any remaining ziti. Bake until top is browned, about 45 minutes. Cool 10 minutes. Run knife around edge of dish without cutting ziti; cover with platter. Invert; remove dish. Serve immediately.

Makes 8 servings.

Chicken-Broccoli Lasagna Rolls
(pictured, page 143)

12 **curly lasagna noodles (about 8 ounces)**

Sauce
3 **tablespoons butter or margarine**
1 **small onion, chopped**
3 **tablespoons all-purpose flour**
1 **cup half-and-half**
1 **can (about 14 ounces) chicken broth**
1½ **cups (6 ounces) shredded Monterey Jack cheese**
¼ **teaspoon salt**

Filling
3 **cups chopped cooked chicken**
2 **packages (10-ounce size) frozen chopped broccoli, thawed and well drained**
2 **large eggs, lightly beaten**
1 **jar (6½ ounces) chopped pimientos, drained**
¾ **cup fresh bread crumbs**
¼ **cup minced parsley**
¼ **teaspoon ground red pepper**
¼ **teaspoon salt**
⅛ **teaspoon ground nutmeg**

1. Cook noodles as package label directs. Drain; lay flat.

2. Make sauce: In medium saucepan, over medium-high heat, melt butter. Add onion; sauté until tender, about 3 minutes. Whisk in flour until blended; cook 1 minute, or until bubbly. Remove pan from heat; whisk in half-and-half and broth until blended. Bring to boiling, stirring until thickened; boil 1 minute. Remove from heat; stir in cheese and salt, stirring until smooth.

3. Make filling: In medium bowl, mix filling ingredients with ¾ cup sauce. Set aside. Pour one-third of remaining sauce into 2-quart shallow baking dish, and set aside.

4. Spread filling mixture over each noodle, dividing evenly. Starting from a short end, roll up noodles, jelly-roll fashion. Place rolls, curly end down, in prepared dish. Top with remaining sauce. Cover with aluminum foil; bake 45 minutes, or until heated through.

Makes 6 servings.

■ To hold cooked pasta for later use, drain and run under cold water in colander. Then toss with 1 tablespoon salad oil and place in plastic bag; seal tight and refrigerate. For use in a recipe, just measure and proceed. To serve, run pasta under very hot tap water in colander.

Pasta and Squash Frittata

(pictured, pages 142 and 143)

3 tablespoons salad oil
1 cup sliced yellow squash
1 cup sliced zucchini
¼ cup chopped onion
4 large eggs
2 cups cooked rotelle pasta
½ cup (2 ounces) shredded Italian fontina cheese
2 tablespoons grated Parmesan cheese
½ teaspoon dried basil leaves, crushed
½ teaspoon salt
⅛ teaspoon pepper
1 jar (12 ounces) spicy red-pepper or marinara sauce, heated
Crisp sesame breadsticks

1. In 10-inch nonstick skillet with ovenproof handle or handle covered with aluminum foil, heat 2 tablespoons oil over medium-high heat. Add yellow squash, zucchini and onion; sauté 3 minutes. Remove pan from heat.

2. In large bowl, with fork, beat eggs lightly. Stir in vegetable mixture, rotelle, cheeses, basil, salt and pepper.

3. Preheat broiler. Set rack 6 inches from heat. In same skillet used to sauté the vegetables, heat remaining 1 tablespoon salad oil over medium-high heat until hot. Add egg mixture; with spatula, spread egg mixture evenly in skillet. Cook 4 minutes, or until underside is golden, shaking pan occasionally to keep frittata moving freely. Place skillet in oven. Cook 10 minutes, or until eggs are set.

4. Carefully slide frittata onto serving dish. Cut into wedges. Spoon some sauce around frittata; pass remainder. Serve with sesame breadsticks.

Makes 4 servings.

Eggplant-Arugula Salad

(pictured, page 142)

4 to 5 small (about 3 ounces each) eggplants
1 red pepper
1 yellow pepper
1 Italian frying pepper
½ small red onion
5 tablespoons olive oil
1 medium clove garlic, crushed
½ cup chopped basil leaves
½ teaspoon salt
½ teaspoon pepper
1 package (8 ounces) small tricolor pasta shells, cooked and drained
3 tablespoons balsamic vinegar
1 jar (1¾ ounces) pine nuts, toasted
1 bunch (4 ounces) arugula, chopped

1. Pare eggplants; cut crosswise into ¼-inch-thick slices. Set aside. Cut red and yellow peppers into thin strips; set aside. Cut Italian pepper and onion crosswise into thin slices; set aside.

2. In large skillet, heat 2 tablespoons oil over medium heat until hot. Cook eggplant in batches until browned on both sides, removing to bowl as it cooks and adding 2 tablespoons oil if needed. In same skillet, in 1 tablespoon oil, sauté peppers and onion until softened, about 5 minutes. Stir in garlic, basil, salt and pepper; transfer to bowl with eggplant. Add remaining ingredients; toss to blend. Serve immediately.

Makes 4 to 6 servings.

Savory Spaghetti Pork Roast

(pictured, page 144)

4 large onions, coarsely chopped
4 large cloves garlic, chopped
4-pound center-cut pork rib roast
1 tablespoon olive oil
1 tablespoon dried oregano leaves, crushed
1 teaspoon salt
1 can (13¾ ounces) condensed chicken broth
1 package (1 pound) spaghetti

1. Preheat oven to 325°F. In bottom of large shallow roasting pan, sprinkle onion and garlic; place roast on top. Brush roast with oil; sprinkle with oregano and salt. Bake 1½ hours. Add broth to pan; cook ½ hour longer, or until meat thermometer inserted in center of roast registers 170°F.

2. Meanwhile, cook spaghetti as package label directs. Drain; set spaghetti aside.

3. Place roast on large heated platter; reserve pan with drippings. Cover roast loosely with aluminum foil. Keep warm.

4. Place roasting pan with drippings over large burner on range top. Add spaghetti; cook, stirring, over medium-high heat, 3 minutes, or until drippings are absorbed. Arrange around roast; if desired, garnish with oregano sprigs.

Makes 8 servings.

■ To dry fresh herbs in a quick, easy way, line a microwave-safe plate with 2 paper towels, one on top of the other. Evenly spread 2 cups of clean, dry leaves or sprigs on towels. Cook herbs on HIGH 4 minutes, turning at least once. Store the dried herbs in a tightly covered container.

■ Whether you bake, broil, or grill meats, be sure that you use tongs, not a fork, to turn the meat. The tine of the fork will pierce the meat, allowing the flavorful juices—those juices that keep the meat moist and succulent—to run out, making the meat tougher.

Plain & Fancy Pasta Cookbook

Escarole Soup

(pictured, pages 144 and 145)

1 pound sweet Italian sausage, casing removed
1 medium onion, chopped
1 large clove garlic, crushed
1 can (28 ounces) whole tomatoes
1 can (46 ounces) chicken broth
½ pound escarole, cleaned and coarsely chopped
1 cup (4 ounces) uncooked small bow-tie egg pasta
1 can (1 pound) cannellini beans, drained
Freshly grated Parmesan cheese

1. In 5-quart Dutch oven, over medium-high heat, brown sausage, breaking it up with a spoon. Add onion and garlic; sauté 3 minutes. Stir in tomatoes and their liquid, breaking up tomatoes with a spoon. Stir in broth. Bring to boiling. Add escarole; simmer, covered, about 15 minutes.

2. Meanwhile, cook pasta as package label directs; drain. Add pasta and beans to soup; heat through. Garnish with Parmesan.

Makes 12 servings.

Lemon Cream Ravioli

(pictured, pages 144 and 145)

1 package (1 pound) frozen ravioli
1 pound asparagus, trimmed and cut into 1½-inch pieces
¼ cup butter or margarine
1 cup heavy cream
1 tablespoon grated lemon peel
½ cup grated Parmesan cheese
1 cup (6 ounces) diced cooked ham
⅛ teaspoon pepper

1. In large pan of boiling salted water, cook ravioli as package label directs. Three minutes before ravioli is cooked, add asparagus to water;

cook until ravioli is done and asparagus is tender-crisp. Drain; place in large bowl.

2. Meanwhile, in small saucepan, over medium heat, cook butter, cream and lemon peel 5 minutes; stir in cheese, ham and pepper. Pour sauce over ravioli; toss to coat. Place on serving platter.

Makes 4 to 6 servings.

Vermicelli Cheese Bake

(pictured, page 145)

1 cup (4 ounces) broken uncooked vermicelli
¼ cup grated Parmesan cheese
¼ cup butter or margarine
¼ cup unsifted all-purpose flour
2 cups milk
2 cups (8 ounces) shredded Cheddar cheese
1 teaspoon dry mustard
¼ teaspoon pepper
6 large eggs, separated
1 cup cubed cooked chicken
1 cup frozen peas, thawed
1 teaspoon salt

1. Cook pasta as package label directs; set aside. Preheat oven to 375°F. Grease 10-cup soufflé dish. Sprinkle with the Parmesan cheese.

2. In large saucepan, over low heat, melt butter. Whisk in flour until blended; cook 1 minute, or until bubbly. Remove from heat; blend in milk. Bring to boiling, stirring until thickened; boil 1 minute. Stir in Cheddar, mustard and pepper until cheese melts. Remove from heat; whisk in egg yolks, one at a time. Stir in pasta, chicken and peas; transfer to large bowl.

3. In bowl of electric mixer, at medium speed, beat egg whites with salt until foamy. Beat at high speed until stiff peaks form when beaters are raised. With rubber spatula, fold egg whites into pasta mixture until

no white streaks remain; pour into dish. Bake 20 minutes; reduce heat to 350°F. Bake 40 minutes, or until center is just set.

Makes 6 to 8 servings.

Sausage and Pasta Roulade

(pictured, page 144)

¼ pound sliced pancetta, diced
½ pound sweet Italian sausage, casing removed
1 large onion, diced
1 medium clove garlic, crushed
1 pound ground beef
¼ cup chopped parsley
1 teaspoon dried oregano leaves, crushed
1 container (15 ounces) marinara sauce
2 (14-by-10-inch-size) sheets fresh pasta
1 package (8 ounces) mozzarella cheese, shredded
2 cups beef broth
1 cup water

1. In large skillet, over medium heat, cook pancetta until almost crisp, about 5 minutes. Add sausage; sauté until cooked, about 10 minutes, breaking it up with a spoon. With slotted spoon, remove sausage mixture to bowl. Discard all but 1 tablespoon fat from skillet.

2. Heat same skillet over medium heat until fat is hot. Add onion and garlic; sauté until softened, about 3 minutes. Stir in beef, breaking it up with a spoon; cook until lightly browned, about 5 minutes. Stir in parsley, oregano and 1 cup of the sauce. Bring to boiling; remove from heat. Stir in sausage mixture. Pour mixture into jelly-roll pan; refrigerate until cool, about 10 minutes.

3. Place pasta sheets on counter. Spread half of filling over each sheet to within 1 inch of edges. Sprinkle each with half the cheese. Beginning with a short side, roll up sheets,

jelly-roll fashion. Place double thickness of cheesecloth on counter. Lift one roulade onto cheesecloth; wrap roulade with cloth. With kitchen string, tie ends. Repeat with second roulade. (Roulades may be prepared to this point up to 3 days before cooking, wrapped in plastic wrap and refrigerated.)

4. In 13-by-9-inch roasting pan placed over large burner on range top, bring broth and water to boiling. Add roulades; cover pan with aluminum foil. Simmer 25 minutes, turning roulades once.

5. Meanwhile, in small saucepan, heat remaining sauce to boiling; keep warm. Remove roulades from pan, immediately remove cheesecloth. Cool roulades slightly before slicing. Serve with sauce.

Makes 6 servings.

Baked Ziti Casserole

Sauce
¼ cup olive or salad oil
1 cup finely chopped onion
1 large clove garlic, crushed
1 can (2 pounds, 3 ounces)
  Italian tomatoes
1 can (6 ounces) tomato paste
1½ cups water
2 tablespoons chopped parsley
1 tablespoon salt
1 tablespoon sugar
1 teaspoon dried oregano leaves
½ teaspoon dried basil leaves
¼ teaspoon pepper
1 package (1 pound) ziti macaroni

Cheese Layer
2 cartons (15-ounce size)
  ricotta cheese
1 package (8 ounces)
  mozzarella cheese, diced
⅓ cup plus 3 tablespoons
  grated Parmesan cheese
2 large eggs
1 tablespoon chopped parsley
1 teaspoon salt
¼ teaspoon pepper

1. Make sauce: In hot oil in 6-quart kettle, sauté onion and garlic until golden brown, about 10 minutes. Add undrained tomatoes, tomato paste, water, parsley, salt, sugar, oregano, basil and pepper; mix well, mashing tomatoes with fork. Bring to boiling; reduce heat. Simmer, covered and stirring occasionally, 1 hour.

2. Preheat oven to 350°F. Cook ziti as package label directs.

3. Make cheese layer: In large bowl, combine ricotta, mozzarella, ⅓ cup Parmesan, the eggs, parsley, salt and pepper. Beat with wooden spoon until blended.

4. Spoon a little sauce into 5-quart casserole. Layer a third of ziti, cheese mixture and remaining sauce. Sprinkle sauce with 1 tablespoon Parmesan. Repeat twice.

5. Bake, uncovered, 45 minutes, or until bubbling in center.

Makes 8 to 10 servings.

Note: If desired, make casserole ahead, and refrigerate. Remove from refrigerator while preheating oven. Bake 60 minutes, or until heated through.

Family-Style Macaroni And Cheese

1 package (8 ounces) rotelle
  macaroni
¼ cup butter or margarine
½ cup chopped green pepper
½ cup chopped red pepper
¼ cup unsifted all-purpose
  flour
½ teaspoon dry mustard
⅛ teaspoon ground red pepper
2 cups milk
1 package (10 ounces) extra
  sharp Cheddar cheese,
  shredded
½ cup grated Parmesan cheese
1 cup cherry tomatoes, halved
1 can (2.8 ounces) French-fried
  onions

1. Prepare macaroni as package label directs. Drain; set aside. Preheat oven to 375°F. In medium saucepan, over medium-high heat, melt butter. Sauté peppers 3 minutes; stir in flour, dry mustard and ground red pepper. Gradually stir in milk; cook, stirring, until mixture thickens. Remove from heat. Add cheeses; stir until mixture is blended.

2. In large bowl, toss cheese sauce with cooked macaroni, cherry tomatoes and ½ cup fried onions. Spoon into shallow 1½-quart casserole. Sprinkle remaining fried onions around edge of dish; bake 5 minutes to heat through.

Makes 4 to 6 servings.

Tortellini With Shrimp

1 package (8 ounces)
  spinach-cheese tortellini
1 package (8 ounces) cheese
  tortellini
¾ cup butter or margarine
1 small onion, sliced
1 medium clove garlic,
  crushed
1 pound shrimp, deveined
  and shelled
½ pound plum tomatoes, cut
  into wedges
¼ pound boiled ham, cut into
  ¼-inch strips
1 cup frozen peas, thawed
½ cup grated Parmesan cheese
Additional Parmesan cheese,
  shredded

1. Cook tortellini as package labels direct; keep warm. In large skillet, melt butter. Sauté onion and garlic 3 minutes. Add shrimp; sauté 3 minutes. Add tomatoes, ham, peas and grated cheese; cook 1 minute.

2. Toss with tortellini; sprinkle with shredded cheese. If desired, garnish with fresh basil; sprinkle with freshly ground pepper.

Makes 4 servings.

McCall's Masterpiece: A Slice of Heaven

Three-Chocolate Mousse

Nonstick cooking spray

Dark-Chocolate Layer
8 ounces bittersweet chocolate, chopped
¼ cup butter
2 tablespoons almond-flavored liqueur
½ cup heavy cream, whipped

White-Chocolate Layer
1¼ cups heavy cream
1½ teaspoons unflavored gelatine
6 ounces white chocolate
½ cup finely chopped almonds

Milk-Chocolate Layer
1 cup fresh raspberries
8 ounces milk chocolate
¼ cup butter
½ cup heavy cream, whipped

Unsweetened cocoa powder
Raspberry Sauce (recipe follows)
Chocolate Filigree (recipe follows)

1. With cooking spray, grease 8½-by-4½-by-2½-inch loaf pan; line with plastic wrap. With dried beans, fill small roasting pan ¾ full. Wedge loaf pan into beans, tilting pan lengthwise.

2. Make dark-chocolate layer: In saucepan, over low heat, melt chocolate with butter; stir in liqueur. Cool; fold in cream. Pour mousse into loaf pan; smooth top. Cover loosely with plastic wrap. Refrigerate both pans until mousse is firm, about 2 hours.

3. Make white-chocolate layer: In saucepan, combine ¾ cup cream and the gelatine. Soak 5 minutes. Add chocolate; heat over low heat, stirring until smooth. Place pan in bowl of ice and water. Cool, stirring occasionally, until mixture is texture of unbeaten egg whites. Remove from ice; stir in almonds. Beat remaining ½ cup cream with rotary beater until stiff peaks form; fold into chocolate mixture. Remove pans from refrigerator; reposition loaf pan in beans so that it is tilted in the opposite direction. Pour mousse into loaf pan; smooth top. Cover loosely with plastic wrap; refrigerate until firm, about 2 hours.

4. Make milk-chocolate layer: In food processor, puree raspberries; strain to remove seeds. In saucepan, over low heat, stir chocolate, butter and puree until mixture is smooth and chocolate is melted. Cool; fold in cream. Remove pans from refrigerator. Set loaf pan level on counter. Pour mousse into loaf pan, smooth top. Cover loosely with plastic wrap; refrigerate until firm, about 2 hours. Mousse can be refrigerated at this point up to 24 hours before serving or wrapped well and frozen up to 1 month before serving.

5. For easy slicing, freeze mousse about 1 hour before slicing. To serve, arrange a dinner fork, rounded side down, and a soup spoon, rounded side up, on a dinner plate. With some unsweetened cocoa powder in a fine sieve, dust plate, sprinkling cocoa over utensils. Carefully remove utensils; repeat on each serving plate. Arrange a slice of mousse to one side of silhouette; if desired, decorate each slice with sauce, chocolate filigree, whipped heavy cream and fresh raspberries.
Makes 10 to 12 servings.

Raspberry Sauce

1 package (10 ounces) frozen raspberries in light syrup, thawed
2 tablespoons cornstarch
3 tablespoons water

In food processor, puree raspberries; strain into small saucepan. In small cup, mix cornstarch with water until blended; stir into raspberry mixture. Bring to boiling, stirring; simmer 1 minute. Cool; refrigerate, covered, until serving.
Makes 1 cup.

Chocolate Filigree

¾ cup chocolate melting wafers, melted

Line baking sheet with waxed paper. With chocolate in pastry bag fitted with number-3 tip, using photograph as a guide, pipe designs onto waxed paper. Set aside until chocolate hardens. Store in covered container in cool place.

■ Almonds take on greater flavor depth and richer aroma when roasted or toasted.

Three-Chocolate Mousse.

Quick & Easy: Eggs, Savory-Style—More Than a Morning Meal

Tex-Mex Strata

½ pound hot Italian sausage
1 jar (6 ounces) roasted red peppers, drained and chopped
1 jar (6 ounces) fried green peppers with onion, drained and chopped
6 slices firm white bread, quartered
1½ cups (6 ounces) shredded Monterey Jack cheese with jalapeños
6 large eggs, beaten
1½ cups milk
1 teaspoon chili powder
½ teaspoon salt

1. In medium skillet, sauté Italian sausage 10 minutes, or until lightly browned. Cool slightly; cut sausage crosswise into thin slices. Place in bowl. Add peppers; toss to combine.
2. Preheat oven to 350°F. Generously grease 2-quart shallow baking dish. Reserve 6 bread quarters; place remainder in prepared dish. Sprinkle with cheese and the sausage mixture; arrange reserved bread on top. Set aside.
3. In medium bowl, beat eggs with milk, chili powder and salt until mixed; pour over bread quarters in dish. Bake 1 hour, or until center is set. Let stand 10 minutes before serving.
Makes 6 servings.

Egg-Salad Croissant-wich

½ package (8-ounce size) Neufchâtel cream cheese, softened
¼ cup low-calorie mayonnaise
1 teaspoon prepared horseradish
¼ cup minced onion
1 teaspoon salt
¼ teaspoon pepper
6 hard-cooked large eggs, chopped
4 medium croissants
Radish or alfalfa sprouts
⅓ cup sunflower seeds
8 pitted black olives, sliced

1. In medium bowl, mix cream cheese, mayonnaise and horseradish until smooth. Stir in onion, salt and pepper. With rubber spatula, fold in eggs. Cover; refrigerate 1 hour to blend flavors, if desired.
2. When ready to serve, slice croissants in half horizontally; sprinkle sprouts on bottom of each. Spread egg mixture over sprouts and sprinkle with sunflower seeds and olives, dividing evenly. Replace croissant tops.
Makes 4 sandwiches.

Tex-Mex Strata, Egg-Salad Croissant-wich.

October

There's something deep-down satisfying about a bowl of soup and a hearty sandwich—the combination is perfect fare for a fall day. Enjoy a double-mushroom and barley soup, chicken pitas, or any of our mix-and-match recipes given below and pictured on the following pages.

Cucumber-Watercress Soup

Shrimp Ratatouille Loaf

Black Bean and Pasta Bowl

Caesar Sandwich   Mexican Cream Soup

Mozzarella in a Carriage   Brie Bisque

Tea Sandwiches   Rosy Cauliflower Soup

Chunky Chicken Pitas   Cioppino

Wild Mushroom and Barley Soup

Stuffed Squash-wiches   Vegetarian Pizza

Soup & Sandwich Cookbook

Choose a classic twosome for a midday meal or midnight supper. We've trimmed a few calories from the chicken pitas by using reduced-calorie ingredients.

Shrimp Ratatouille Loaf

(pictured, page 157)

1 (1 pound) eggplant
¼ pound zucchini
1 medium green pepper
¼ cup olive oil
1 medium onion, chopped
3 medium cloves garlic, crushed
1 can (1 pound) whole tomatoes
1 teaspoon salt
½ teaspoon basil leaves, crushed
½ teaspoon crushed red-pepper flakes
⅛ teaspoon freshly ground pepper
2 tablespoons tomato paste
1 tablespoon red-wine vinegar
1 large round loaf French bread
1 pound large shrimp, peeled and deveined with tails removed

1. Cut eggplant, zucchini and pepper into ¾-inch cubes. In large skillet, heat oil over medium-high heat until hot. Add cubed vegetables, the onion and garlic; sauté 5 minutes. Stir in tomatoes and their liquid, salt, basil, pepper flakes, pepper, tomato paste and vinegar, breaking up tomatoes with a spoon. Simmer, covered, 20 minutes, stirring occasionally.

2. Meanwhile, cut off top of bread. Hollow out loaf, leaving ½-inch shell, reserving inside for another use.

3. Stir shrimp into vegetable mixture in skillet; cook, covered, 4 minutes, or until shrimp turn pink. Fill bread with shrimp mixture. Replace bread top.

Makes 6 to 8 servings.

■ To give new crunch to stale pretzels, crackers or chips, just heat in a 325° oven for five to ten minutes, and cool.

Page 157: Cucumber-Watercress Soup, Shrimp Ratatouille Loaf.

Pages 158 and 159: (Clockwise from top left) Black Bean and Pasta Bowl, Caesar Sandwich, Mexican Cream Soup, Mozzarella in a Carriage, Brie Bisque, Tea Sandwiches.

Pages 160 and 161: (Clockwise from left) Rosy Cauliflower Soup, Chunky Chicken Pitas, Cioppino, Wild Mushroom and Barley Soup, Stuffed Squash-wiches, Vegetarian Pizza.

Cucumber-Watercress Soup

(pictured, page 157)

2 European cucumbers
2 tablespoons butter or margarine
2 leeks, white parts only, chopped
4 cups chicken broth
1 package (8 ounces) cream cheese
1 bunch watercress, leaves only
1 tablespoon lemon juice
5 drops hot-red-pepper sauce
Dill sprigs
Sour cream

1. Pare, seed and chop cucumbers. Melt butter in 3-quart saucepan. Add leeks; sauté 5 minutes. Add broth and cucumbers. Cover; simmer 30 minutes.

2. Slice cream cheese. With slotted spoon, remove half the vegetables to food processor with some broth. Puree, adding several slices of cream cheese and some watercress. Remove puree to a bowl and repeat with remaining vegetables, cream cheese and watercress. Return puree to saucepan; over low heat, stir soup until cream cheese melts.

3. Remove pan from heat. Stir in lemon juice and pepper sauce. Chill thoroughly. Ladle soup into bowls, dividing evenly; serve with dill and sour cream.

Makes 6 servings.

Brie Bisque

(pictured, page 158)

1½ pounds brie cheese
2 cans (about 14 ounces each) chicken broth
2 tablespoons butter or margarine
1 package (6 ounces) fresh Cremini mushrooms (or 6 ounces shiitake mushrooms)
3 medium carrots, pared and julienned
2 medium shallots, minced
2 cups light cream
½ teaspoon cracked pepper
2 tablespoons dry sherry
Watercress sprigs
Baguette Croutons (recipe follows)

1. Trim off and discard rind from brie. In 5-quart Dutch oven, bring broth to boiling. Stir in brie until melted and mixture is smooth. Strain through sieve placed over large bowl, discard any solids.

2. In same pan, over medium-high heat, melt butter. Add mushrooms, carrots and shallots; sauté until tender, about 5 minutes. Stir in broth mixture, the cream, pepper and sherry. Bring to boiling; simmer, covered, 10 minutes. Ladle bisque into bowls; garnish each with watercress sprig and sprinkle with some croutons.

Makes 8 servings.

Baguette Croutons

1 baguette loaf French bread
½ cup olive oil
4 medium cloves garlic, sliced

With serrated knife, cut baguette into ½-inch cubes. In 12-inch skillet, heat oil and garlic over medium heat 3 minutes, or until hot. With slotted spoon, remove garlic; add bread cubes. Sauté until lightly browned, about 3 minutes.

Makes about 2 cups.

Black Bean and Pasta Bowl

(pictured, page 158)

1 cup dried black beans
2 tablespoons salad oil
1 large onion, chopped
2 large cloves garlic, crushed
2 cans (about 14 ounces each) chicken broth
1 can (28 ounces) whole tomatoes, cut up and undrained
2 teaspoons sugar
¼ teaspoon pepper
2 tablespoons red wine
1 tablespoon bottled hot salsa
1 cup uncooked elbow macaroni
1 large red pepper, chopped
2 green onions, chopped
2 tablespoons chopped cilantro (fresh coriander) leaves

1. In 3-quart saucepan, cover beans with water. Bring to boiling; boil, covered, 2 minutes. Turn off heat; let stand 1 hour. Drain.

2. In 5-quart saucepan, heat oil over medium-high heat. Add onion and garlic; sauté until onion is softened, about 3 minutes. Add beans and the chicken broth; bring to boiling. Simmer, covered, 1½ hours, or until beans are tender. Add tomatoes and their liquid, the sugar, pepper, wine and salsa. Simmer, covered, 15 minutes.

3. Meanwhile, cook pasta as package label directs; drain. Add pasta and red pepper to soup. Simmer 5 minutes. Sprinkle each serving with some green onion and cilantro.

Makes 10 servings.

Mozzarella in a Carriage

(pictured, page 159)

3 tablespoons unsalted butter or margarine
4 flat anchovies, rinsed, patted dry with paper towels and chopped
1 tablespoon capers, chopped
1 small clove garlic, crushed
¼ cup finely chopped red pepper
4 large eggs
⅓ cup fine dry bread crumbs
8 slices homemade-style white bread
8 slices smoked mozzarella cheese
½ teaspoon grated lemon peel
1 teaspoon lemon juice
2 tablespoons chopped parsley
¼ cup olive oil

1. In small skillet, over low heat, melt butter. Add anchovies, capers and garlic; sauté 5 minutes. Stir in red pepper; keep warm.

2. Preheat oven to 350°F. In large shallow bowl, with fork, beat eggs. Place bread crumbs on sheet of waxed paper. Make sandwiches with bread and mozzarella, dividing cheese evenly. Dip each sandwich in egg until coated; drain. Coat both sides with bread crumbs.

3. Stir lemon peel, lemon juice and parsley into anchovy mixture; transfer to small serving bowl. Cover to keep warm. In same skillet, heat oil over medium-high heat until hot. Add sandwiches; cook until browned on each side, about 6 minutes in all. Drain on paper towels. Place on baking sheet; heat in oven 5 minutes. Serve hot with anchovy mixture.

Makes 4 servings.

Soup & Sandwich Cookbook

Caesar Sandwich

(pictured, page 159)

1 can (2 ounces) flat anchovy
  fillets, rinsed and patted dry
1 medium clove garlic, crushed
1 tablespoon Dijon mustard
1 tablespoon olive oil
2 tablespoons unsalted butter
  or margarine, softened
1 (12-inch) loaf pumpernickel
  bread, cut in half
  horizontally
¼ cup bottled Caesar or
  favorite Italian-style salad
  dressing
½ head romaine lettuce,
  separated into leaves
¼ pound thinly sliced
  prosciutto
2 hard-cooked large eggs,
  sliced
¼ cup shredded Parmesan
  cheese
¼ cup chopped walnuts

1. In food processor, puree anchovies and garlic; add mustard, oil
and butter. Process until smooth.
Spread mixture over cut side of bottom half of loaf of bread. Remove
some of inside of top half of loaf,
leaving ½-inch shell. (Reserve bread
for other use.) Drizzle or brush salad
dressing over cut side of the top half
of loaf of bread.

2. Over anchovy mixture, layer:
lettuce, prosciutto, eggs, Parmesan
and walnuts. Place top of bread over
all. Secure with wooden skewers or
picks. Cut crosswise into slices. Remove skewers to serve.
Makes 8 servings.

■ If a recipe requires softened
butter, but you forgot to take it
out of the refrigerator, it will be
easier to cream if you shred it
first with a vegetable parer.

■ If you have a recipe that calls
for pine nuts (pignolis) but can't
find any, try a less expensive al-
ternative: blanched almonds.

Mexican Cream Soup

(pictured, page 159)

2 cans (15½-ounce size) pinto
  beans, drained
2 cans (about 14 ounces each)
  chicken broth
1 medium onion, finely
  chopped
1 large clove garlic, crushed
1 tablespoon chili powder
1 teaspoon ground cumin
½ cup sour cream
Chopped toasted pine nuts
Chives

1. In 4-quart saucepan, mix
beans, broth, onion, garlic, chili
powder and cumin. Bring to boiling;
simmer, covered, 30 minutes. With
slotted spoon, remove beans and
onion to food processor; puree. Stir
puree into broth mixture in saucepan. Heat through; pour into tureen.

2. In small bowl, stir sour cream
until of pourable consistency. (If desired, add 1 tablespoon milk to thin
slightly.) Spoon sour cream into
soup; with skewer or wooden pick,
swirl decoratively through soup, but
do not blend in. Sprinkle with pine
nuts; garnish with chives.
Makes 6 servings.

Rosy Cauliflower Soup

(pictured, page 160)

2 tablespoons cider vinegar
2-pound head cauliflower, cut
  into flowerets
2 tablespoons olive oil
1 Spanish onion, sliced
2 small cloves garlic, crushed
¼ teaspoon crushed
  red-pepper flakes
2 tablespoons tomato paste
½ teaspoon ground cumin
¼ teaspoon salt
4 cups chicken broth
½ cup cilantro (fresh
  coriander) leaves
1 cup (4 ounces) grated
  Monterey Jack cheese

1. In large bowl, combine 2
quarts water and the vinegar. Add
cauliflower; soak 10 minutes. Drain.

2. In 4-quart saucepan, heat oil
over medium heat. Add onion, garlic
and pepper flakes; sauté 15 minutes,
or until onion is tender. Stir in tomato paste, cumin and salt; cook,
stirring, 1 minute. Stir in broth and
cauliflower; bring to boiling. Simmer, covered, 15 minutes.

3. Pour soup mixture through
large sieve or colander placed over
large bowl. Place solids in electric
blender; puree. Return broth to
saucepan; stir in puree and ¼ cup
cilantro. Ladle soup into bowls, dividing evenly; sprinkle each with
some cheese and remaining cilantro.
Makes 8 servings.

Tea Sandwiches

(pictured, page 158)

Beef
2 tablespoons butter or
  margarine, softened
1 teaspoon prepared
  horseradish
1 tablespoon whole-grain
  Dijon mustard
6 slices marbled rye
  bread
6 thin slices rare roast beef
¼ cup mixed sprouts
4 radishes, trimmed and
  thinly sliced

1. In small bowl, mix butter,
horseradish and mustard until
blended. Trim crusts from bread;
cut each slice into 2 squares. Cover
bread with damp paper towels.

2. Cut beef to size of bread
squares. Spread each bread square
on one side with butter mixture,
dividing evenly. On buttered side of
each bread square, place beef, then
sprouts and radishes, dividing
evenly. Cover with damp paper
towels until serving.
Makes 12 sandwiches.

Shrimp

1 can (4¼ ounces) tiny shrimp
¼ cup shredded carrots
1 tablespoon minced red
pepper
¼ cup mayonnaise
½ teaspoon curry powder
1 teaspoon chutney
1 tablespoon finely chopped
toasted almonds
6 slices (6-by-4-inch) challah
(egg bread)
1 tablespoon mayonnaise
2 leaves Boston lettuce
12 cilantro (fresh coriander)
leaves

1. Drain shrimp; rinse with cold water. Pat dry with paper towels. Set aside 24 shrimp; finely chop remainder. In small bowl, combine chopped shrimp, carrots, pepper, ¼ cup mayonnaise, curry powder, chutney and almonds.

2. Trim crusts from bread; cut each slice into two triangles. Using 1 tablespoon mayonnaise, spread one side of each triangle, dividing evenly. Tear lettuce into pieces same size as bread triangles. Top mayonnaise-covered side of triangles with lettuce and then shrimp mixture, dividing evenly; garnish each with two whole shrimp and a cilantro leaf. Cover with damp paper towels until serving.
Makes 12 sandwiches.

Cucumber

12 slices whole-wheat bread
3 ounces sliced smoked
salmon
1 package (3 ounces) cream
cheese, softened
1 teaspoon grated lemon peel
½ cup watercress leaves, finely
chopped
12 thin slices unpared
European cucumber

1. With 2½-inch heart-shaped cookie cutter, cut out a heart from center of each bread slice. (Reserve crusts for bread crumbs.) Cover with damp paper towels; set aside.

With 1-inch heart-shaped cookie cutter, cut out 12 hearts from salmon slices.

2. In small bowl, mix cream cheese, ½ teaspoon lemon peel and the watercress until blended. Finely chop remaining salmon; stir into cream-cheese mixture.

3. Spread one side of each bread heart with cream-cheese mixture, dividing evenly; top each with a cucumber slice and one salmon heart. Sprinkle each with some of remaining lemon peel. Cover with damp paper towels until serving.
Makes 12 sandwiches.

Chunky Chicken Pitas
(pictured, pages 160 and 161)

2 cups shredded cooked
chicken breasts
½ cup diced celery
½ cup halved seedless red
grapes
½ cup chopped pistachios

Dressing
½ cup reduced-calorie
mayonnaise
½ cup reduced-calorie sour
cream
2 tablespoons snipped fresh
dill
1 tablespoon chopped onion
½ teaspoon salt
¼ teaspoon freshly ground
pepper
1 tablespoon tarragon vinegar

6 large pita breads
Alfalfa sprouts
Sliced cherry tomatoes

1. In large bowl, combine chicken, celery, grapes and pistachios. Set aside.

2. In food processor, mix dressing ingredients until blended. Pour over chicken mixture; toss to coat.

3. Cut off and discard ½ inch from one side of each pita; open

pocket and fill with chicken salad, dividing evenly. Top with sprouts and tomatoes, dividing evenly.
Makes 6 servings.

Wild Mushroom and Barley Soup
(pictured, page 161)

½ cup uncooked barley
3 slices bacon, diced
¼ cup chopped shallots
1 cup sliced mushrooms
1 cup sliced shiitake
mushrooms, stems
removed
1 teaspoon salt
½ teaspoon ground white
pepper
5 cups water
1 cup half-and-half
2 tablespoons chopped
parsley

1. Rinse barley; place in small bowl. Cover with warm water; soak 30 minutes. Drain; set aside.

2. In 4-quart saucepan, over medium heat, cook bacon until crisp; with slotted spoon, remove to plate. Drain off all but 1 tablespoon bacon fat. To fat in pan, over medium heat, add shallots; sauté 3 minutes. Add all mushrooms; sauté 5 minutes, or until mushrooms release their liquid. Reduce heat to low; cook mushrooms 10 minutes, stirring often. Add soaked barley, salt, pepper and water. Bring soup to boiling; simmer, covered, 45 minutes. Stir in half-and-half and cooked bacon; heat through but do not boil. Sprinkle soup with parsley.
Makes 6 servings.

■ To add extra flavor to just about any dish, chop parsley and onion in a food processor; then freeze the mixture in a small plastic container. It's ready to use whenever you need it.

Cioppino

(pictured, page 161)

18 littleneck clams, scrubbed
2 tablespoons olive oil
1 medium onion, chopped
1 green pepper, chopped
2 medium cloves garlic, crushed
1/3 cup finely chopped fresh basil leaves
1/4 cup finely chopped celery leaves
2 tablespoons chopped parsley
1/2 teaspoon salt
1 can (28 ounces) crushed Italian tomatoes
1 1/4 cups Chianti wine
1 tablespoon Worcestershire sauce
1/4 teaspoon hot-red-pepper sauce
1 pound haddock or cod fillet, cut into 2-inch chunks
1/2 pound large shrimp, peeled and deveined with tails intact

1. Place clams in 5-quart Dutch oven; cover with 1 inch water. Bring to boiling. Cover; simmer 5 minutes, or until clams open. (Discard any clams that do not open.) With slotted spoon, remove clams from pot. Line sieve with double thickness of cheesecloth; place over glass measure. Pour enough cooking liquid from clams through cheesecloth to measure 1 cup; discard remaining liquid. Set cooked clams and strained liquid aside.

2. In same Dutch oven, heat oil over medium-high heat until hot. Add onion, pepper and garlic; sauté 3 minutes, or until vegetables are softened. Add basil, celery, parsley, salt, reserved clam liquid, the tomatoes, wine, Worcestershire and pepper sauce. Bring to boiling; simmer, covered, 1 hour.

3. Stir in haddock and shrimp; bring to boiling. Simmer 3 minutes, stirring gently, until fish is just firm and shrimp is pink. Add clams and their shells; heat through.

Makes 6 servings.

Stuffed Squash-wiches

(pictured, page 161)

1 large (8 ounces) yellow squash
1 large (8 ounces) zucchini
1 teaspoon salt
1 cup (4 ounces) shredded fontina cheese
1 ounce thinly sliced prosciutto, slivered
1/4 cup slivered fresh basil leaves
2 sun-dried tomatoes, finely chopped
1 large egg
1/2 cup seasoned fine dry bread crumbs
1 tablespoon grated Parmesan cheese
1/2 cup olive oil

1. Trim off and discard ends of squash and zucchini; cut each into 1/4-inch-thick slices. Place 12 larger slices of each flat on double-thickness paper towels; sprinkle with 1/2 teaspoon salt on each side. Cover with double-thickness paper towels, a large baking sheet and then a weight (such as several cans or a bag of flour). Let stand 30 minutes.

2. In small bowl, mix fontina, prosciutto, basil and tomatoes. In small shallow bowl, with fork, beat egg. On sheet of waxed paper, combine bread crumbs and Parmesan. Brush salt from squash and zucchini; arrange same-size slices in pairs. Form 1 tablespoon of the fontina mixture into a ball; flatten slightly. Place between a pair of squash and zucchini slices. Repeat with remaining fontina mixture and squash and zucchini slices. Dip each "sandwich" into egg; drain slightly. Dip into bread-crumb mixture to coat both sides. Place on baking sheet; refrigerate 15 minutes.

3. In a large skillet, heat oil over medium heat until hot. In oil, cook sandwiches, six at a time, until browned on both sides, about 4 minutes in all. Drain on paper towels; place on platter. If desired, garnish with sprig of fresh basil. Serve immediately.

Makes 6 appetizer servings.

Vegetarian Pizza

(pictured, pages 160 and 161)

Pizza Dough
1 1/2 cups unsifted all-purpose flour
1/2 cup whole-wheat flour
1 package fast-rising or regular dry yeast
1 teaspoon salt
1/2 teaspoon sugar
2/3 cup warm (120° to 130°F) water
2 tablespoons salad oil

Topping
3 tablespoons salad oil
2 cups broccoli flowerets
1 cup sliced mushrooms
1 cup diced yellow squash
1 small red onion, thinly sliced and separated into rings
1 small red pepper, julienned
1/2 teaspoon salt

Cornmeal
1/2 cup prepared pizza sauce
1 package (8 ounces) mozzarella cheese, shredded

1. Make dough: In large bowl of electric mixer, combine 1/2 cup all-purpose and the whole-wheat flours, yeast, salt and sugar. With mixer at low speed, pour water and oil into flour mixture. Beat at medium speed 3 minutes, scraping bowl with rubber spatula. With wooden spoon, gradually add remaining 1 cup all-purpose flour; stir until dough leaves side of bowl. On lightly floured surface, knead dough until smooth and elastic, about 5 minutes. Place in lightly greased bowl; turn dough over to bring up greased side. Cover bowl with towel; let dough rise in warm place (85°F), free from drafts, until doubled, about 45 minutes.

2. Meanwhile, make topping: In large skillet, heat oil over medium-high heat until hot. Add broccoli, mushrooms, squash, onion, pepper and salt; sauté 3 minutes, or until vegetables are tender. Set aside.

3. Preheat oven to 500°F. Lightly sprinkle cornmeal on each of 2 baking sheets. Punch down dough; divide into 8 equal pieces. On lightly floured surface, with floured rolling pin, roll out each piece of dough to a 4½–5-inch round. Place rounds on baking sheets. Spread each with pizza sauce to within ½ inch of edges, dividing evenly; sprinkle each with vegetable topping and mozzarella, dividing evenly. Bake 10 minutes, or until crust is browned.
Makes 8 servings.

Lentil-Chickpea Stew

3 medium onions, chopped
1 small clove garlic, minced
1 tablespoon olive or salad oil
1 cup water
4 stalks celery, cut into 1-inch pieces
½ pound carrots, cut into ½-inch slices
1 teaspoon ground cumin
1 teaspoon ground coriander
½ teaspoon curry powder
¼ teaspoon ground cardamom
¼ teaspoon ground cinnamon
Dash ground red pepper
1 cup dried lentils, washed and sorted
3 cups chicken broth
1 can (19 ounces) chickpeas, drained
¼ cup slivered almonds

1. In large skillet, over medium heat, sauté onions and garlic in oil until onions are tender.

2. Add water and remaining ingredients except chickpeas and almonds. Simmer, covered, over medium-low heat, 45 minutes, or until lentils are tender. Stir in chickpeas and almonds.
Makes 6 servings.

Greek Lemon Soup

4 cups chicken broth
⅓ cup orzo (rice-shaped pasta)
¾ pound boneless chicken breasts, skinned and cut into thin strips
2 large eggs
3 tablespoons lemon juice
1 tablespoon chopped fresh dill
1 tablespoon chopped parsley

1. In microwave-safe 2-quart casserole, place broth. Cover with plastic wrap; turn back one corner to vent. Cook on HIGH 8 to 10 minutes, or until boiling. Add orzo; cook, covered, on HIGH 7 minutes. Add chicken breasts; cook, covered, on HIGH 5 minutes longer, until orzo and chicken breasts are tender.

2. In medium bowl, beat eggs with lemon juice. Whisk in some of the hot broth; return to casserole. Cook, covered, on MEDIUM 3 minutes; stir in dill and parsley.
Makes 4 to 6 servings.

Cabbage-Bean Soup

1½-pound fully cooked smoked boneless pork-shoulder butt
9 cups water
1 large onion, quartered
2 sprigs parsley
1 small clove garlic, crushed
½ teaspoon salt
1 bay leaf
4 peppercorns
1 pound red new potatoes, washed and cut into ¼-inch-thick slices
1 pound carrots, pared and sliced on diagonal
1 head (2 pounds) green cabbage, coarsely chopped
2 cans (1-pound size) white kidney beans, drained

1. In 8-quart kettle, place pork and 6 cups water. Add onion, parsley, garlic, salt, bay leaf and peppercorns. Bring to boiling. Reduce heat; simmer, covered, 1 hour.

2. Add remaining 3 cups water, the sliced potatoes, carrots and cabbage; cook, covered, 25 minutes, or until potato is just tender.

3. Remove pork from kettle; slice. Stir in white kidney beans; simmer 5 minutes more. Return pork to kettle and remove bay leaf before serving.
Makes 8 servings.

Fresh Plum-Tomato Soup

1 medium onion, chopped
1 medium clove garlic, minced
2 tablespoons olive or salad oil
2 pounds fresh plum tomatoes, coarsely chopped
2 tablespoons tomato paste
1 teaspoon sugar
½ teaspoon salt
¼ teaspoon paprika
¼ cup heavy cream
4 large fresh basil leaves
4 fresh mint leaves

1. In microwave-safe, deep 2-quart casserole, combine onion, garlic and oil. Cover with plastic wrap; turn back one corner to vent. Cook on HIGH 4 minutes, or until onion is tender. Add tomatoes; cover, and vent. Cook on HIGH 8 minutes, or until tomatoes are very tender, stirring once after 4 minutes.

2. In food mill set over medium bowl, puree tomato mixture; discard tomato skin and seeds remaining in mill. Return tomato mixture to same casserole. Stir in tomato paste, sugar, salt and paprika. Cover, and vent. Cook on HIGH 6 minutes, or until mixture begins to boil. Stir in cream; let stand 2 minutes.

3. Stack basil leaves; beginning at stem end, tightly roll up leaves. With sharp knife, cut rolled leaves crosswise into 1/16-inch-wide strips. Repeat with mint leaves. Serve soup hot or cold, sprinkled with basil and mint strips.
Makes 4 servings.

McCall's Masterpiece: Ultimate Shrimp Rolls

Shrimp Chinoiserie

24 medium shrimp, shelled
  and deveined with tails intact
Salad oil
1 tablespoon minced garlic
1 tablespoon minced ginger
  root
½ cup finely chopped green
  onions
2 tablespoons shredded carrot
2 tablespoons minced celery
¼ pound prosciutto, minced
¼ teaspoon freshly ground
  black pepper
2 teaspoons soy sauce
1½ teaspoons balsamic vinegar
2 tablespoons chopped cilantro
  (fresh coriander) leaves
8 (9-inch) egg-roll wrappers
Ginger Soy Sauce (recipe
  follows)
Bourbon Duck Sauce (recipe
  follows)

1. Remove tails from and chop 8 shrimp; set aside. Butterfly remaining shrimp: With small sharp knife, cut each shrimp nearly through on outside curve, leaving tails intact; spread each shrimp open and flatten slightly. Set aside.

2. In large skillet, heat 1 tablespoon oil over medium heat until hot. Add garlic and ginger; sauté 30 seconds, or until fragrant. Add onions, carrot and celery; sauté 2 minutes, or until tender. Stir in chopped shrimp; sauté 2 minutes, or just until shrimp are pink. Remove pan from heat. Stir in prosciutto, pepper, soy sauce and vinegar. Cool slightly; stir in cilantro. Set aside.

3. With kitchen shears, trim corners of each egg-roll wrapper to make a 9-inch round. (See *Note*.) Cut each round in half. Place 1 butterflied shrimp, cut side down, about ½ inch from one end of each half-wrapper, with tail hanging over edge of straight side. Place 2 teaspoons vegetable mixture on top of each shrimp. With pastry brush, lightly brush water over edges of wrappers. Using photograph as a guide, turn wrapper end nearest shrimp over shrimp and topping and, keeping shrimp flat, roll up in remaining wrapper, aligning curved wrapper ends, pressing out any air between layers and lightly pinching edges together to seal. Place on baking sheet; cover with damp paper towels and plastic wrap. Refrigerate until ready to cook.

4. Line clean baking sheet with paper towels. Preheat oven to 250°F. In wok or deep skillet, heat 2 inches oil to 350°F on deep-fat thermometer. Fry wrapped shrimp, a few at a time, 3 minutes, or until golden brown. Place on prepared baking sheet; keep warm in oven while frying remaining shrimp. Serve immediately with Ginger Soy Sauce and Bourbon Duck Sauce.

Makes 8 appetizer servings.

Note: For an extra treat, fry trimmings when frying wrapped shrimp. Drain; sprinkle with salt.

Ginger Soy Sauce

2 teaspoons salad oil
1 tablespoon minced
  ginger root
1 cup low-sodium soy
  sauce

In small saucepan, heat oil. Add ginger; sauté 30 seconds, or until fragrant. Stir in soy sauce; heat through. Keep warm.

Makes about 1 cup.

Bourbon Duck Sauce

2 teaspoons salad oil
½ cup finely chopped green
  onions
½ cup finely chopped red
  pepper
2 teaspoons minced garlic
2 teaspoons minced ginger
  root
2 tablespoons bourbon
  whiskey
1 cup bottled duck sauce

In small saucepan, heat oil. Add onions and pepper; sauté 3 minutes, or until tender. Add garlic and ginger; sauté 30 seconds, or until fragrant. Stir in bourbon; bring to boiling. Boil 1 minute. Stir in duck sauce; cool to room temperature.

Makes about 1 cup.

■ When using fresh herbs instead of dried, use three times the recommended amount. And, by the way, to allow herb flavor to fully develop, be sure to simmer the food at least 30 minutes.

Shrimp Chinoiserie.

Lite Eating: Fresh Fruit and Fabulous

Mosaic Fruit Terrine

Nonstick cooking spray
2 cans (5½-ounce size) peach
   nectar
1 envelope unflavored gelatine
1 pint strawberries, hulled and
   sliced
½ pint blueberries
½ pint raspberries
½ cup seedless green grapes
½ cup seedless red grapes
1 navel orange, peeled,
   skinned and cut into sections

Light Vanilla Sauce
3 tablespoons sugar
2 teaspoons cornstarch
1 large egg yolk
¾ cup skim milk
1 teaspoon vanilla extract

1. Grease 6-cup loaf pan with cooking spray; line pan with plastic wrap. Set aside.

2. Place nectar and gelatine in saucepan. Let stand 5 minutes. Over low heat, dissolve gelatine, stirring. Place fruit in bowl; add gelatine mixture. Toss to coat. Pour into loaf pan. Cover; refrigerate overnight.

3. Make sauce: In small bowl, combine sugar and cornstarch; beat in egg yolk and 1 tablespoon milk. Place remaining milk in saucepan; heat until almost boiling. Blend some hot milk into yolk mixture; blend yolk mixture into hot milk in pan. Over low heat, cook, stirring, until mixture boils. Remove from heat; stir in vanilla. Pour into bowl; cover with plastic wrap, placing wrap directly on surface of sauce. Refrigerate until cool.

4. To serve, invert terrine onto cutting board. Remove plastic. With electric knife, cut terrine into 12 slices. Serve with sauce.

Makes 12 servings, 70 calories each.

Apple-Champagne Sorbet

2 cups prepared applesauce
1 cup champagne or apple
   juice
2 tablespoons apple jelly
2 to 4 drops red food
   color
2 tablespoons lemon
   juice
1 tablespoon water
1 apple, cored, cut into 12
   slices

1. In bowl, mix applesauce, champagne and 1 tablespoon jelly; with food color, tint light pink. Freeze at least 2 hours.

2. Thaw frozen mixture slightly; break into chunks. Place chunks in food processor; process until slushy. Transfer to bowl. Freeze about 30 minutes.

3. In skillet, heat remaining jelly, the lemon juice and water until boiling. Add apple slices. Over low heat, poach slices 3 minutes, or until tender. Drain slices. Scoop sorbet into 6 dessert cups, dividing evenly; arrange 2 apple slices over sorbet in each cup. If desired, garnish each with mint sprig.

Makes 6 servings, 89 calories each.

Berry Cream Pie

Nonstick cooking spray
6 phyllo-pastry leaves
2 cups sliced strawberries
1 cup blueberries
1 cup raspberries
1 tablespoon lemon juice
2 large egg whites
3 tablespoons sugar
2 cups frozen nondairy
   whipped topping, thawed

1. Preheat oven to 350°F. With cooking spray, grease 9-inch pie plate; lay one phyllo leaf in pie plate, allowing edges to hang over outside of plate. Lightly spray phyllo inside plate only. Repeat with remaining phyllo to line plate. Bake 15 minutes or until golden; cool.

2. In bowl, mix berries with lemon juice; refrigerate 30 minutes. In bowl of electric mixer, at high speed, beat egg whites until soft peaks form when beaters are raised. Beat in sugar, 1 tablespoon at a time; beat until stiff. Fold in nondairy topping; gently fold in berries. Place in phyllo shell.

Makes 8 servings, 74 calories each.

Counterclockwise from top: Berry Cream Pie, Mosaic Fruit Terrine, Apple-Champagne Sorbet.

Micro-Way: Happy Halloween Desserts

Bewitched Cake

1 package (18.5 ounces) yellow
   cake mix
1 tablespoon pumpkin-pie
   spice
1 can (1 pound) pumpkin
3 large eggs
¼ cup salad oil
¼ cup water
1 cup mini chocolate pieces
2 cans (1-pound size) chocolate
   frosting
¼ cup marzipan
Yellow and red food colors

1. Grease 2 glass 8-inch-square
baking dishes. Line each with 2
sheets waxed paper; grease. Cover
corners with aluminum foil. In large
bowl of electric mixer, beat first 6
ingredients 2 minutes. Stir in chocolate; pour into baking dishes, dividing evenly. Place one dish on
inverted bowl; cook on MEDIUM 8
minutes, rotating dish every 2 minutes. Remove foil; cook on HIGH 4
minutes, rotating dish after 2 minutes. Let stand 5 minutes. Repeat for
second layer. Invert layers onto
rack; cool.

2. Place one layer on plate. Frost
top; add second layer and frost top
and sides. Tint marzipan yellow. On
waxed paper, roll out 2 tablespoons
marzipan; cut out moon and stars.
With red color, tint scraps and remaining marzipan orange. Roll out;
cut out witch. Decorate cake with
marzipan shapes.

Makes 12 servings.

*Bewitched Cake, Pumpkin
Scream Pie.*

Spider's Treat.

Spider's Treat

1 package (10 ounces) large
   marshmallows
⅓ cup butter or margarine, cut
   up
½ cup creamy peanut butter
6 cups presweetened
   chocolate-flavored puffed
   cereal
1 can (1 pound) vanilla
   frosting
¼ cup peanut-butter pieces
1 teaspoon salad oil
1 large red gumdrop
Red or black string licorice

Grease pizza pan. In glass bowl,
cook marshmallows and butter on
HIGH 2 minutes. Add peanut butter;
cook on HIGH 2 minutes. Stir in
cereal. Press into pan. Frost when
cool. In glass bowl, melt peanut-butter pieces with oil on MEDIUM 1
minute; with mixture in icing bag
fitted with small plain tip, pipe web
over frosting. Attach gumdrop spider with licorice legs.

Makes 12 servings.

Pumpkin Scream Pie

1 envelope unflavored gelatine
¾ cup light-brown sugar
1½ teaspoons pumpkin-pie
   spice
½ cup milk
3 large egg yolks
1 can (1 pound) pumpkin
1 container (8 ounces) frozen
   nondairy whipped topping,
   thawed
9-inch chocolate-cookie crust

In glass bowl, mix gelatine, sugar
and spice. Stir in milk and egg yolks;
let stand 1 minute. Cook on ME-
DIUM 6 minutes, stirring every 2
minutes. Stir in pumpkin. Place bowl
in ice water; chill 15 minutes, until
thickened. Fold in 2 cups topping;
spoon into crust. Chill 2 hours. Decorate with remaining topping.

Makes 8 servings.

November

French-bread stuffing and continental side dishes give our traditional holiday turkey an elegant turn. For smaller gatherings, we've put a new twist on the traditional, starting with a seafood pasta and starring capon with a fruity rice stuffing.

Mussel Bisque

Turkey With French-Bread Stuffing

Stuffed-Tomato Tart   Glazed Broccoli Mélange

Cranberry Crunch Muffins

Warm Seafood Salad

Tropical Stuffed Capon

Mushrooms Scandia   Onion Triangles

Green Bean and Jicama Salad

Cauliflower With Red-Pepper Sauce

Fruited Hazelnut Cake   Pecan-Pumpkin Tart

Apricot Lace Cups

Thanksgiving Cookbook

Excellent with either of the main-meal menus that follow, our family-favorite desserts are festive with nuts, cranberries and bits of dried fruit.

**TRADITIONAL
TURKEY MENU**

MUSSEL BISQUE
TURKEY WITH FRENCH-BREAD
STUFFING
STUFFED-TOMATO TART
GLAZED BROCCOLI MÉLANGE
CRANBERRY CRUNCH MUFFINS
DESSERT OF CHOICE:
FRUITED HAZELNUT CAKE
PECAN-PUMPKIN TART
APRICOT LACE CUPS

---

*Page 175: (Clockwise from top)
Fruited Hazelnut Cake, Pecan-
Pumpkin Tart, Apricot Lace Cups.*

*Pages 176 and 177: (Clockwise
from top left) Glazed Broccoli
Mélange, Cranberry Crunch
Muffins, Mussel Bisque, Turkey
With French-Bread Stuffing,
Stuffed-Tomato Tart.*

*Pages 178 and 179: (Clockwise
from top left) Cauliflower With
Red-Pepper Sauce, Onion
Triangles, Warm Seafood Salad,
Green Bean and Jicama Salad,
Tropical Stuffed Capon,
Mushrooms Scandia.*

Mussel Bisque

(pictured, page 177)

2 tablespoons butter or
  margarine
2 large shallots, chopped
1 medium onion, cut into
  strips
1 can (about 14 ounces)
  chicken broth
1 cup dry white wine
½ teaspoon dried thyme
  leaves
½ bay leaf
⅛ teaspoon freshly ground
  pepper
2 dozen mussels,
  scrubbed
½ cup crème fraîche
2 large egg yolks
⅛ teaspoon saffron threads

1. In 5-quart saucepan, melt butter over medium-high heat. Add shallots and onion; sauté 3 minutes. Add chicken broth, white wine, thyme, bay leaf and ground pepper. Bring to boiling; add mussels. Cover; simmer 5 minutes.

2. With slotted spoon, remove mussels to bowl, discarding any unopened mussels; keep warm. Pour broth through sieve double-lined with cheesecloth into another bowl; discard solids. Return broth to saucepan; whisk in remaining ingredients. Simmer bisque, whisking, 5 minutes, or until slightly thickened. Add mussels.

Makes 4 servings.

Turkey With French-Bread Stuffing

(pictured, pages 176 and 177)

Stuffing
12 cups cubed French bread
½ cup butter or margarine
4 large leeks, sliced and rinsed
3 large cloves garlic, crushed
2 celery stalks, thinly sliced
½ pound shiitake mushrooms,
  sliced
1 large carrot, pared and
  shredded
½ cup chopped pistachios
½ cup sun-dried tomatoes
⅓ cup chopped parsley
1 tablespoon chopped fresh
  rosemary leaves
1 tablespoon chopped fresh
  sage leaves
1 tablespoon chopped fresh
  thyme leaves
¼ teaspoon freshly ground
  pepper
1½ cups chicken broth

14- to 16-pound fresh turkey
5 cups water
1 medium onion, quartered
2 tablespoons butter or
  margarine
½ teaspoon seasoned pepper
½ teaspoon salt
⅓ cup unsifted all-purpose
  flour

1. Make stuffing: Preheat oven to 325°F. Arrange bread cubes in one layer on two jelly-roll pans. Bake,

stirring occasionally, until toasted, about 15 minutes. Place in large bowl. In large skillet, over medium heat, melt half the butter. Add leeks and garlic; sauté until tender, about 10 minutes. Add to bread. In same skillet, over medium-high heat, melt remaining butter. Add celery and mushrooms; sauté 4 minutes. Add carrot; sauté 1 minute. Add, with remaining stuffing ingredients, to bread; toss to combine.

2. Remove giblets and neck from turkey. Set aside liver; place remaining giblets and the neck, the water and onion in medium saucepan. Bring to boiling; simmer 2 hours. Strain, reserving giblets and broth; cool. Meanwhile, remove excess fat from turkey. Rinse turkey; pat dry.

3. Preheat oven to 325°F. Lightly spoon stuffing into neck cavity of turkey. Bring neck skin over stuffing; secure with poultry pins. Spoon some of remaining stuffing into body cavity; do not pack. (Place extra stuffing in greased baking dish; cover and bake last 30 minutes turkey is in oven.) Close cavity with poultry pins; lace with string. Tie legs together; pin wings to breast.

4. Place turkey, breast side up, on rack in large open roasting pan. In small bowl, combine butter, seasoned pepper and salt; spread over turkey. Insert meat thermometer into thickest portion of thigh, away from bone. Roast, uncovered, 5 hours, or until meat thermometer registers 170°F. After 1 hour, add 1 cup giblet broth to pan. When turkey turns golden, cover loosely with aluminum-foil tent.

5. Place turkey on warm serving platter. Remove poultry pins and string. Let stand 15 minutes for easier carving. If desired, garnish platter with fresh herbs, cranberries and small squashes.

6. Skim off and discard fat from pan juices. Blend flour with 2 cups broth from giblets. Add to pan. Bring to boiling, stirring to loosen any browned bits. Simmer, stirring until thickened, about 5 minutes. If desired, sauté and chop liver; add to gravy with chopped giblets.

Makes 12 servings.

Stuffed-Tomato Tart
(pictured, page 176)

3 medium tomatoes
   (14 ounces)
1 teaspoon coarse salt
½ package (17¼-ounce size)
   frozen puff pastry, thawed

Filling
2 tablespoons butter or
   margarine
4 large shallots, finely chopped
2 cups sliced mushrooms
½ cup fresh bread crumbs
¼ teaspoon salt
⅛ teaspoon pepper

Custard
1 large egg
½ cup heavy cream
1 teaspoon minced fresh
   tarragon leaves
¼ teaspoon salt

2 teaspoons Dijon mustard
½ cup shredded Gruyère cheese

1. In boiling water in saucepan, blanch tomatoes about 1 minute; place in bowl of ice and water until cold. Remove and discard skins; halve tomatoes crosswise. With grapefruit spoon, remove pulp. Sprinkle insides with coarse salt, dividing evenly; let stand 45 minutes.

2. Meanwhile, preheat oven to 400°F. On floured surface, with floured rolling pin, roll pastry to 10-by-16-inch rectangle. Transfer to 13¾-by-4-by-1-inch tart pan with removable bottom. Press lightly to line pan with pastry; trim off excess. Refrigerate 10 minutes. Line tart with aluminum foil; fill with aluminum pie weights or dry beans. Bake 20 minutes. Remove foil and weights; bake tart shell 5 minutes or until inside is golden brown. If pastry rises unevenly or bubbles, prick with fork. Cool tart shell in pan on wire rack 10 minutes.

3. Make filling: In large skillet, over medium heat, melt butter. Add shallots; sauté until tender, about 5 minutes. Add mushrooms; sauté 5 minutes. Over medium-high heat, sauté mixture until moisture evaporates. Remove pan from heat; stir in bread crumbs, salt and pepper. With paper towels, dry tomatoes; spoon filling mixture into each, dividing evenly.

4. In bowl, with fork, mix custard ingredients until well blended.

5. Assemble tart: Reduce oven temperature to 350°F. Place tart pan on jelly-roll pan. With pastry brush, spread mustard over bottom of tart shell. Sprinkle Gruyère over mustard. Using photograph as a guide, arrange tomatoes in tart shell. Pour custard around tomatoes. Bake until custard is set, about 35 minutes. Cool tart in pan 10 minutes before serving. If desired, garnish with tarragon sprigs.

Makes 8 servings.

■ Remember, if you purchase a frozen turkey, you'll need to thaw it for a minimum of three days in the refrigerator before it's ready to go into the oven.

Thanksgiving Cookbook

Glazed Broccoli Mélange

(pictured, page 176)

¼ cup butter or margarine
1 tablespoon sugar
1 teaspoon salt
¼ cup beef broth
1 package (12 ounces) baby carrots, pared
¾ pound rutabagas, pared and diced
1½ pounds broccoli, cut into flowerets with stems pared and sliced crosswise into ½-inch pieces
1 can (10 ounces) whole peeled chestnuts, drained and rinsed
1 red pepper, cut into 1-inch cubes

1. In large skillet, melt butter. Add sugar and salt; stir to dissolve sugar. Add broth, carrots and rutabagas; bring to boiling. Simmer 4 minutes.

2. Add broccoli, chestnuts and red pepper; heat to boiling. Simmer, covered, 7 minutes, or until vegetables are tender-crisp. Remove lid; boil 2 minutes to reduce liquid.

Makes 6 servings.

Cranberry Crunch Muffins

(pictured, page 177)

1 cup cranberries, coarsely chopped
1 cup chopped pecans
2 teaspoons grated orange peel
2 cups unsifted all-purpose flour
1 tablespoon baking powder
¾ cup firmly packed light-brown sugar
⅔ cup orange juice
2 large eggs
⅓ cup salad oil

1. Preheat oven to 400°F. Line mini-muffin pans with paper liners. (See *Note*.)

2. In small bowl, mix cranberries, pecans and orange peel. In large bowl, mix flour and baking powder. In medium bowl, mix remaining ingredients. With fork, stir juice mixture into flour mixture just until dry ingredients are moistened. (Batter will be lumpy.) Fold cranberry mixture into batter.

3. Spoon batter into prepared muffin pans. Bake 12 minutes, or until golden. Remove from pan; cool on wire rack.

Makes 48 muffins.

Note: Allow 1 tablespoon batter for each; bake in batches.

CONTEMPORARY CAPON MENU

WARM SEAFOOD SALAD
TROPICAL STUFFED CAPON
MUSHROOMS SCANDIA
GREEN BEAN AND
JICAMA SALAD
CAULIFLOWER WITH
RED-PEPPER SAUCE
ONION TRIANGLES
DESSERT OF CHOICE:
FRUITED HAZELNUT CAKE
PECAN-PUMPKIN TART
APRICOT LACE CUPS

Warm Seafood Salad

(pictured, page 179)

2 tablespoons salad oil
4 large leeks, sliced and rinsed
4 carrots, pared and sliced diagonally
1 green pepper, cubed
¾ pound sea scallops
¾ pound medium shrimp, shelled and deveined with tails intact
½ pound tomato and basil penne pasta, cooked
4 plum tomatoes, seeded and diced
½ teaspoon salt
¼ teaspoon freshly ground pepper
¼ teaspoon crushed red-pepper flakes
¾ cup bottled red-wine salad dressing
1 cup dry white wine
12 small mussels, scrubbed
¼ cup minced parsley

1. In large skillet, heat oil over medium heat. Add leeks; sauté 5 minutes. Add carrots and green pepper; sauté 5 minutes, or until vegetables are tender-crisp. Stir in scallops and shrimp; cook, covered, 4 minutes, or just until cooked through. Stir in next 6 ingredients.

■ With just a few tricks, you can turn nutritional, low-calorie vegetables into eye-catching garnishes. To make Turnip-and-Carrot Flowers, you'll need turnips, carrots and capers. First, wash a medium turnip; pare. Cut turnip crosswise into ⅛-inch-thick slices. With the tip of a paring knife, divide each turnip slice into eighths by cutting out thin slivers from the center section to the edge. Be careful not to cut through the center of the turnip. Trim each eighth to a point; place turnip pieces in a bowl of ice water to which a little lemon juice has been added. Cover, and refrigerate. Next, repeat the procedure, using a large carrot. When you're ready to use the vegetables, drain all flowers well on paper towels. Secure a carrot flower to the center of a turnip flower with part of a wooden pick. Last, place a caper in the center. Now you're ready to garnish a platter or cheese board.

2. Meanwhile, in large saucepan, heat wine to boiling. Add mussels; cook over medium-high heat, covered, 6 minutes. Drain; discard any unopened mussels. Add to leek mixture; sprinkle with parsley. Serve salad hot or warm.

Makes 12 first-course or 6 main-course servings.

Tropical Stuffed Capon

(pictured, page 178)

8-pound capon
1 can (8 ounces) crushed
    pineapple in natural juices
1 jar (12 ounces) red-pepper or
    red-currant jelly
2 tablespoons butter or
    margarine
1 cup chopped onions
3 cups cooked brown rice
¾ cup currants
¾ cup chopped macadamia
    nuts
2 tablespoons chopped
    crystallized ginger
½ cup chicken broth
Nonstick cooking spray

1. Preheat oven to 325°F. Remove giblets and neck from capon; set aside for another use. Remove and discard excess fat. Wash capon; pat dry with paper towels.

2. Drain pineapple, pouring juice into small saucepan. Add jelly to juice; set aside. Reserve pineapple.

3. In large skillet, over medium-high heat, melt butter. Add onions; sauté until tender, about 3 minutes. Add pineapple, the rice, currants, macadamia nuts, ginger and broth; heat through. Spoon mixture into neck cavity of capon. Bring neck skin over stuffing; secure with poultry pins. Spoon some of remaining stuffing into body cavity; do not pack. (Place extra stuffing in greased baking dish; cover and bake last 30 minutes capon is in oven.) Close body cavity with poultry pins; lace

with string. Tie legs together. Pin wings to breast.

4. Grease rack in roasting pan with cooking spray; place capon, breast side up, on rack. Insert meat thermometer into thickest portion of thigh, away from bone. Heat jelly mixture until jelly melts, stirring until blended; brush some mixture over capon. Roast capon, uncovered, basting every 30 minutes with jelly mixture, until thermometer registers 170°F.

5. Place capon on warm serving platter. Remove pins and string. Let stand 15 minutes for easier carving. If desired, garnish with pineapple and papaya slices, lime twists and parsley.

Makes 6 servings.

Mushrooms Scandia

(pictured, page 178)

4 cups water
1 tablespoon plus 2 teaspoons
    lemon juice
12 very large mushrooms,
    about 3 inches in diameter,
    with stems removed
4 cups broccoli flowerets and
    stems, pared and sliced
    crosswise into ½-inch pieces
1 can (10¾ ounces) condensed
    cream-of-broccoli soup
½ cup instant-mashed-potato
    granules
¼ cup grated Parmesan cheese
5 tablespoons unsalted butter
    or margarine
¼ teaspoon ground white
    pepper
⅛ teaspoon ground nutmeg
1 tablespoon snipped fresh dill
    or 1 teaspoon dried dillweed

1. In medium saucepan, bring water and 1 tablespoon lemon juice to boiling. Add mushroom caps; boil 2 minutes. Line baking sheet with paper towels; with slotted spoon, remove mushrooms to baking sheet

to drain. To boiling water, add broccoli; cook until tender-crisp, about 8 minutes. Drain; place in food processor. Add soup, potato granules, Parmesan, 3 tablespoons butter, the pepper, nutmeg and remaining lemon juice. Puree; stir in dill.

2. Preheat oven to 450°F. Place mushrooms, stem side up, in lightly buttered shallow baking dish. With pastry bag fitted with large star tip, pipe filling into mushroom caps. Bake until golden brown, about 10 minutes. Melt remaining butter; drizzle over filling.

Makes 12 servings.

Green Bean and Jicama Salad

(pictured, page 179)

Vinaigrette
¼ teaspoon salt
⅛ teaspoon pepper
3 tablespoons balsamic vinegar
1 tablespoon lemon juice
¾ cup salad oil

1½ pounds green beans,
    trimmed and halved
¾ pound jicama, pared and
    julienned
1 pint red cherry tomatoes,
    halved
1 large head radicchio
3 tablespoons chopped
    pistachios

1. In food processor, combine salt, pepper, vinegar and lemon juice; with motor running, pour in oil in a thin, steady stream until dressing is smooth.

2. In saucepan of boiling salted water, cook green beans 3 minutes, or until tender-crisp. Drain. Place in large bowl of ice and water until cold; drain. Place in bowl with jicama, tomatoes and vinaigrette; toss.

3. Line bowl with radicchio leaves; add salad. Sprinkle with nuts.

Makes 6 servings.

Cauliflower With Red-Pepper Sauce

(pictured, page 178)

3 large sweet red peppers (see *Note*)
4 cups water
1 tablespoon vinegar
1 tablespoon salt
3-pound head cauliflower, trimmed
¼ cup butter or margarine
⅓ cup finely chopped onion
2 large cloves garlic, crushed
1 tablespoon all-purpose flour
½ cup half-and-half
⅛ teaspoon ground red pepper

1. Roast the sweet red peppers: Quarter and seed peppers; place, cut sides down, on broiler pan. Broil 8 inches from heat 15 minutes, or until skin is charred. Place peppers in plastic bag; seal. Let stand 15 minutes, or until peppers are cool enough to handle.

2. Meanwhile, in 5-quart Dutch oven, bring water, vinegar and 1 teaspoon salt to boiling. Add cauliflower, stem side down. Return water to boiling; cover, reduce heat to medium-low and cook 15 minutes. With 2 large spoons, turn cauliflower; cook, covered, 5 minutes longer, or until cauliflower is easily pierced with a fork. Drain in colander; keep warm.

3. Meanwhile, in medium skillet, over medium-high heat, melt butter. Add onion and garlic; sauté until golden, about 3 minutes. Blend in flour. Cook 1 minute, stirring, until bubbly. Remove from heat. Gradually blend in half-and-half; add remaining salt and the ground red pepper. Bring to boiling, stirring, until thickened and smooth; simmer 1 minute.

4. Remove skin from peppers and discard; place peppers in food processor. Puree. Add onion mixture; process until blended. Gradually blend into sauce in skillet; heat to boiling.

5. Place cauliflower on large serving platter; spoon some pepper sauce on top. Pass remaining sauce. If desired, garnish with mâche (lamb's lettuce) and fresh cherry peppers.

Makes about 6 servings.

Note: Or use 2 jars (7-ounce size) roasted red peppers, drained, and omit step 1; since peppers are already skinned, disregard instructions to do so in step 4.

Onion Triangles

(pictured, page 179)

¼ cup butter or margarine
2 large onions, thinly sliced
1 bunch green onions, sliced
¼ pound mushrooms, thinly sliced
½ teaspoon dried rosemary leaves
2 cups unsifted all-purpose flour
2 teaspoons baking powder
½ teaspoon salt
¼ cup shortening
1 cup milk
2 tablespoons chopped parsley
½ cup sour cream
1 large egg yolk

1. Preheat oven to 425°F. Grease 13-by-9-by-2-inch pan. In large skillet, over medium-high heat, melt butter. Add onions; sauté 5 minutes. Add green onions, mushrooms and rosemary; sauté 5 minutes. Cool slightly.

2. In medium bowl, combine flour, baking powder and salt. With pastry blender or two knives, cut in shortening until mixture resembles coarse crumbs. With fork, stir in milk and parsley. With floured hands, pat dough into pan; spread onion mixture on top. In bowl, blend sour cream and egg yolk; spread over onion mixture. Bake 25 minutes, until golden. Cut into 2-inch triangles.

Makes 40 triangles, or 12 servings.

Fruited Hazelnut Cake

(pictured, page 175)

Cake

3½ cups unsifted all-purpose flour
1 tablespoon pumpkin-pie spice
2 teaspoons baking powder
½ teaspoon salt
1½ cups butter or margarine, softened
2 cups granulated sugar
1 teaspoon vanilla extract
4 large eggs
1 cup milk
½ cup chopped toasted hazelnuts

Topping

1¾ cups heavy cream
¼ cup confectioners' sugar
2 tablespoons hazelnut-flavored liqueur
½ cup chopped dried apricots
½ cup chopped dried figs
½ cup chopped toasted hazelnuts

1. Preheat oven to 325°F. Grease and flour 12-cup Bundt pan.

2. In bowl, mix flour, spice, baking powder and salt. In large bowl of electric mixer, at medium speed, beat butter until light and fluffy. Gradually beat in sugar; add vanilla. Beat in eggs, one at a time, beating until blended. Alternately add flour mixture and milk, beginning and ending with flour and adding one-third of milk at a time. Stir in hazelnuts. Spoon batter into prepared pan, spreading evenly. Bake 1 hour and 5 minutes, or until cake tester inserted into cake comes out clean. Cool in pan 10 minutes; invert onto wire rack to cool completely.

3. Make topping: In large bowl of electric mixer, at medium-high speed, beat cream with sugar and liqueur until stiff peaks form when beaters are raised. Spread mixture over cake; using photograph as a guide, decorate with dried fruits and hazelnuts.

Makes 12 servings.

Pecan-Pumpkin Tart

(pictured, page 175)

Crust
½ package (19-ounce size)
    pecan shortbread cookies,
    crushed
1 cup coarsely chopped pecans
2 tablespoons butter or
    margarine, melted

Filling
3 large eggs
1 can (16 ounces) pumpkin
½ cup dark-brown sugar
¾ teaspoon ground cinnamon
½ teaspoon ground allspice
½ teaspoon salt
¼ teaspoon ground ginger
½ cup heavy cream
12 pecan halves

Hard Sauce (recipe follows)

1. Preheat oven to 375°F. In bowl, with fork, mix crust ingredients. Pour into 9-inch square tart pan with removable bottom. With fork, press evenly over bottom and sides of pan. Bake 5 minutes, or until golden. Cool on wire rack.

2. Place eggs in bowl; whisk lightly until blended. Add remaining ingredients except nuts; mix until blended. Place tart pan on jelly-roll pan. Pour filling into crust; using photograph as a guide, arrange 3 pecan halves over filling in corners. Bake 50 minutes, or until set. Cool on wire rack. Serve with Hard Sauce.
    Makes 9 servings.

Hard Sauce

½ cup confectioners' sugar
¼ cup unsalted butter,
    softened
2 teaspoons brandy

In small bowl, mix sauce ingredients until blended. Spoon into serving bowl or place in pastry bag fitted with star tip; pass with or pipe over tart.
    Makes about ½ cup.

Apricot Lace Cups

(pictured, page 175)

Lace Cookie Cups
¼ cup sugar
¼ cup butter or margarine
3 tablespoons molasses
⅓ cup finely chopped walnuts
¼ cup unsifted all-purpose
    flour
¼ teaspoon ground ginger

Apricot Mousse
1 cup dried apricots
½ cup plus 3 tablespoons sugar
1 cup water
1¼ cups heavy cream

Cranberries
Mint sprigs

1. Make cookies: Preheat oven to 350°F. Line 3 large baking sheets with parchment paper. In small saucepan, bring sugar, butter and molasses to boiling. Remove from heat; stir in nuts, flour and ginger. Place two large spoonfuls of batter on one baking sheet and three spoonfuls of batter on each remaining baking sheet, allowing space between spoonfuls and at edges of sheet for batter to spread. Bake cookies, one sheet at a time, 9 minutes, or until bubbly and browned. Cool on baking sheet on wire rack 2 minutes, or until cookies are firm enough to remove but still pliable. With metal spatula, remove from paper. Immediately place each upside down on overturned, 2-inch-diameter glass; press gently to ruffle edges. (If cookies harden too quickly to remove or shape, place in hot oven to soften.) Set aside. Remove cups from glasses when cooled; store in airtight container until serving.

2. Make mousse: In small saucepan, bring apricots, ½ cup sugar and the water to boiling. Cover; simmer 15 minutes. Pour into food processor; puree. Cool. In small bowl of electric mixer, at high speed, beat cream with remaining sugar until

stiff peaks form when beaters are raised. With rubber spatula, fold in apricot puree, blending slightly so that swirls of each mixture remain distinct. Refrigerate until serving.

3. To serve, fill cups with mousse, dividing evenly. Garnish each with a few cranberries and a mint sprig.
    Makes 8 servings.

Orange Chiffon Cake

2 cups unsifted all-purpose flour
1½ cups granulated sugar
1 tablespoon baking powder
1 teaspoon salt
½ cup salad oil
5 large egg yolks
1 cup fresh orange juice
6 tablespoons grated orange peel
1 teaspoon vanilla extract
1 cup egg whites (7 to 8), at
    room temperature
½ teaspoon cream of tartar
3 cups confectioners' sugar
2 tablespoons butter or
    margarine, melted

1. Preheat oven to 325°F. In bowl, combine first four ingredients. Make a well in center; add oil, egg yolks, ¾ cup orange juice, 3 tablespoons orange peel and the vanilla. Beat until smooth; set aside.

2. In large bowl of electric mixer, at high speed, beat egg whites with cream of tartar until stiff peaks form when beaters are raised. Pour flour mixture gradually over egg whites, folding with rubber spatula until no white streaks remain. Pour into ungreased 10-inch tube pan; bake 1 hour, or until wooden pick inserted in center of cake comes out clean. Invert cake in pan over neck of a bottle; let stand 1½ hours, or until completely cold. Carefully invert onto serving dish; remove pan.

3. Meanwhile, in bowl, blend confectioners' sugar with melted butter and remaining orange juice and orange peel; drizzle over cake.
    Makes 12 servings.

McCall's Masterpiece: Herbal Pasta

Herb-Layered Pasta

2 cups unsifted all-purpose flour, plus additional for rolling pasta
3 tablespoons freshly grated Parmesan cheese
1½ teaspoons salt
4 large eggs
½ cup packed Italian parsley leaves
½ cup dill sprigs
12 basil leaves
Shallot Butter (recipe follows)

1. In medium bowl, combine 2 cups flour, the Parmesan and ½ teaspoon salt. Make a well in center of flour mixture; break eggs into well. With fork, beat eggs until mixed; gradually incorporate flour mixture into eggs to form a dough. With hands, form dough into ball; knead gently 5 minutes. Wrap in plastic wrap; let rest 10 minutes.

2. Divide dough into four parts. Keep each part wrapped in plastic wrap while working with remainder. With some flour, lightly coat one portion of pasta on all sides. With hands, pat pasta into flat rectangle with one side smaller than width of pasta machine rollers. With rollers adjusted to widest setting, roll dough through machine. Fold pasta sheet lengthwise into thirds; with rollers adjusted to next widest setting, roll dough through machine. Repeat 2 more times, using next-to-the-last setting (¹⁄₁₆-inch opening) for final rolling.

3. Place pasta sheet on lightly floured surface; with long side of dough facing you, cover top side of right half with one-fourth of herbs, placing leaves flat and ½ inch apart. With pastry brush dipped in water, brush top side of left side of dough; fold dampened side over side of dough with leaves, aligning edges and pressing out air bubbles. Press all over to seal. Dust dough lightly with flour; roll dough through machine using next-to-the-last setting. Trim off and discard edges of dough; with pizza cutter, cut dough into 2½-inch squares. Set aside. Repeat, using remaining dough and herbs.

4. In 6-quart pan or Dutch oven, bring 4 quarts water to boiling. Add remaining salt and the pasta. Boil until pasta is al dente, about 3 minutes. Pour through colander; drain. Return pasta to empty pan; add Shallot Butter. Toss gently to coat. Serve immediately.

Makes 8 appetizer or side-dish servings.

Shallot Butter

¼ cup butter or margarine
2 large shallots, minced
½ teaspoon salt
¼ teaspoon freshly ground pepper

In small skillet, over medium heat, melt butter. Add shallots; sauté until tender, about 4 minutes. Stir in salt and pepper; keep warm.

Makes about ¼ cup.

Herb-Layered Pasta.

Lite Eating: Soups That Make a Meal

California Gingered Soup

1 tablespoon salad oil
½ pound firm tofu, cubed
4 green onions, sliced
3 medium cloves garlic, crushed
1 tablespoon minced ginger
   root
3 cups water
1 can (about 14 ounces)
   chicken broth
4 ounces capellini pasta, cooked
1 package (16 ounces) frozen
   mixed vegetables (broccoli,
   red pepper, bamboo shoots
   and mushroom combination)
2 tablespoons dark sesame oil
2 tablespoons soy sauce
½ teaspoon salt

In 5-quart Dutch oven, heat oil over medium-high heat. Add tofu, onions, garlic and ginger; stir-fry 3 minutes, until onions are tender. Stir in remaining ingredients; bring to boiling. Simmer, covered, 5 minutes.

Makes 4 servings, 270 calories each.

■ Don't throw away those celery leaves—they have a wonderful flavor! Chop them with parsley and use on broiled fish or in casseroles, or add them to soup.

California Gingered Soup.

Manhattan Oyster Chowder

2 tablespoons salad oil
3 medium potatoes, pared and
   diced
3 celery stalks, chopped
1 large leek, rinsed and diced
2 medium cloves garlic, crushed
1 can (16 ounces) crushed
   tomatoes
1 bottle (8 ounces) clam juice
½ cup dry white vermouth
¾ teaspoon dried thyme leaves
1 yellow pepper, julienned
1 pint shucked oysters with
   liquor

In 5-quart Dutch oven, heat oil over medium heat. Add potatoes, celery, leek and garlic; sauté 5 minutes. Stir in tomatoes, clam juice, vermouth and thyme. Bring to boiling; simmer, covered, 20 minutes. Add pepper; simmer 10 minutes. Stir in oysters and the liquor; simmer 2 minutes. If desired, sprinkle with chopped chives.

Makes 4 servings, 265 calories each.

Manhattan Oyster Chowder,
Midwest Lentil Soup.

Midwest Lentil Soup

1 tablespoon salad oil
2 pounds boneless chicken breasts, skinned
1 medium onion, chopped
¾ cup dried lentils, rinsed
1 can (about 14 ounces) chicken broth
3 cups water
2 large tomatoes, seeded and diced
1 yellow summer squash, diced
2 carrots, pared and thinly sliced
1 green pepper, diced
½ teaspoon dried basil leaves

In 5-quart Dutch oven, heat oil over medium-high heat. Add chicken and onion; sauté 5 minutes, until browned. Add lentils, broth and the water. Bring to boiling; simmer, covered, 20 minutes. Add remaining ingredients. Bring to boiling; simmer, covered, 10 minutes, until vegetables are tender. Remove chicken; julienne. Stir chicken into soup.

Makes 6 servings, 235 calories each.

Micro-Way: Elegant First Courses

Mushrooms à la Grecque

1 pound button mushrooms
½ cup olive oil
1 large lemon
¼ cup tarragon vinegar
2 large cloves garlic, crushed
1 bay leaf
½ teaspoon dried thyme leaves
1 can (14 ounces) hearts of
  palm, diagonally sliced
1 teaspoon salt
⅛ teaspoon pepper

In glass bowl, mix mushrooms and oil. Cover; cook on HIGH 3 minutes. Grate lemon peel to make

1 teaspoon; add to mushrooms with 3 tablespoons juice from lemon and remaining ingredients. Cover; cook on HIGH 5 minutes. Chill. If desired, serve on lettuce-lined platter.

Makes 4 servings.

Red Lentils Vinaigrette

1 cup dry red lentils
1 bay leaf
½ teaspoon dried thyme leaves
3 cups water

Dressing
⅓ cup olive oil
3 tablespoons lemon juice
2 large cloves garlic, crushed
½ teaspoon salt
⅛ teaspoon pepper
1 tablespoon coarse Dijon-style
  mustard

1 small green or red pepper,
  diced
1 celery stalk, diced
1 large carrot, shredded
1 small red onion, finely
  chopped

In very large glass bowl, combine lentils, bay leaf, thyme and water. Cover; cook on HIGH 15 minutes, or until lentils are tender, stirring every 5 minutes. Discard bay leaf; drain lentils. In large bowl, blend dressing ingredients; stir in lentils and remaining ingredients. Serve warm or chilled; if desired, serve on platter lined with endive leaves.

Makes 8 servings.

Squash Timbales

¼ cup butter or margarine
1 (1-pound) butternut squash,
  pared, seeded and shredded
4 green onions, sliced
2 tablespoons orange juice
½ cup (2 ounces) shredded
  Swiss cheese
½ teaspoon salt
¼ teaspoon ground ginger
¼ teaspoon pepper
3 large eggs
¾ cup half-and-half

1. With 2 tablespoons butter, grease six 6-ounce glass custard cups. In large glass bowl, mix remaining butter, the squash, onions and orange juice. Cover tightly; cook on HIGH 6 minutes, stirring after 3 minutes. Stir in cheese, salt, ginger, and pepper.

2. In small bowl, whisk eggs with half-and-half until well blended; stir into squash mixture. Spoon into prepared cups. Place cups in a circle in microwave; cook on MEDIUM 10 minutes, rotating cups every 4 minutes. Cover cups with waxed paper; let stand 10 minutes. Remove waxed paper; invert onto serving dish. If desired, garnish with green onions and peppers.

Makes 6 servings.

■ One of the nicest things about a microwave is the variety of products you can use in it. You can heat a roll on a napkin or reheat a meal on a dinner plate (instead of warming up food in pans that have to be washed). You can use plastic, paper, glass, ceramic and china dishes that can go from the freezer to the microwave to the table— even into the dishwasher.

■ To test whether a dish or utensil is microwave-safe, place it in the microwave and cook on HIGH for 15 seconds. If the dish or utensil is very warm to the touch, it should not be used in the microwave oven.

Clockwise from left: Red Lentils Vinaigrette, Mushrooms à la Grecque, Squash Timbales.

December

Enjoy a special gala dinner this year by choosing a menu from our holiday cookbook. Our collection ranges from scallop-sandwich appetizers to Yule-log cake, with a host of delicious dishes in between. Special cause for celebration—our dazzling array of deluxe Noël desserts.

Shrimp Fajitas in Lettuce

Oysters à la Ross   Curried-Chicken Puffs

Endive Mediterranée   Burrito Bundles

Scallop Sandwich Beurre Blanc

Leek Tartlets   Cucumber Rolls

Avocado-Phyllo Stars   Chicken Quenelle Tureen

Peppered Rib Roast

Broccoli Medley   Tomatoes Florentine

Holiday Salad Vinaigrette

Double Chocolate Mousse Bombe

Babas au Rhum   Bourbon Pecan Truffles

Cranberry Cream Tart   Pears en Croûte

Macadamia Macaroons   Winter-Fruit Strudel

Bûche de Noël   Hazelnut Cream Cake

Holiday Parties Cookbook

Starting here, our toast to the season—grand and glorious recipes like these elegant cocktail hors d'oeuvres.

Oysters à la Ross
(pictured, page 193)

1 tablespoon butter or
    margarine
1 bulb fennel (6 ounces), diced
1 small red pepper, diced
1 cup heavy cream
¼ cup Pernod
¼ teaspoon salt
18 oysters on the half shell

Page 193: (Clockwise from top) Oysters à la Ross, Shrimp Fajitas in Lettuce, Curried-Chicken Puffs, Endive Méditerranée, Burrito Bundles, Leek Tartlets, Cucumber Rolls, (center of front platter) Avocado-Phyllo Stars.

Pages 194 and 195: (Clockwise from top right) Peppered Rib Roast, Tomatoes Florentine, Horseradish-Cream Sauce, Holiday Salad Vinaigrette, Scallop Sandwich Beurre Blanc, Bûche de Noël, Chicken Quenelle Tureen, (center) Broccoli Medley.

Pages 196 and 197: (Clockwise from top right) Cranberry Cream Tart, Hazelnut Cream Cake, Winter-Fruit Strudel, Pears en Croûte, Macadamia Macaroons, Bourbon Pecan Truffles, Double Chocolate Mousse Bombe, (center) Babas au Rhum.

1. Preheat oven to 475°F. In 10-inch skillet, over medium heat, melt butter. Add fennel and pepper; sauté 5 minutes. With slotted spoon, remove vegetables to bowl. To drippings in pan, add heavy cream and the liqueur; bring to boiling. Boil 4 minutes, or until sauce is reduced to about ¾ cup. Stir in salt.

2. Arrange oysters in broiler pan; top each with about 1 teaspoon cream sauce and then 1 teaspoon vegetable mixture. Bake 5 minutes, or until oysters are hot and edges curl. If desired, serve on sea-salt-lined platter garnished with chives.
Makes 18 servings.

■ Aluminum foil is the key to easy cleanup after baking. Simply line pans or sheets with foil—no need to grease or flour—and, when you remove from oven, just throw away the foil!

■ Toasted walnuts add an unusual flavor to any holiday dish. Bake the shelled nuts at 350°F in a shallow baking pan for 12 minutes or until golden. In a real rush? Microwave! Spread 1 cup walnut pieces in a glass pie plate. Cook on HIGH 5 minutes, stirring every 2 minutes.

Shrimp Fajitas in Lettuce
(pictured, page 193)

Dipping Sauce
2 tablespoons minced green
    onions
¼ cup soy sauce
2 tablespoons rice vinegar

Filling
½ pound sweet Italian sausage,
    casing removed
½ green pepper, diced
½ red pepper, diced
½ pound medium shrimp,
    peeled, deveined and diced
2 teaspoons grated gingerroot
⅛ teaspoon crushed
    red-pepper flakes

20 leaves radicchio

1. Mix sauce ingredients. Set sauce aside.
2. Make filling: In large skillet, over medium heat, sauté sausage and green and red peppers 8 minutes, or until sausage is browned, breaking up sausage with a spoon. Stir in shrimp, ginger and pepper flakes; sauté 2 minutes, or until shrimp is just cooked.
3. Spoon about 2 tablespoons shrimp mixture into each radicchio leaf. To eat, roll radicchio leaves around shrimp filling and dip fajitas into sauce.
Makes 20 fajitas.

Cucumber Rolls

(pictured, page 193)

12-inch European-style cucumber
2 packages (5-ounce size)
   garlic-and-herb cheese spread
1 green onion, minced
1 tablespoon minced parsley
1 large carrot, shredded

1. Cut off ½ inch from ends of cucumber. Using a mandoline or vegetable peeler, cut cucumber lengthwise into about 24 thin slices; dry with paper towels.

2. In bowl, combine cheese, green onion and parsley; spread 2 teaspoons mixture over length of each cucumber slice. Sprinkle with carrot; roll up, jelly-roll fashion. Place rolls, seam sides down, on serving dish. Cover with plastic wrap; refrigerate until serving.

Makes 24 rolls.

Curried-Chicken Puffs

(pictured, page 193)

2 tablespoons salad oil
1 carrot, finely chopped
1 celery stalk, finely chopped
1 onion, finely chopped
1 tablespoon ground coriander
   seeds
1 teaspoon mustard seeds
1 teaspoon turmeric
½ teaspoon ground ginger
⅛ teaspoon ground red pepper
½ pound boneless chicken
   breast, skinned and finely
   chopped
1 tablespoon all-purpose flour
¼ teaspoon salt
½ cup chicken broth
3 tablespoons plain yogurt
1 package (17¼ ounces) frozen
   puff pastry, thawed
1 large egg yolk, beaten
Cilantro (fresh coriander) leaves

1. In large skillet, heat oil over medium-high heat. Add carrot, celery, onion, coriander, mustard seeds, turmeric, ginger and ground pepper; sauté 5 minutes. Stir in chicken, flour and salt; sauté 2 minutes, or until chicken is cooked. Stir in chicken broth; bring to boiling. Simmer, stirring, 5 minutes, or until thickened. Remove pan from heat; cool. Whisk in yogurt.

2. Preheat oven to 400°F. Place one sheet pastry on floured surface. With short side of pastry facing you, cut pastry lengthwise into 5 equal strips and then crosswise into 5 strips to make 25 equal rectangles. Place rectangles on baking sheet; repeat with remaining pastry sheet. Brush top of each rectangle with some egg yolk; top each rectangle with a cilantro leaf. Bake 10 minutes, or until puffed. Cool on wire racks. Split each pastry rectangle in half almost all the way through; spoon about 2 teaspoons chicken mixture into each.

Makes 50 servings.

Avocado-Phyllo Stars

(pictured, page 193)

1 avocado, peeled, pitted and
   mashed
2 green onions, minced
1 small tomato, seeded and
   diced
⅓ cup grated Parmesan cheese
¼ teaspoon hot-red-pepper
   sauce
½ cup lump crabmeat
8 sheets phyllo pastry
¼ cup butter or margarine,
   melted

1. In bowl, mix first five ingredients; fold in crab.

2. Preheat oven to 375°F. On work surface, place 1 sheet phyllo with long side facing you; brush with some butter. Top with second sheet phyllo; repeat with butter and phyllo to make 4 layers. Cut phyllo stack lengthwise into 5 equal strips and then crosswise into fourths to make 20 equal rectangles of stacked phyllo. Place about 1 teaspoon avocado mixture in center of top of each stack; bring opposite corners of phyllo over mixture on each stack, pinching all corners together on top. Place on baking sheet. Repeat with remaining phyllo, butter and avocado mixture, using some of remaining butter to brush cut-pastry edges. Bake 8 minutes, or until lightly browned.

Makes 40 servings.

Endive Mediterranée

(pictured, page 193)

6 ounces Gorgonzola or other
   blue cheese
⅓ cup chopped walnuts
24 Belgian endive leaves
1 large Bartlett pear, halved
   and cored
1 ounce thinly sliced
   prosciutto

1. In bowl, mix cheese and nuts; spoon 1 teaspoon mixture onto each endive leaf. Cut pear lengthwise into 12 slices; cut each slice crosswise in half. Place one piece pear over cheese mixture on each endive leaf.

2. Cut prosciutto into ½-inch-wide strips; roll up each strip, jelly-roll fashion. Arrange one roll of prosciutto on each piece of pear. Place filled leaves on dish. Cover with plastic wrap; chill until serving.

Makes 24 servings.

Burrito Bundles
(pictured, page 193)

6 (7- to 8-inch) flour tortillas
½ pound lean ground beef
2 teaspoons chili powder
½ teaspoon ground cumin
¼ teaspoon salt
½ cup bottled mild salsa
½ cup frozen corn kernels,
  thawed
½ cup (2 ounces) shredded
  Monterey Jack cheese with
  jalapeños
1 bunch chives

1. Using 3-inch-round cookie cutter, cut out 4 rounds from each tortilla. Cover with damp paper towels; set aside.

2. In large skillet, over high heat, sauté beef with chili powder, cumin and salt until beef is browned. Stir in salsa and corn. Remove pan from heat; stir in cheese.

3. Preheat oven to 400°F. Place about 1 tablespoon beef mixture in center of each tortilla round. Using photograph as a guide, fold two opposite sides of each round over filling. Tie a chive around each tortilla bundle to hold together. Arrange bundles on baking sheet; bake 10 minutes, or until hot.

Makes 24 servings.

Leek Tartlets
(pictured, page 193)

Pastry
2 cups unsifted all-purpose
  flour
2 tablespoons sesame seeds
¼ cup cold butter or
  margarine
1 tablespoon shortening
5 to 6 tablespoons ice water

Filling
3 tablespoons butter or
  margarine
1 pound leeks, white part only,
  sliced and rinsed
1 small red onion, finely
  chopped
1 small red pepper, finely
  chopped
1 can (10¾ ounces) condensed
  cream-of-broccoli
  soup
1 cup (4 ounces) shredded
  Swiss cheese
2 large eggs, beaten

1. Make pastry: In bowl, mix flour and sesame seeds. With pastry blender or two knives, cut in butter and shortening until crumbly. Sprinkle 5 tablespoons ice water over mixture; with fork, toss until mixture holds together (add more water, 1 teaspoon at a time, if necessary). Divide in half; shape each into a disk. Wrap in plastic wrap; refrigerate 20 minutes.

2. Meanwhile, prepare filling: In skillet, over medium heat, melt butter. Add leeks, onion and pepper; sauté 15 minutes, or until vegetables are tender. Transfer to bowl; cool. Stir in remaining ingredients.

3. Preheat oven to 350°F. On floured surface, with floured rolling pin, roll out one pastry disk to ¼-inch thickness. Arrange 9 oval (3¾-inch-long) or 9 round (3½-inch-diameter) tartlet pans on baking sheet; using rolling pin, lift pastry over pans. Press pastry into pans; remove excess. Repeat with remaining pastry and 9 more pans, rerolling trimmings if necessary.

4. Fill pastry shells with leek mixture. Bake 20 minutes, or until puffed.

Makes 18 servings.

Bûche de Noël
(pictured, page 194)

Meringue Mushrooms (recipe
  follows)
Marzipan Holly and Berries
  (recipe follows)

Cake
1 cup sifted cake flour
¾ teaspoon baking powder
¼ teaspoon salt
6 large eggs
1 cup granulated sugar
1¼ teaspoons vanilla extract
2 tablespoons confectioners'
  sugar

Filling
1 cup heavy cream
2 teaspoons instant espresso
  powder
1 package (12 ounces)
  semisweet-chocolate pieces
2 tablespoons rum

Frosting
1½ cups heavy cream
½ cup unsweetened cocoa
  powder
⅓ cup confectioners' sugar

**Additional unsweetened cocoa
  powder**

1. Up to a week before serving, make Mushrooms and Marzipan.

2. Make cake: Preheat oven to 375°F. Grease 17¼-by-11½-by-1-inch jelly-roll pan; line with waxed paper. Grease and flour paper. Onto another sheet of waxed paper, sift flour, baking powder and salt. In large bowl of electric mixer, at medium speed, beat eggs until foamy. At high speed, beat in granulated sugar, 1 tablespoon at a time, beating until mixture is thick, about 5 minutes. Beat in vanilla. With rubber spatula, fold flour mixture into egg mixture, using an under-and-over motion, until just combined. Spread batter evenly in prepared pan. Bake 10 minutes, or until cake top springs back when touched.

■ Keep beef in its unopened package in the refrigerator, and use within four days (within two days for ground beef). Wrap cooked beef in aluminum foil, and use within five days.

3. Sprinkle a clean kitchen towel with the confectioners' sugar. With metal spatula, loosen cake around edges of pan; invert cake onto towel. Remove pan; peel off paper from cake. Starting at one short end, roll up cake with towel; cool.

4. Prepare filling: In small heavy pan, heat cream and espresso powder until boiling. Place chocolate in blender or food processor; pour in hot cream mixture. Puree. Pour into bowl; stir in rum. Refrigerate, stirring occasionally, until cold and thick enough to spread.

5. Unroll cake. Spread filling over inside curl of cake; roll up without the towel. Place cake, seam side down, on serving plate.

6. Make frosting: In small bowl of electric mixer, at high speed, beat frosting ingredients until stiff. For knots on the bûche, cut a 1-inch-thick slice on the diagonal from each end of the cake; place cut sides on side of the bûche. With metal spatula, spread frosting over cake, making barklike lines. Insert wooden picks into slices to hold in place. Refrigerate until serving.

7. To serve, place about 2 tablespoons cocoa powder in fine sieve; sprinkle over meringue mushrooms to resemble dirt. Arrange mushrooms and Marzipan Holly and Berries on and around bûche.

Makes 14 servings.

Meringue Mushrooms

2 large egg whites, at room temperature
¼ teaspoon cream of tartar
½ cup sugar
2 squares (1-ounce size) semisweet chocolate, melted

1. Preheat oven to 250°F. Line 2 baking sheets with aluminum foil or parchment paper.

2. In small bowl of electric mixer, at low speed, beat egg whites and cream of tartar until foamy. At high speed, beat in sugar, 1 tablespoon at a time, until stiff. Spoon meringue into pastry bag fitted with small plain tip. Pipe twenty (1½-inch-diameter) round mushroom caps onto foil on one sheet. Wet finger with water, and smooth points. Onto second prepared sheet, pipe twenty (1½-inch-long) mushroom stems. Bake 30 minutes, or until pieces are firm and dry. Cool completely before removing from foil.

3. With tip of paring knife, make a small hole in flat side of each mushroom cap; place a small amount of melted chocolate in each hole. Insert a stem into each cap; set aside to dry. Store in a cool, dry place.

Makes 20 servings.

Marzipan Holly and Berries

1 package (7 ounces) marzipan
Green and red food color
Granulated sugar

In small bowl, tint all but 2 tablespoons marzipan with green color. Tint remaining marzipan with red color. On work surface lightly sprinkled with sugar, roll out green marzipan to ⅛-inch thickness. Using small holly-leaf-shape cutter, cut out leaves, rerolling and cutting scraps. With knife, score veins in leaves. With hands, roll bits of red marzipan into berries. Store in cool, dry place.

Makes about ⅔ cup.

■ Making meringues for the holidays? We came up with this trick: Grind granulated sugar in the food processor, using on-and-off spurts for a few seconds. This sugar will dissolve very quickly in egg whites—and meringues won't have a gritty taste. (There's also another use for this handy trick: You can use this ground sugar in place of superfine sugar in beverages.)

Chicken Quenelle Tureen
(pictured, page 194)

¼ cup butter or margarine
1 medium head escarole, rinsed and torn into 3-inch pieces
1 small leek, white part only, thinly sliced and rinsed
1 yellow pepper, cubed
3 cans (about 14-ounce size) chicken broth
1 can (16 ounces) whole tomatoes, undrained
⅓ cup arborio (Italian short-grain) rice
1 cup water
1¾ teaspoons salt
¾ pound boneless chicken breasts, skinned and cut into 1-inch pieces
½ cup packed parsley leaves
1 cup fine dry bread crumbs
⅛ teaspoon ground nutmeg
2 large eggs
2 tablespoons milk
2 teaspoons grated onion
1½ teaspoons anchovy paste
1 teaspoon lemon juice
2 tablespoons grated Romano cheese

1. In 5-quart Dutch oven, over medium heat, melt butter. Add escarole, leek and pepper; sauté 5 minutes. Add chicken broth, tomatoes and their liquid, rice, water and 1 teaspoon salt. Bring to boiling; simmer, covered, 20 minutes, or until rice is tender.

2. Meanwhile, make quenelles: In food processor, finely chop chicken and parsley. Add remaining ¾ teaspoon salt and remaining ingredients except cheese; process just until mixed. Shape mixture into 1-inch balls.

3. Drop quenelles into simmering soup; return to boiling. Cook 5 minutes or until quenelles are cooked. Sprinkle with cheese.

Makes 14½ cups.

Broccoli Medley
(*pictured, page 194*)

1 bunch (1¾ pounds) broccoli
2 tablespoons salad oil
¼ pound mushrooms, quartered
1 onion, thinly sliced into rings
1 red pepper, julienned
1 can (8 ounces) whole water chestnuts, drained
¾ teaspoon salt
¼ cup rice vinegar
1 tablespoon dark sesame oil
2 tablespoons toasted sliced almonds

1. Trim broccoli; cut into flowerets. Pare stems; cut crosswise into ½-inch pieces. In ½ inch boiling salted water in skillet, cook broccoli 3 minutes, or until tender-crisp; drain. Place in serving dish; keep warm.

2. In same skillet, heat salad oil over medium-high heat. Add mushrooms, onion and pepper; sauté 3 minutes, or until tender-crisp. Add water chestnuts, salt, vinegar and sesame oil; bring to boiling. Pour mixture over broccoli; sprinkle with almonds.

Makes 8 servings.

■ If scallops seem strong or old in aroma, add 1 tablespoon lemon juice, sherry or brandy to the dish or add a generous dash of ground ginger.

■ You don't have to worry about meat mishaps. *If your roast is too rare,* arrange end slices on platter and return roast to oven, or slice and broil rare slices to desired doneness. *If meat is overcooked,* dip slices into gravy and arrange on platter. It's also a good idea to keep parsley on hand to add color; then just chop and sprinkle over meat.

Scallop Sandwich Beurre Blanc
(*pictured, page 194*)

1 pound baking potatoes
About ½ cup salad oil
¼ cup plus 1 tablespoon butter (sauce will not thicken if margarine is used)
¼ cup minced red pepper
2 tablespoons minced onion
½ pound sea scallops, cut horizontally in half or, if large, into thirds
¼ teaspoon salt
¼ cup plus 1 tablespoon dry white wine
1 shallot, sliced
1½ teaspoons green peppercorns, drained
4 teaspoons heavy cream

1. Scrub, pare and shred potatoes. Place in large bowl of cold water to prevent discoloration. Drain; place on clean kitchen towel. Roll potatoes in towel; squeeze dry.

2. Preheat oven to 250°F. In large skillet, heat 3 tablespoons oil over medium heat. For each of 16 pancakes, drop about 2 tablespoons potatoes into hot oil; flatten with pancake turner. Cook 3 minutes, or until bottom is golden; turn pancake. Cook other side until golden. Remove to baking pan; keep warm in oven while cooking remaining pancakes, adding oil as needed.

3. In same skillet, over medium-high heat, melt 1 tablespoon butter. Add pepper and onion; sauté 3 minutes, or until tender. Add scallops and salt; sauté 5 minutes, or until scallops are just cooked. Add 1 tablespoon wine; cook until wine evaporates. Remove pan from heat.

4. In saucepan, over medium-high heat, bring remaining wine and the shallot to boiling; cook until reduced to 1 tablespoon. Strain through fine sieve; discard shallot. Return wine to pan; add peppercorns. Over low heat, whisk in remaining butter, 1 tablespoon at a time, until butter is just melted and

mixture is thick. Remove pan from heat; whisk in cream and then scallop mixture.

5. For each serving, place one pancake on serving dish; top with some scallop mixture. Cover with another pancake.

Makes 8 servings.

Peppered Rib Roast
(*pictured, page 195*)

2 tablespoons green peppercorns (not in brine)
2 tablespoons white peppercorns
1 tablespoon whole allspice
12- to 14-pound rib roast (6 ribs)
Horseradish-Cream Sauce (recipe follows)

1. Preheat oven to 325°F. Place spices in plastic bag; crush with rolling pin.

2. Place roast, fat side up, in large roasting pan. Insert meat thermometer through fat into thickest part of meat (point of thermometer should not rest on fat or bone). Press spices onto roast. Cook, uncovered, until thermometer registers 135°F for rare or 160°F for medium-well, about 4 hours. Let roast stand on carving platter, loosely covered with foil, 10 minutes (roast will continue to cook while standing). Serve with Horseradish-Cream Sauce.

Makes 16 servings.

Horseradish-Cream Sauce
(*pictured, page 195*)

1 jar (4 ounces) prepared white horseradish
½ cup mayonnaise
½ cup sour cream
2 tablespoons minced parsley
1 shallot, minced
¼ teaspoon salt
1 tablespoon Dijon mustard
½ cup heavy cream, whipped

In bowl, whisk all ingredients except whipped cream. Fold in cream. Cover; refrigerate. Whisk just before serving.

Makes about 2½ cups.

Tomatoes Florentine
(pictured, page 195)

6 large tomatoes
1 teaspoon dried fines herbs, crushed
1 teaspoon salt
½ teaspoon pepper
2 tablespoons olive oil
1 medium onion, finely chopped
¼ cup pine nuts
1 medium clove garlic, crushed
1 package (10 ounces) frozen chopped spinach, thawed and squeezed dry
½ cup uncooked white rice
¼ cup chopped parsley
½ cup water
½ cup dry white wine

1. Cut off tomato tops by inserting tip of paring knife into each ½ inch from top at an angle and continuing around tomato zigzag fashion. Chop and reserve tops. Scoop out pulp from each tomato. Discard seeds; chop and reserve pulp.

2. Place tomatoes in baking dish; sprinkle inside of each with mixture of fines herbs, ½ teaspoon salt and ¼ teaspoon pepper, dividing evenly.

3. In skillet, heat olive oil over medium-high heat. Add onion, pine nuts and garlic; sauté 5 minutes, or until onions are tender. Stir in spinach, chopped tomato, the remaining salt and pepper, the rice, chopped parsley, water and white wine. Simmer, uncovered, 30 minutes, or until rice is cooked.

4. Preheat oven to 350°F. Fill each tomato with rice mixture. Bake 20 minutes, or until tomatoes and filling are hot.

Makes 6 servings.

Holiday Salad Vinaigrette
(pictured, page 195)

1 pound green beans, trimmed
1 medium red apple, cored
1 ripe avocado, pitted and peeled
1 medium red Bartlett pear, cored
2 tablespoons lemon juice
Red-leaf lettuce leaves
Boston lettuce leaves
2 navel oranges, peeled and sectioned
Champagne grapes
Honey-Mustard Vinaigrette (recipe follows)

1. In ½ inch boiling salted water in saucepan, cook green beans 3 minutes, or until tender-crisp. Drain; place in bowl of ice and water until cool. Drain; pat dry.

2. Cut apple, avocado and pear lengthwise into thin wedges; brush with lemon juice. On platter, arrange lettuce leaves, green beans and fruits. Pass dressing separately.

Makes 8 servings.

Honey-Mustard Vinaigrette

1 tablespoon minced parsley
1 teaspoon salt
⅛ teaspoon freshly ground pepper
¾ cup salad oil
¼ cup red-wine vinegar
2 tablespoons honey
1 tablespoon prepared mustard

In jar with tight-fitting lid, combine ingredients. Shake until blended.

Makes about 1¼ cups.

■ Store chocolate tightly wrapped or covered in a cool, dry place or in the refrigerator.

Macadamia Macaroons
(pictured, page 196)

1 cup toasted macadamia nuts
1¼ cups sugar
1 can (8 ounces) almond paste
2 large egg whites
1 teaspoon grated lemon peel
3 squares (1-ounce size) semisweet chocolate, melted
3 ounces white chocolate, melted

1. Preheat oven to 425°F. Line 2 baking sheets with parchment paper or aluminum foil.

2. In food processor, grind nuts with ¼ cup sugar. In bowl, mix almond paste, egg whites, lemon peel and remaining sugar; beat in nut mixture. Place in pastry bag fitted with ½-inch star tip. Pipe 1½-inch rosettes onto baking sheets. Bake 8 minutes, or until golden. Cool on wire racks. Dip half of each macaroon into one of the chocolates.

Makes 4 dozen.

Bourbon Pecan Truffles
(pictured, page 196)

2⅓ cups sifted confectioners' sugar
½ cup plus 3 tablespoons European-style unsweetened cocoa powder
Dash salt
⅓ cup unsalted butter, melted
2 tablespoons bourbon
2 tablespoons heavy cream
½ teaspoon vanilla extract
¾ cup chopped pecans

1. In bowl, mix sugar and ½ cup cocoa powder. Stir in next five ingredients until blended. Stir in nuts. Cover with plastic wrap; chill 2 hours, or until firm.

2. With hands, form truffle mixture into 1-inch balls. On sheet of waxed paper, roll balls in remaining cocoa powder. Place in airtight container; chill until serving.

Makes about 3 dozen.

Babas au Rhum

(pictured, page 196)

½ cup raisins
1 tablespoon dark rum
2¼ cups unsifted all-purpose
  flour
¼ cup sugar
1 package fast-rising or regular
  dry yeast
¼ teaspoon salt
½ cup milk
⅓ cup butter or margarine
2 large eggs, at room
  temperature

Rum Syrup
1½ cups sugar
1½ cups water
¾ cup dark rum

1. In small bowl, mix raisins and rum; let stand 30 minutes.

2. In large bowl of electric mixer, combine 1½ cups flour, the sugar, yeast and salt. In small saucepan, heat milk and butter until butter melts and mixture is 120° to 130°F. With mixer at low speed, pour milk mixture and eggs into flour mixture. Beat at medium speed 3 minutes, scraping bowl with rubber spatula. With wooden spoon, stir in soaked raisins and remaining flour. Cover bowl with a kitchen towel; let stand in a warm place (85°F), free from drafts, until doubled in bulk, about 45 minutes.

3. Meanwhile, grease 5 (4-inch) mini Bundt or 10 (2½- to 3-inch) muffin pans.

4. Stir down dough; spoon into prepared pans, dividing evenly (dough should fill pans halfway). Cover with kitchen towel; let rise until dough reaches ½ inch from top of pan, about 30 minutes.

5. Preheat oven to 350°F. Bake babas 20 minutes, or until golden. Cool in pans.

6. Meanwhile, make syrup: In medium saucepan, bring sugar and water to boiling, swirling pan to dissolve sugar. Boil 10 minutes. Stir in rum; simmer 1 minute.

7. Remove babas from pans; place in shallow dish. With skewers, pierce babas thoroughly. Pour syrup over babas, turning babas and basting with syrup to coat and soak well. Cover with plastic wrap; let stand at room temperature, occasionally turning and basting with syrup, until all syrup is absorbed, about 1 hour.
  Makes 5 (4-inch) babas.

Double Chocolate Mousse Bombe

(pictured, page 196)

1 package (10¾ ounces) frozen
  pound cake, thawed
½ cup chocolate-wafer cookie
  crumbs
¼ cup crushed bittersweet
  almond-flavored Italian
  cookies
1 tablespoon almond-flavored
  liqueur
¾ cup milk
3 tablespoons orange-flavored
  liqueur
2 envelopes unflavored gelatine
13½ ounces white chocolate,
  chopped
4 large egg whites
⅓ cup sugar
1½ cups heavy cream

Ganache
6 squares (1-ounce size)
  semisweet chocolate
⅔ cup heavy cream

1. Day before serving: Line 2½-quart bowl with aluminum foil. Cut cake crosswise into ¼-inch-thick slices; line prepared bowl to within ½ inch of top with cake slices, cutting some into triangles to fit.

2. In small bowl, combine all cookie crumbs and almond-flavored liqueur; set aside. In top of double boiler, combine milk, orange-flavored liqueur and gelatine; let soak 1 minute. Place over hot, not boiling, water; heat, stirring, until

gelatine dissolves. Add 12 ounces white chocolate; stir until melted. Pour into large bowl; cool.

3. In large bowl of electric mixer, at low speed, beat egg whites until foamy. At high speed, beat in sugar, 1 tablespoon at a time, until stiff peaks form when beaters are raised. Stir about ½ cup meringue mixture into gelatine mixture; with rubber spatula, fold in remaining meringue. In clean large bowl of electric mixer, at high speed, beat 1½ cups cream until stiff; with rubber spatula, fold into gelatine mixture. Spoon about 4 cups mousse into cake-lined bowl; sprinkle with cookie-crumb mixture. Spoon remaining mousse on top. Cover; refrigerate overnight, or until firm.

4. Day of serving, make ganache: In small saucepan, combine ganache ingredients. Over low heat, cook, stirring, until smooth. Refrigerate until thick but still pourable, about 1 hour. Invert bombe onto 8-inch cardboard cake round; remove foil. Place bombe (on cake round) on wire rack over baking sheet. Pour ganache over bombe, spreading smoothly with spatula. Melt remaining 1½ ounces white chocolate; with spoon, drizzle over bombe. Chill 1 hour, or until ganache and chocolate are firm. Place on serving dish. If desired, decorate with sweetened whipped cream.
  Makes 16 to 20 servings.

■ Did you know that extra egg whites can be kept in a sealed jar in your refrigerator for up to one year? You can also freeze, defrost and refreeze them. A helpful note: One egg white is approximately an eighth of a cup, or about two tablespoons.

■ A substitution for 1 cup milk: 1 cup skim milk plus 2 tablespoons butter or margarine.

Cranberry Cream Tart
(pictured, page 197)

Pastry
1 cup unsifted all-purpose flour
2 tablespoons sugar
6 tablespoons cold butter or margarine
1 large egg yolk

Filling
1 package (8 ounces) cream cheese, softened
½ can (15-ounce size) chestnut puree
¾ cup confectioners' sugar
¼ cup butter or margarine, softened
¼ cup brandy
1 teaspoon vanilla extract

¼ cup seedless raspberry jam
2 tablespoons granulated sugar
2 tablespoons water
2½ cups cranberries

1. Make pastry: In food processor, mix flour, sugar and butter. Using pulse motion, process just until mixture is crumbly. Add egg yolk; process just until mixture holds together. Turn out into 9-inch tart pan with removable bottom; pat to line pan with pastry. Refrigerate 15 minutes.

2. Preheat oven to 400°F. Line pastry shell with aluminum foil; spoon pie weights over foil. Bake 10 minutes; carefully lift out foil and weights. Bake 4 minutes longer, or until golden. Cool pastry in pan on wire rack.

3. Make filling: In food processor, combine filling ingredients; process until blended. Spread over cooled pastry shell; chill until firm.

4. In small saucepan, combine jam, sugar and water; bring to boiling. Add cranberries; cook, stirring constantly, 5 minutes, or until mixture is thickened but still has some whole berries. Cool completely.

5. Spread cooled cranberry mixture over chestnut cream. If desired, garnish tart with sweetened whipped cream, sugared cranberries and chocolate leaves.

Makes 8 servings.

Hazelnut Cream Cake
(pictured, page 197)

Cake
6 large eggs, at room temperature
1 cup sugar
2 teaspoons vanilla extract
1½ cups unsifted cake flour
1 teaspoon instant espresso powder
½ cup finely ground toasted hazelnuts
6 tablespoons butter or margarine, melted

½ cup hazelnut-flavored liqueur
1¾ cups seedless raspberry jam
Lemon Frosting (recipe follows)

1. Make cake: Preheat oven to 350°F. Line 15½-by-10½-by-1-inch jelly-roll pan with aluminum foil; grease and flour foil. In large bowl of electric mixer, at low speed, beat eggs until foamy. At high speed, beat until lemon-colored. Gradually beat in sugar; beat 5 minutes, or until mixture forms a ribbon when beaters are raised and sugar is dissolved. Beat in vanilla. On sheet of waxed paper, combine flour and espresso powder; sift one-fourth of mixture at a time over egg mixture and fold in just until blended before adding more flour mixture. Fold in nuts. Spoon about ½ cup batter into small bowl; fold in melted butter until blended. Fold butter mixture into remaining batter; spread into prepared pan. Bake 18 minutes, or until cake top springs back when touched. Cool in pan on wire rack.

2. Assemble cake: With long side of cooled cake facing you, cut cake crosswise into 4 equal rectangles. Cut each rectangle crosswise in half to make 8 equal rectangles. Place one rectangle on serving platter; brush with some liqueur and spread with ¼ cup jam. Top with another cake layer; repeat layering with remaining liqueur, jam and cake. Reserve ¾ cup frosting; with metal spatula, spread remainder over cake. Using pastry decorating comb, make ridges in frosting on sides of cake. With reserved lemon frosting in pastry bag fitted with star tip, decorate top of cake.

Makes 16 servings.

Lemon Frosting

1 cup butter or margarine, softened
4 cups confectioners' sugar
1 teaspoon grated lemon peel
2 tablespoons fresh lemon juice
1 tablespoon milk

In large bowl of electric mixer, at high speed, beat ingredients until blended.

Makes 2¾ cups.

■ Cakes freeze better without icing or filling. For best results, place cooled, baked layers in freezer bags or plastic wrap then seal and freeze. Keep in mind that cakes with uncooked frosting can be frozen successfully, while cakes with cooked frostings or whipped-cream toppings do not freeze well.

Winter-Fruit Strudel

(pictured, page 197)

1 cup pitted prunes, halved
½ cup brandy
5 medium Granny Smith apples
   (2 pounds), pared and cored
2 cups cranberries
1 cup sugar
⅔ cup chopped walnuts
½ cup fine dry bread crumbs
1 teaspoon ground cinnamon
1 teaspoon grated lemon peel
¼ teaspoon ground nutmeg
1 tablespoon lemon juice
½ pound phyllo pastry (about
   12 leaves)
¾ cup butter or margarine,
   melted

1. In saucepan, simmer prunes and brandy, covered, 10 minutes. Cool mixture.

2. Thinly slice apples; place in large bowl with prunes, the cranberries, sugar, ½ cup walnuts, ⅓ cup bread crumbs, the cinnamon, lemon peel, nutmeg and lemon juice. Mix well. In small bowl, combine remaining bread crumbs and walnuts; set aside.

3. Grease large jelly-roll pan. Preheat oven to 375°F. Cover phyllo with plastic wrap to keep from drying out. On work surface, overlap 2 sheets waxed paper to make a 17-by-15-inch rectangle. With long side facing you, place 1 sheet phyllo on waxed paper; brush lightly with some melted butter. Place another sheet phyllo so that it overlaps first sheet and covers the waxed paper; brush with some butter. Repeat with remaining pastry and butter, sprinkling bread crumb–walnut mixture between the last 2 pastry sheets.

4. Spoon fruit mixture over one long half of the pastry rectangle, leaving a 1-inch border on 3 sides. Fold the short sides of the rectangle over the filling; beginning with filled long side, roll up strudel, jelly-roll fashion, using waxed paper to roll strudel and to transfer, and place it, seam side down, on prepared pan.

Brush strudel with remaining butter. Bake 45 minutes, or until golden. Cool on baking sheet on rack. If desired, before serving, sift confectioners' sugar over strudel.

Makes 12 servings.

Pears en Croûte

(pictured, page 197)

Pastry
½ cup butter or margarine,
   softened
½ package (8-ounce size)
   cream cheese, softened
1 cup unsifted all-purpose
   flour

3 tablespoons sugar
¼ teaspoon ground cinnamon
2 pears, pared, halved and
   cored
1 large egg
1 tablespoon heavy cream

Caramel Sauce
½ cup sugar
1 cup heavy cream

1. Make pastry: In bowl, blend butter and cream cheese; stir in flour. Shape into a disk; wrap in plastic wrap. Refrigerate 2 hours.

2. Place 3 tablespoons sugar and cinnamon in plastic bag. Place pear halves, one at a time, in bag; shake to coat with sugar mixture.

3. Grease baking sheet. On floured surface, with floured rolling pin, roll out pastry to 16-inch round; cut into 4 wedges. On each wedge, place a pear half, rounded side down and small end facing toward point of pastry wedge. Bring edges of each pastry wedge together, pinching off excess; pinch edges together to seal each pear inside pastry. Place pastry-wrapped pears, seam side down, on prepared baking sheet. Reroll pastry scraps; cut out leaves and strips for vines. With sharp knife, score veins on leaves. Place pastry vine and leaf

pieces on pastry-wrapped pears. Freeze on baking sheet 15 minutes.

4. Preheat oven to 350°F. In custard cup, blend egg with 1 tablespoon cream; with pastry brush, brush pastry-wrapped pears. Bake 45 minutes, or until browned. Cool pears slightly on baking sheet on wire rack.

5. Meanwhile, make sauce: In large heavy skillet, over medium-high heat, melt sugar. Lower heat to medium; heat sugar, stirring, until caramel colored. In small saucepan, heat cream until very hot. Remove skillet from heat; carefully stir in hot cream. Cook, stirring, 3 minutes, or until smooth and thickened. To serve, pour some warm sauce onto each of 4 serving dishes; arrange a warm pastry-wrapped pear on top. Pass remaining sauce.

Makes 4 servings, 1 cup sauce.

Christmas Angel Food Cake

Strawberry-Cream Filling
2 packages (10-ounce size)
   frozen strawberry halves,
   thawed
Water
1 envelope unflavored gelatine
½ cup sugar
1 tablespoon lemon juice
Dash salt
Red food color (optional)

1 (10-inch) angel-food cake
   (made from a packaged mix)
1½ cups heavy cream, beaten
   until stiff
10 strawberries
Strawberry Sauce (recipe
   follows)

1. Day before, make strawberry-cream filling: Drain strawberries, reserving syrup; add water to syrup to make 1½ cups. Sprinkle gelatine over syrup in small saucepan to soften. Place over low heat, stirring until gelatine is dissolved.

2. In large bowl, combine strawberries, the sugar, lemon juice, salt and if desired, a few drops red food color; mix well. Stir gelatine into strawberry mixture.

3. Set in pan of ice and water. Let stand, stirring occasionally, 20 to 30 minutes, or until mixture thickens and mounds slightly.

4. Meanwhile, using knife with a serrated edge, cut cake in half crosswise; cut one half into 1½-inch cubes (freeze other cake half for another use). Lightly grease inside of 10-inch Bundt pan or 10-inch tube pan.

5. When filling is completely cool but not set, using rubber scraper, fold in whipped cream until well combined. Add cake cubes; mix lightly. Turn into prepared pan; smooth top with spatula. Refrigerate, covered, overnight, until thoroughly chilled and set.

6. To unmold: Run metal spatula around edge of pan. Invert cake onto serving dish; shake to loosen cake from pan. If cake does not come out, let stand a few minutes; shake again.

7. Decorate with whole strawberries. Serve with Strawberry Sauce. Makes 12 servings.

Strawberry Sauce

**1 package (10 ounces) frozen
  sliced strawberries, thawed
Water
2 tablespoons sugar
1 tablespoon cornstarch**

1. Drain strawberries, reserving syrup. Add water to syrup to measure 1 cup.

2. In small saucepan, combine sugar and cornstarch. Gradually add strawberry syrup, stirring until smooth. Over low heat, slowly bring to boiling, stirring, until mixture is thickened and translucent.

3. Remove from heat. Stir in strawberries. Refrigerate until cold. Makes 1½ cups.

Decadent Mocha-Bourbon Cake

**1 package (about 18 ounces)
  chocolate-fudge cake mix
¼ cup unsweetened cocoa
  powder
1 tablespoon instant-coffee
  powder
1 cup water
½ cup salad oil
¼ cup bourbon
3 large eggs**

**Mocha Filling
1½ cups unsalted butter,
  softened
4 large egg yolks
1 cup sugar
½ cup water
2 squares (1-ounce size)
  semisweet chocolate, melted
2 to 4 tablespoons bourbon
1 tablespoon instant-coffee
  powder**

**Chocolate Glaze (recipe
  follows)
Candied violets**

1. Up to one week ahead, prepare cake layers: Preheat oven to 350°F. Grease and flour three 9-inch round cake pans; set aside.

2. In large bowl of electric mixer, combine cake mix, cocoa and coffee. Add water, oil, bourbon and eggs. Beat at low speed just until mixture is moistened. Beat at medium speed 2 minutes. Pour cake mixture into pans.

3. Bake 20 minutes, or until wooden pick inserted in center comes out clean. Cool in pans 5 minutes. Remove cakes from pans; cool completely.

4. Make filling: In large bowl of electric mixer, at low speed, beat butter until creamy; set aside. In bowl of electric mixer, beat egg yolks at high speed 5 minutes, or until thick and lemon-colored; set filling aside.

5. In 1-quart saucepan, combine sugar and water; bring to boiling.

Continue to boil, without stirring, until mixture reaches the soft-ball stage, 234°F on a candy thermometer. Remove from heat. Gradually pour sugar syrup in a thin stream into egg yolks, beating constantly at low speed. Continue to beat 5 minutes, or until thickened and cooled. Gradually beat egg-yolk mixture into butter. Blend in chocolate.

6. In small bowl, combine 2 tablespoons bourbon and instant coffee; mix to dissolve coffee. Blend coffee mixture into butter mixture. Do not refrigerate.

7. Assemble cake: Brush tops of two cake layers with remaining 2 tablespoons bourbon, if desired. Spread ¾ cup mocha filling on each of two layers. Stack layers, filling sides up; top with remaining layer. With knife, trim sides to make even. Use ¾ cup filling to smooth sides. Refrigerate 30 minutes. (Do not refrigerate remaining filling.)

8. Place cake on rack set over jelly-roll pan. Pour chocolate glaze over top and spread on sides. Reuse any glaze that drips into pan. Chill 10 minutes, or until glaze sets. Place cake on serving plate. Place remaining ¾ cup filling in pastry bag fitted with a small shell tip. Pipe around filling around base of cake and on top. Garnish with candied violets. Chill until ready to serve.

Makes 12 servings.

Chocolate Glaze

**½ cup water
¼ cup sugar
4 squares (1-ounce size)
  semisweet chocolate**

In small saucepan, combine water and sugar. Bring to boiling, stirring, until sugar dissolves. Add chocolate; stir until chocolate melts. Simmer 1 minute, or until mixture thickens enough to coat back of spoon. Cool 30 minutes before using.

Makes about 1 cup.

McCall's Masterpiece: Fine Art Cookies

Truly elevated examples of the holiday baker's art—the finest cookies ever made.

From left: Mint Stick, Florentine, Holiday Bell, Cinnamon Star, Honey Ginger Crisp, Christmas Ornament Ball, Pretty Package Cookie, Lemon Sable, Sugar-and-Spice Cane, Coffee Kiss, Anise Rosette, Gingerbread Child, Fantasy Spritz.

McCall's Masterpiece

Mint Sticks

(pictured, page 208)

¾ cup butter or margarine, softened
½ cup sugar
1 large egg yolk
½ teaspoon mint extract
1¾ cups unsifted all-purpose flour
¼ teaspoon baking powder
1 tube (4.25 ounces) white decorating icing
2 tubes (.68-ounce size) red decorating gel

1. Preheat oven to 325°F. In bowl of electric mixer, at medium speed, beat butter with next three ingredients until blended. On waxed paper, combine flour and baking powder; with wooden spoon, stir into butter mixture until blended.

2. Shape 1 tablespoon dough into 4-inch log; place on ungreased baking sheet. Repeat with remaining dough. Bake 12 minutes, or until firm but not browned. Cool on baking sheet 1 minute. Transfer to wire rack; cool completely. Using photograph as a guide, decorate with icing and gel.
Makes 2 dozen.

Florentines

(pictured, page 208)

½ cup plus 2 tablespoons butter or margarine, softened
¾ cup confectioners' sugar
1 large egg
1 teaspoon brandy extract
1¾ cups unsifted all-purpose flour
½ cup granulated sugar
3 tablespoons honey
2 tablespoons heavy cream
1¼ cups toasted slivered almonds
1 cup chopped mixed candied fruit

1. In small bowl of electric mixer, at medium speed, beat ½ cup butter and the confectioners' sugar until blended. Beat in egg and brandy extract. With wooden spoon, stir in flour until blended.

2. Preheat oven to 350°F. On floured surface, with floured rolling pin, roll half the dough to ³⁄₁₆-inch thickness. With 2-inch round crinkle cutter, cut out dough; place cookies 1 inch apart on ungreased baking sheet. Repeat with remaining dough, rerolling scraps. Bake 12 minutes, or until edges start to brown. Transfer to wire racks; cool.

3. In saucepan, bring granulated sugar, honey, cream and remaining butter to boiling, stirring to dissolve sugar. Simmer 5 minutes. Off heat, stir in nuts and fruit. Spoon heaping teaspoon of mixture on center of each cookie. Cool.
Makes 56 cookies.

Holiday Bells

(pictured, page 208)

1 cup butter or margarine, softened
⅔ cup sugar
1 large egg
¼ cup maple syrup
2¾ cups unsifted all-purpose flour
1 teaspoon baking powder
¼ teaspoon red food color
½ cup finely chopped walnuts
Green candy sprinkles

1. In bowl of electric mixer, at medium speed, beat butter and sugar until blended. Beat in egg and syrup. On waxed paper, combine flour and baking powder; with wooden spoon, stir into butter mixture until blended. Wrap 1 cup dough in plastic wrap; set aside. Tint remaining dough with red food color. Wrap 2 tablespoons red dough in plastic wrap; chill. Add walnuts to remaining red dough. On lightly floured baking sheet, shape into a 12-inch-long log. Press along length on one side to shape as for the top of a bell (log will be cut crosswise into bell-shaped cookies). Chill dough on floured baking sheet 1 hour.

2. On sheet of waxed paper, with floured rolling pin, roll reserved 1 cup dough into 12-by-8-inch rectangle. With long side of dough facing you, place chilled bell-shaped log lengthwise on rectangle; wrap rolled dough around log, lightly pressing doughs together. Press green candy sprinkles onto uncolored dough. Cover with plastic wrap; freeze 1 hour.

3. Preheat oven to 350°F. Grease 3 baking sheets. With sharp knife, cut dough crosswise into ¼-inch-thick slices. Place 2 inches apart on baking sheets. Form reserved red dough into 42 small balls; press one ball onto each bell for clapper. Bake 9 minutes, or until set and edges just start to brown. Transfer cookies to wire racks; cool.
Makes 3½ dozen.

Cinnamon Stars

(pictured, page 208)

½ cup butter or margarine, softened
¾ cup plus 2 tablespoons sugar
2 large egg yolks
1 tablespoon milk
½ teaspoon vanilla extract
1½ cups unsifted all-purpose flour
1 teaspoon baking powder
1 large egg white, lightly beaten
¼ cup finely chopped pecans
Silver dragées
½ teaspoon ground cinnamon

1. In bowl of electric mixer, at medium speed, beat butter and ¾ cup sugar until blended. Beat in eggs, milk and vanilla. On waxed paper, combine flour and baking powder; with wooden spoon, stir into butter mixture until blended. Halve dough; shape into disks. Wrap in plastic wrap; chill 3 hours.

2. Preheat oven to 350°F. Grease 3 baking sheets. On floured surface, with floured rolling pin, roll out half the dough to ⅛-inch thickness. With 3-inch star-shaped cutter, cut out dough. Transfer to baking sheets; repeat with remaining dough, rerolling scraps. Brush cookies with egg white; sprinkle centers with pecans and press a dragée onto each point. Combine remaining sugar and the cinnamon; sprinkle over cookies. Bake 5 minutes, or until golden brown. Transfer to wire racks; cool. Makes 5 dozen.

Honey Ginger Crisps
(pictured, page 208)

½ cup butter or margarine, softened
¼ cup granulated sugar
2 tablespoons light-brown sugar
1 large egg
¼ cup honey
¼ cup molasses
2 cups unsifted all-purpose flour
¾ cup whole-wheat flour
1 teaspoon ground ginger
½ teaspoon baking soda
1 tube (4.25 ounces) green decorating icing
1 tube (4.25 ounces) red decorating icing
1 tube (4.25 ounces) white decorating icing

1. In bowl of electric mixer, at medium speed, beat butter with sugars until blended. Beat in egg, honey and molasses until blended. On waxed paper, combine flours with ginger and baking soda; with wooden spoon, stir into butter mixture until blended. Divide dough in half; shape into disks. Wrap in plastic wrap; chill 2 hours.

2. Preheat oven to 350°F. Grease 2 large baking sheets. On floured surface, roll out one-half of dough to ⅛-inch thickness. With 3-inch

round crinkle cutter, cut out dough; using ½-inch round crinkle cutter, cut out center of each round. Place large rounds 1 inch apart on baking sheets; repeat with remaining dough, rerolling scraps. Bake 9 minutes, or until lightly browned. Transfer to wire racks; cool. Decorate cookies with icing.
Makes 4 dozen.

Christmas Ornament Balls
(pictured, page 209)

Cookie Dough
¾ cup butter, softened
1½ cups sugar
2 large eggs
2 teaspoons vanilla extract
3 cups unsifted all-purpose flour
2½ teaspoons baking powder

Icing
3 cups confectioners' sugar
¼ teaspoon cream of tartar
2 large egg whites

Food colors
Candy decorations

1. Make dough: In large bowl of electric mixer, at medium speed, beat butter and sugar. Beat in eggs and vanilla. On waxed paper, mix flour and baking powder; stir into butter mixture. Divide dough into thirds; shape into disks. Wrap in plastic wrap; refrigerate 3 hours.

2. Preheat oven to 375°F. Grease 3 large baking sheets. On floured surface, with floured rolling pin, roll out one-third of dough to ⅛-inch thickness. Using 3- and 4-inch round cutters, cut out dough; place cookies on prepared baking sheets. Repeat with remaining dough, rerolling scraps. Bake 6 minutes, or until edges begin to brown. Transfer to wire racks to cool.

3. Beat icing ingredients until stiff. Tint with food colors, using a

separate bowl for each color. Decorate with icing and candies.
Makes about 3 dozen.

Pretty Package Cookies
(pictured, page 209)

Cookie Dough
¾ cup butter, softened
1½ cups sugar
2 large eggs
1 teaspoon grated orange peel
2 teaspoons orange extract
3 cups unsifted all-purpose flour
2½ teaspoons baking powder

Icing
1½ cups confectioners' sugar
¼ teaspoon cream of tartar
1 large egg white

Blue food color
Silver dragées

1. Make dough: In large bowl of electric mixer, at medium speed, beat butter and sugar. Beat in eggs, grated orange peel and orange extract until blended. On sheet of waxed paper, combine flour and baking powder; beat into butter mixture. Divide dough in half; shape into disks. Wrap in plastic wrap; refrigerate 3 hours.

2. Preheat oven to 350°F. Grease 3 baking sheets. On floured surface, with floured rolling pin, roll out half of dough to ⅛-inch thickness. Cut into 3-inch squares; place 1 inch apart on baking sheets. Repeat with remaining dough, rerolling scraps. Bake 9 minutes, or until edges brown. Transfer to racks; cool.

3. Beat icing ingredients until stiff. Beat in blue food color to desired shade. With icing in pastry bag fitted with small tip, pipe icing ribbon and bow on each cookie to resemble a package; while icing is wet, attach dragées to bows.
Makes about 3 dozen.

McCall's Masterpiece

Lemon Sables

(pictured, page 209)

Cookie Dough
½ cup butter or margarine, softened
¾ cup confectioners' sugar
3 large egg yolks
1½ teaspoons grated lemon peel
1 tablespoon lemon juice
1½ cups unsifted all-purpose flour

Icing
About 2½ cups confectioners' sugar
2 large egg whites

Food color

1. In bowl of electric mixer, at medium speed, beat butter and sugar until blended. Beat in egg yolks, lemon peel and lemon juice until blended. With wooden spoon, stir in flour until blended. Divide dough in half; shape into disks. Wrap in plastic wrap; chill 4 hours.

2. Preheat oven to 350°F. Grease large baking sheet. On floured surface, with floured rolling pin, roll out one-half of dough into a ⅛-inch-thick rectangle. Using assorted shapes of 3-inch cookie cutters, cut out dough; place 1 inch apart on baking sheet. Repeat with remaining dough, rerolling scraps. Bake 9 minutes, or until edges begin to brown. Transfer to wire racks; cool.

3. In bowl, with wooden spoon, mix 2½ cups sugar and egg whites until smooth. With metal spatula, spread icing over cookies. Let stand 15 minutes to dry. Add additional sugar to remaining icing to stiffen to piping consistency; tint with food color. Use to decorate cookies.
Makes 2 dozen.

Sugar-and-Spice Canes

(pictured, page 209)

½ package (17¼-ounce size) frozen puff pastry, thawed
¼ cup ground pecans
½ teaspoon ground cinnamon
1 tablespoon green decorating sugar
1 tablespoon red decorating sugar
1 large egg yolk
1 teaspoon water

1. Line 2 baking sheets with parchment paper. On floured surface, with floured rolling pin, roll out pastry to 12-inch square. In each of 2 custard cups, combine half the pecans with half the cinnamon. Stir green sugar into mixture in 1 cup; stir red sugar into mixture in other custard cup.

2. In clean custard cup, mix egg yolk with water; with pastry brush, spread half the mixture over pastry. Sprinkle pastry with green-sugar mixture, pressing it lightly over one side of pastry. Turn over; brush with remaining yolk mixture. Sprinkle with red-sugar mixture, pressing it lightly into pastry.

3. Cut pastry crosswise in half; cut each half crosswise into ½-inch-wide strips. Twist each strip so green and red colors alternate; bend one end to form a cane. Place canes 1 inch apart on prepared baking sheets. Refrigerate 20 minutes.

4. Preheat oven to 400°F. Bake one sheet of canes at a time, 7 minutes, or until golden brown. Transfer to wire racks to cool.
Makes 46 canes.

Coffee Kisses

(pictured, page 209)

¾ cup butter or margarine, softened
½ cup granulated sugar
1 teaspoon instant coffee powder
2 tablespoons hot water
1 large egg
1½ cups unsifted all-purpose flour
1 cup confectioners' sugar
1 tablespoon coffee-flavored liqueur
Candy sprinkles

1. Preheat oven to 375°F. In small bowl of electric mixer, at medium speed, beat ½ cup butter with the granulated sugar until light and fluffy. In custard cup, dissolve coffee powder in hot water; beat coffee mixture and egg into butter mixture. With wooden spoon, stir in flour until blended.

2. Place dough in pastry bag fitted with ½-inch star tip. Pipe 1-inch stars 1 inch apart onto ungreased baking sheets. Bake 8 minutes, or until edges begin to brown. Transfer to wire racks to cool.

3. In bowl, with wooden spoon, mix confectioners' sugar with remaining butter and the liqueur until blended. Press cookies together with mixture with flat sides inside; squeeze so filling oozes slightly. Place sprinkles on waxed paper; roll edges of kisses in sprinkles.
Makes 27 filled cookies.

Anise Rosettes

(pictured, page 209)

½ cup unsifted all-purpose flour
1 tablespoon granulated sugar
½ cup milk
1 large egg
1 tablespoon anise-flavored liqueur
1 tablespoon salad oil plus enough for deep frying
Confectioners' sugar

■ Take the mess out of measuring honey or molasses. Warm the measuring cup or spoon by rinsing it with hot water before you add the honey or molasses. The liquid won't stick, so that your measurement will be more accurate, and cleanup will be easier.

1. In bowl, whisk together first 5 ingredients and 1 tablespoon oil. Line baking sheet with paper towels.

2. In 3-quart saucepan, heat 2 inches oil to 375°F on deep-fat thermometer. Place mold end of rosette iron in hot oil for 1 minute. Dip mold into batter to coat to top edge only (do not cover entire mold with batter); place mold with batter in hot oil. Cook until golden.

3. Drain rosette on the mold over pan; place on prepared baking sheet. Remove rosette from mold, using fork if necessary. Repeat with remaining batter, preheating the mold in hot oil each time. Place some confectioners' sugar in fine sieve; sprinkle over rosettes.

Makes 2 dozen.

Gingerbread Children

(pictured, page 209)

Cookie Dough
2 packages (about 14-ounce size) gingerbread cake and cookie mix
⅓ cup chopped currants
1 tablespoon minced crystallized ginger
⅔ cup warm water

Icing
3 cups confectioners' sugar
¼ teaspoon cream of tartar
2 large egg whites

Food colors
Candies for decoration

1. In bowl, mix cookie ingredients. Divide dough in half. Shape into disks; wrap in plastic wrap. Chill 4 hours, or until firm enough to roll.

2. Preheat oven to 350°F. Grease 2 or 3 large baking sheets. On floured surface, with floured rolling pin, roll out one-half of dough to ³⁄₁₆-inch thickness. With floured 9-inch gingerperson cutter, cut out about 4 cookies; place 1 inch apart on prepared baking sheets. Repeat with remaining half of dough, rerolling scraps. Bake 10 minutes. Cool cookies on baking sheets 2 minutes; carefully transfer to wire racks to cool completely.

3. Meanwhile, in small bowl of electric mixer, at medium speed, beat icing ingredients until stiff peaks form when beaters are raised. Divide icing into small bowls; with food colors, tint icing in each bowl as desired. Place each color icing in separate pastry bag fitted with decorating tip; use to decorate cookies and to attach candies.

Makes 10 gingerbread children.

Fantasy Spritz

(pictured, page 209)

1 cup butter or margarine, softened
⅔ cup sugar
1 large egg
1 teaspoon vanilla extract
2½ cups unsifted all-purpose flour
Green food color
Red food color

1. Preheat oven to 400°F. In large bowl of electric mixer, at medium speed, beat butter and sugar until light and fluffy. Beat in egg and vanilla. With wooden spoon, stir in flour until blended.

2. Divide dough into thirds. Place one-third in bowl and tint green; place another third in bowl and tint red. Keep one-third uncolored.

3. On work surface, roll each third into a rope; place ropes together lengthwise in cookie press fitted with favorite disk. Press out dough onto ungreased baking sheets. Bake 7 minutes, or until set. Transfer to wire racks to cool.

Makes about 6 dozen.

Blondies

¾ cup butter or margarine
1½ cups lightly packed light-brown sugar
2 large eggs
1 teaspoon vanilla extract
2 cups unsifted all-purpose flour
1 package (6 ounces) semisweet-chocolate pieces
1 cup chopped walnuts

1. Grease and flour 13-by-9-by-2-inch baking pan. Preheat oven to 350°F.

2. In 3-quart saucepan, over medium heat, melt butter. With wooden spoon, stir in brown sugar until well blended; remove from heat. Stir in eggs and vanilla until combined. Gradually stir in flour until mixed. Stir in chocolate and walnuts. Pour into baking pan.

3. Bake 20 to 25 minutes. Cool completely in pan on wire rack. Cut into 12 (3-inch) squares; cut each square in half diagonally.

Makes 2 dozen triangles.

■ If you're caught short of confectioners' sugar while making cake or cookie frosting, try this simple trick: Combine 1 cup granulated sugar with 1 tablespoon cornstarch in the electric blender, and process at high speed for several minutes, until sugar is powdery.

■ Need to store cookies? Empty coffee or shortening cans make excellent containers for storing batches of homemade cookies. Separate layers of cookies with paper toweling. To take cookies along in lunch boxes, use small cans with plastic lids to keep cookies fresh.

Storybook Christmas Houses

Take a page from a beloved fairy tale to create holiday enchantment. Our trio of Christmas showpieces suits varying degrees of skill, from a chocolaty tower you can make with your children to a woodsy cottage and a palatial castle for the more expert to undertake.

Rapunzel's Tower

TOWER PATTERN PIECES
(page 243)
A, B, C, D (description
provided), E, F, G, H

PROPS AND SUPPORTS
Marker; ruler; tracing paper;
scissors; X-acto knife; 2
(40-by-32-inch) sheets,
¼-inch-thick foam-core
board; custard cups; small
paintbrush; 4 disposable
pastry bags; pastry tips: Nos.
3 (two), 19 and 352; 1 sheet
thin white cardboard; fork;
tweezers; waxed paper; small
metal spatula; sharp knife;
glue; tape; tall juice cans

1 recipe Royal Icing, page 220

Water

Food paste colors: pink, sky
blue, yellow, green

DECORATIONS
2 tablespoons sugar crystals; 1
egg white; 3 pounds
chocolate melting wafers,
melted (melt only 2 cups at a
time); 3 packages (1-pound
size) chocolate-covered
peanut and nougat candy
bars (1¾-by-1-inch size); ¼
pound white chocolate,
melted; 4 packages (12-ounce
size) candy-coated chocolate-
covered peanuts; red
cinnamon candies

1. With marker, ruler and tracing
paper, trace pattern pieces; enlarge
to scale. Label all pieces; cut out
with scissors. For castle base, with
X-acto knife and ruler, cut out 28-
by-15-inch piece foam-core board.
For pattern piece D (tower walls),
cut four 5-by-12-inch pieces foam-
core board. On remaining foam-core
board, outline all remaining pattern
(Continued on page 218)

*Rapunzel lets down her golden hair from a chocolate-covered tower
paved with candy-bar bricks. The door to the castle is studded with
candy-covered peanuts. Instructions, above. (Skill level: beginner.)*
Houses designed and executed by Pat Darling.

pieces except G and H. Cut out foam-core pieces with X-acto knife.

2. Make window (continue to work on castle while icing dries): Place 2 tablespoons icing in custard cup; thin to painting consistency with a few drops of water. With paintbrush, cover F foam-core piece with thinned icing. Let dry overnight. Next day, with marker, using photograph as a guide, lightly outline pattern piece H on icing on window. With 2 tablespoons icing in pastry bag fitted with number-3 tip, cover marker lines. Let dry 10 minutes. In custard cup, with 1 teaspoon icing and pink food color, tint icing flesh-pink; thin to painting consistency with a few drops of water. With paintbrush, paint face on Rapunzel. Let dry 10 minutes. With 1 teaspoon icing in clean custard cup and blue food color, tint icing blue; thin to painting consistency with a few drops of water. With clean paintbrush, paint dress on Rapunzel. Let dry 10 minutes.

3. Make doves: On thin white cardboard, outline 4 G pattern pieces; cut out with scissors. Place sugar crystals in custard cup. Place egg white in another custard cup; with fork, beat just until thinned. With paintbrush, cover one side of each cardboard dove with egg white so that only 2 doves face in same direction; dip egg-white-coated sides in sugar crystals. With tweezers, transfer doves to sheet of waxed paper; let dry 1 hour.

4. With metal spatula, spread melted chocolate over one side of one A foam-core piece, top half of one side of other A foam-core piece, over top of one side of each B piece

and over one side of 2 D pieces. (If you wish to cover remaining exterior of tower and castle, you will need additional chocolate for melting.) While chocolate is wet, using photograph as a guide, attach C to completely chocolate-covered side-A piece. Let dry 1 hour.

5. With sharp knife, cut each candy bar crosswise into 6 pieces; cut about 15 cut pieces crosswise in half. With metal spatula and melted chocolate, using photograph as a guide and working in one small section at a time, attach one cut side of each candy-bar piece to chocolate on door side of A piece and each chocolate-covered D piece, staggering candy pieces and arranging smaller cut pieces in a continuous arch around door. (If you are covering all sides, you will need additional candy bars.) Let dry 1 hour.

6. With metal spatula and melted white chocolate, cover C. While chocolate is wet, using photograph as a guide, attach candy-coated peanuts to C.

7. Make tower: With glue and tape, attach long sides of all D pieces, joining chocolate-covered pieces at one seam. Let dry 1 hour. With melted chocolate, using photograph as a guide, attach F (window) to one chocolate-covered D piece so that second chocolate-covered D piece is at left seam. Place ¼ cup icing in custard cup; with yellow food color, tint icing yellow. Place in pastry bag fitted with number-3 tip; using photograph as a guide, pipe hair and a braid on Rapunzel. With paintbrush and remaining blue icing, paint arm extending down from window. Let dry 1 hour.

Opposite page: Little Red Riding Hood follows a gumdrop path to Grandma's cottage in the woods. No wolves are lurking here, though, behind trees covered with tasty pretzels and spearmint candies. The cottage's puff-pastry roof, thatched with shredded wheat, drips frosting icicles. Instructions begin on page 222. (Skill level: intermediate.)

8. With glue and tape, attach long sides of E foam-core pieces to form tower roof. Let dry 1 hour.

9. On ¾ of one side of foam-core base (allow room for tower), using photograph as a guide, assemble castle frame from foam-core pieces, propping up sides with tall juice cans: Glue and tape one side of chocolate-covered A piece with door to long side of each B piece so that chocolate-covered tops of B pieces are inside the castle. With glue and tape, attach remaining long side of each B piece to remaining A piece so that chocolate-covered top of A is inside the castle. Let pieces dry 1 hour.

10. Stand tower next to castle so that window faces toward front of castle. With metal spatula, spread melted chocolate over top edge of tower; while chocolate is wet, attach tower roof. Let dry 1 hour.

11. Finish castle: Place 1½ cups icing in pastry bag fitted with number-19 tip. Using photograph as a guide, cover edge of window and each seam of tower roof with a zig-zag line of icing; pipe stars over sides of tower roof. In small bowl, with green food color, tint ½ cup icing green. Place in pastry bag fitted with number-352 tip; using photograph as a guide, pipe green-icing leaves over window side of tower and door side of castle. While icing is wet, attach doves to leaves around

Pages 216 and 217: Cinderella glides down the stairs of a palace truly fit for royalty. The frosted towers, sparkling with a sugar-crystal coating, are topped with pebbly nonpareil-covered turrets. Instructions begin on page 220. (Skill level: advanced.)

(Continued on page 220)

tower window and on tower roof; with tweezers, attach red cinnamon candies to leaves. Let dry 2 hours.

If desired, spread salt around castle for snow and scatter colored candy-coated chocolate-covered peanuts in snow.

Royal Icing

3 large egg whites, at room temperature
1 package (1 pound) confectioners' sugar (sift if lumpy)
½ teaspoon cream of tartar

In small bowl of electric mixer, combine all ingredients. Beat at high speed until stiff peaks form when beaters are raised. (Add more sugar if necessary.) Cover with a damp cloth or moist paper towel, or place plastic wrap directly on icing surface. If you have filled pastry bags with icing, cover tips with plastic wrap. Store excess icing in sealed container in refrigerator.

Makes about 2 cups.

Note: To prepare icing for decoration, use wooden picks to add dots of paste colors to icing until desired color is achieved. If painting with icing, place a small amount of icing in a custard cup. Color; thin with drops of water until icing is spreadable with a paintbrush. If too thin, add more icing.

■ If you forgot whether a refrigerated egg is raw or cooked, carefully spin it on a counter. If the egg wobbles, it's raw; if it twirls evenly, it's cooked.

■ To keep fine white-flour "dust" from clinging to the sides of home-baked chocolate cakes, "flour" your pans with cocoa instead—it even adds flavor.

Cinderella's Castle

(pictured, pages 216 and 217)

PATTERN PIECES
(page 244)
A, A1, A2, A3, B, B1, B2, C, C1, C2, D

PROPS AND SUPPORTS
Marker; ruler; tracing paper; scissors; X-acto knife; 2 (40-by-32-inch) sheets, ¼-inch-thick foam-core board; tape; waxed paper; 5 disposable pastry bags; pastry tips: Nos. 3 (three), 19 (two) and 101; 3 custard cups; small paintbrush; plastic wrap; 2 roasting pans; teaspoon; wooden picks; 3 cardboard cylinders from inside paper-towel rolls; 2 (2-inch-diameter) cardboard cylinders from inside wrapping-paper rolls; 1 (1¼-inch-diameter) cardboard cylinder from inside wrapping-paper roll; small metal spatula; glue; 1 sheet opalescent cellophane; tall juice cans; tweezers; white china marker; colored construction paper

About 10 recipes Royal Icing, page 220 (make in separate, double batches before using)

Water

Food paste colors: sky blue, pink, yellow, brown

DECORATIONS
5 pounds sugar crystals; 4 cups sugar nonpareils; 4 small ice cream cones; 5 sugar cones; 2 packages (6-ounce size) unhulled pumpkin seeds; sugar cubes; sugar tablets; silver dragées

1. With marker, ruler and tracing paper, trace pattern pieces; enlarge to scale. Label all pieces; cut out with scissors. With X-acto knife and ruler, cut out 18½-by-30-inch piece foam-core board for base. On remaining foam-core board, outline all pattern pieces. Cut out foam-core pieces with X-acto knife. On remaining whole foam-core board, with ruler and marker, outline 1-by-6-inch, 1-by-7-inch, 1-by-8-inch, 1-by-9-inch, 1-by-10-inch, 1-by-11-inch, 1-by-12-inch, 1-by-13-inch and 1-by-14-inch rectangles for stairs; cut out with X-acto knife. Cut out 1-by-3-inch support piece from foam-core board for Cinderella.

2. Begin to make Cinderella (continue to work on castle while icing dries): Tape D pattern piece to work surface. Tape a sheet of waxed paper over pattern. With ⅓ cup icing in pastry bag fitted with number-3 tip, outline pattern. Let icing outline stand 10 minutes to harden. Place 2 tablespoons icing in custard cup; thin to painting consistency with a few drops of water. With paintbrush, paint in outline of dress except for center of front panel. Let dry overnight. Next day, with 2 tablespoons icing in custard cup and blue food color, tint icing blue. Place 1 teaspoon blue icing in another custard cup; thin to painting consistency with a few drops of water (place remaining unthinned blue icing in pastry bag fitted with number-3 tip; cover with plastic wrap to prevent icing from hardening, and set aside). With paintbrush, paint center panel on front of dress blue. With 1 teaspoon icing in another custard cup and pink food color, tint icing flesh-pink; thin to painting consistency with a few drops of water. With clean paintbrush, paint face and arms on Cinderella. Let dry 10 minutes. With 1 tablespoon icing in another custard cup and yellow food color, tint icing yellow. Place in pastry bag fitted with number-3 tip; use to pipe hair on Cinderella. Let dry overnight. Next day, with 1 tablespoon white icing in pastry bag fitted with number-101 tip, pipe ruffle at end of white portion of dress.

With blue icing in pastry bag fitted with number-3 tip, pipe ruffle at end of blue portion of dress and pipe ribbon in hair. With dot of pink food color on tip of clean paintbrush, paint mouth on face. With dot of brown food color on tip of clean paintbrush, paint eyes on face. Let dry overnight. Next day, carefully remove waxed paper; with icing, attach reserved foam-core support piece. Let stand 10 minutes, or until icing hardens. Set aside.

3. Place sugar crystals in large roasting pan. Place 1 drop of water on teaspoon; with wooden pick, stir in enough blue food color to tint blue. Add tinted water to sugar; stir to color sugar evenly. Repeat with additional water and food color until sugar is desired intensity of blue. Set aside, stirring occasionally, until sugar is dry. In another roasting pan, place 3 cups nonpareils; tint blue as for sugar crystals.

4. With ruler, marker and X-acto knife, measure and cut 2 of the cardboard cylinders from paper-towel rolls to 9½-inch lengths. Cut 2-inch diameter cardboard cylinder into 2 (8-inch) lengths, 1 (9-inch) length, and 1 (5-inch) length. Cut 1¼-inch-diameter cardboard cylinder into 1 (5-inch) length. Make windows: With ruler, marker and X-acto knife, using photograph as a guide, cut 1-by-1¾-inch opening 1½ inches from one end of each of the 8-inch-long cylinders.

5. With X-acto knife, cut off wide end of one ice cream cone. With metal spatula, cover cone with white icing; while icing is wet, roll cone in white nonpareils. Place on sheet of waxed paper; set aside to dry. Without removing wide ends, cover 2 more ice cream cones and 2 sugar cones with icing and white nonpareils; set aside to dry.

6. Make stairs: With glue, using photograph as a guide, attach foam-core rectangles to each other, placing ¼ inch of one long side of smallest (1-by-6-inch) rectangle onto ¼ inch of one long side of next larger (1-by-7-inch) rectangle, so that there is ¾ inch overhang on one long side. Repeat with remaining rectangles so that the bottom stair is the 1-by-14-inch-rectangle. With metal spatula, spread a thin layer of white icing over top side of stairs; while icing is wet, sprinkle with blue sugar crystals. Shake off excess. Place stairs on waxed paper; let dry.

7. Cut cellophane to 1 inch larger than door and window openings of A (castle front); with tape, attach to one side of foam-core A.

8. In bowl, with blue food color, tint 6 recipes Royal Icing light blue. (Keep icing tightly covered with plastic wrap when not using.)

9. With metal spatula and some blue icing, cover remaining ice cream and sugar cones; while icing is wet, roll in blue nonpareils. Place on sheet of waxed paper; set aside to dry. Spread some blue icing on center portion (with windows and door) of foam-core A piece (side without tape and cellophane). Sprinkle with blue sugar crystals; gently shake off excess. (To cover all sides of castle, you will need additional colored icing and sugar.) Generously spread icing on front portion not covered with crystals. While icing is wet, using photograph as a guide, attach pumpkin seeds, flat side down, to resemble a stone wall. With blue icing in pastry bag fitted with number-3 tip, using photograph as a guide, attach sugar cubes around door. Let dry 2 hours.

10. Cover outside of cardboard cylinders with blue icing and sprinkle with blue sugar crystals, shaking off excess. On each 9½-inch cylinder, with blue icing, using photograph as a guide, attach a double ring of sugar cubes placed 2½ inches from one end. On 5-inch-long, 2-inch-diameter cylinder, and the 11-inch cardboard cylinder, attach a single ring of sugar cubes 2 inches from one end. Place on waxed paper; let dry.

11. On foam-core base, using photograph as a guide, assemble castle frame from foam-core pieces, propping sides up with tall juice cans: Glue and tape each short side of A (front) to one long side of one A1 (side) piece. Glue and tape A3 (roof) to A and A1 pieces, placing roof ½ inch below top edge of frame pieces. Glue and tape A2 (back) to A1 and A3 pieces. Glue and tape castle frame to foam-core base. Let dry 2 hours.

12. Assemble square tower: Glue and tape each short side of one C (tower front) piece to one side of one C1 (tower side) piece. Glue and tape C2 (roof) piece to C and C1 pieces, with roof ½ inch below top edge of frame pieces. Glue and tape remaining C piece (tower back) to C1 and C2 pieces. Let dry 1 hour.

13. Glue one end of 5-inch-long, 2-inch-diameter cardboard cylinder to roof on right side of castle. Glue one end of 5-inch-long, 1¼-inch-diameter cardboard cylinder on roof of square tower. Let dry 1 hour.

14. With metal spatula, generously spread blue icing on roof and side walls of castle and square tower, on B1 pieces and around base of cardboard cylinders. While icing is wet, using photograph as a guide, attach pumpkin seeds, flat side down, to walls to resemble stone walls. Let dry 2 hours.

15. Glue and tape one short side of each B1 (central tower side) piece to central tower front of A, and glue and tape base of each B1 piece to castle roof. Glue and tape long side of each B2 (central tower roof) piece to sloping sides of B (tower back) for roof. Top of central tower is open. Glue and tape B to castle roof and B2 pieces to central tower front of A. With metal spatula, cover roof of central tower with white icing. While wet and using additional icing, attach white cone with wide end removed to front of central tower. Let dry 2 hours.

(Continued on page 222)

16. With blue icing in pastry bag fitted with number-3 tip, using photograph as a guide, attach square tower to roof and central tower of castle, sugar tablets to top edge of castle and square tower walls, and stairs to front of castle at door. Let dry 2 hours.

17. Using photograph as a guide, glue cardboard cylinders to foam-core base, placing one 9½-inch cylinder at each side of door, one cylinder with a window on each side of base of stairs, the 11-inch cylinder at left corner of castle and the 9-inch cylinder at right corner of castle. With blue icing in pastry bag with number-3 tip, pipe icing around bases of cylinders to cover tape. Let dry 2 hours. With icing, using photograph as a guide, attach cones to cylinders. Let dry 2 hours.

18. With ¾ cup blue icing in pastry bag fitted with number-19 tip, using photograph as a guide, decorate front of castle along each side where sugar crystals end and window openings on towers with a continuous border of icing stars, making an arch at top of each window. While icing is wet, with tweezers, attach a dragée to center of each star around windows.

19. With 3 cups white icing in pastry bag fitted with number-19 tip, using photograph as a guide, decorate door opening, window openings on castle front and wide end of each cone with a continuous border of stars, adding rows of stars on cones. Decorate roof of central tower with wavy lines. While icing is wet, with tweezers, attach a dragée to center of each star.

20. Finish scene: With china marker, color 9 wooden picks. Cut out 9 triangles from construction paper for flags; with tape, attach 1 flag to 1 pointed end of each wooden pick. With X-acto knife, make a tiny hole in end of each cone; insert a flag in each hole. Put Cinderella on stairs. If desired, put sugar crystal mounds around scene.

Grandma's Cottage
(pictured, page 219)

PATTERN PIECES
(pages 242 and 243)
A, A1, A2, B, B1, B2, C, D

PROPS AND SUPPORTS
Marker; ruler; tracing paper; scissors; X-acto knife; 2 (40-by-32-inch) sheets, ¼-inch-thick foam-core board; tape; waxed paper; 5 disposable pastry bags; pastry tips: Nos. 3 (two), 19, 101 and 352; custard cup; paintbrush; glue; tall juice cans; metal spatula; rolling pin; 19-inch, ¼-inch-thick wooden dowel; 2 baking sheets; pastry brush; wire rack; 2 (12-inch) and 1 (9-inch) Styrofoam cones
About 10 recipes Royal Icing, page 220 (make in separate, double batches before using)

Water

Food paste colors: red, leaf green

DECORATIONS
2 brown candy-coated chocolate candies; 25 chocolate melting wafers; 2 rectangular wheat crackers; 7 sugar hearts; flour; 5 packages (17¼-ounce size) frozen puff pastry, thawed; 2 large egg whites, beaten; 1 large biscuit shredded wheat; 2 oval biscuit wafers topped with chocolate and pecans; 3 packages (22-ounce size) tiny fish-shaped pretzels; 2 packages (5-ounce size) spearmint-leaf candies; red cinnamon candies; chocolate candy sprinkles; sugar; 1 box (7½ ounces) pumpernickel cracker sticks; gumdrops

1. With marker, ruler and tracing paper, trace pattern pieces; enlarge to scale. Label pieces; cut out with scissors. With X-acto knife and ruler, cut out 21-by-24-inch piece foam-core board for base. On remaining foam-core board, outline pattern pieces. Cut out foam-core pieces with X-acto knife. Cut out 4-by-1-inch support piece from foam-core for Red Riding Hood.

2. Begin to make Red Riding Hood (continue to work on the cottage while icing figure dries): Tape D pattern piece to work surface. Tape a sheet of waxed paper over pattern. With ⅓ cup icing and red food color, tint icing red. Place in pastry bag fitted with number-3 tip; pipe outline of pattern. Let stand 10 minutes to harden. Place 2 tablespoons remaining red icing in custard cup; thin to painting consistency with a few drops of water. With paintbrush, paint in outline. Let dry overnight. Next day, with remaining red icing in pastry bag fitted with number-3 tip, pipe in folds at neckline of collar and hood; with ⅓ cup white icing in pastry bag fitted with number-101 tip, pipe ruffles over bottom edge of skirt. Pipe 2 dots of icing at edge of skirt; while icing is wet, attach 2 brown candy-coated chocolate candies for shoes. Let stand 4 hours, or until icing hardens. Carefully remove waxed paper; with icing, attach reserved foam-core support piece to back of figure at an angle. Let stand 10 minutes, or until icing hardens. Set Red Riding Hood aside.

3. On foam-core board base, using photograph as a guide, assemble cottage frame from foam-core pieces: Glue and tape one short side of each A piece (front and back) to one side of each A1 piece (side), using tall juice cans to support structure. With icing in pastry bag fitted with number-3 tip, attach cottage frame to base (allow room at center of one long side for cottage vestibule).

4. Make cottage roof: With glue and tape, attach A2 pieces (roof) to

cottage frame. Let stand until glue and base icing dry, about 2 hours. With metal spatula and icing, lightly coat outside of walls, the A2 piece facing vestibule and one side of C piece, applying icing more heavily in some areas for rough stucco effect. (To cover all sides of cottage, you will need additional icing and more puff pastry for thatching.) Let stand until dry, about 2 hours.

5. Meanwhile, in small bowl in microwave oven, heat chocolate wafers on MEDIUM 2 minutes, or until melted. With metal spatula and melted wafers, coat one side of B and B1 pieces. While chocolate is still wet, attach smooth side of C (door) to center of (5½-inch side of) B (vestibule front), aligning straight short side of C with edge. With icing, using photograph as a guide, attach crackers to C. With red icing in pastry bag fitted with number-3 tip, pipe dots of icing around top edge of crackers. With icing, attach 2 sugar hearts, points touching, to each cracker. Let stand 30 minutes, or until hardened.

6. Assemble vestibule: With glue and tape, attach one long side of each B1 piece (side) to B piece (front), spacing B1 pieces 5¼ inches apart and with chocolate on outside. Glue and tape remaining long side of each B1 piece to center of cottage front. With icing in pastry bag fitted with number-3 tip, pipe icing over seams. Let stand until glue and icing dry, about 2 hours. Meanwhile, make vestibule roof: With glue and tape, attach B2 pieces to cottage and vestibule frames. With icing in pastry bag fitted with number-3 tip, pipe icing over seams. Let stand until glue and icing dry, about 2 hours.

7. Make puff-pastry thatching: Preheat oven to 375°F. On floured surface, with floured rolling pin, roll out one sheet puff pastry to 13-inch square. With X-acto knife and ruler, cut pastry crosswise to make 1-inch-wide strips. With 3 strips, twist pastry around dowel to cover, joining strips by pressing short ends together. Place on large baking sheet. With index finger, press along length of half of one side of each remaining strip; for thatching effect, with X-acto knife, cut pressed portion of pastry crosswise at close intervals and occasionally removing a sliver of pastry. Place strips on another large baking sheet. Continue to make "thatched" strips with remaining pastry. Brush all pastry with egg white; bake 20 minutes, or until golden brown. Cool on baking sheets on wire rack; slide metal spatula under pastry to loosen from sheets. Cool pastry completely on wire rack.

8. With icing, attach thatched pastry strips to cottage and vestibule roofs, beginning at bottom of roof and stacking strips like shingles; cut strips to fit with X-acto knife. With X-acto knife, separate pieces of shredded wheat biscuit; insert shreds in between "thatching." With icing in pastry bag fitted with number-19 tip, using photograph as a guide, pipe a thick line of icing over roof seams of cottage and vestibule and along side edges of pastry on roof; while icing is wet, attach twisted-pastry-covered dowel to cottage roof.

9. With icing, using photograph as a guide, attach plain side of each cookie to center of each side of front of cottage for windows. With icing, attach mouth side of fish-shaped pretzels around edge of cookie except at bottom of each cookie and leaving a space at top curve of each candy; with icing, attach a candy heart in the space.

10. With icing in pastry bag fitted number-19 tip, using photograph as a guide, pipe zigzag strips around door and edges of vestibule and front seams of cottage. While icing is wet, using photograph as a guide, attach mouth side of fish-shaped pretzels to zigzag decoration on vestibule. With icing, attach a candy heart to vestibule above pretzels around door.

11. With metal spatula and some icing, cover one 12-inch Styrofoam cone. With icing in pastry bag fitted with number-19 tip, attach fish-shaped pretzels to cone, beginning at base of cone and placing tails of fish facing toward top, and layering until all of cone is covered. Repeat with remaining 12-inch cone and pretzels; repeat with 9-inch cone, using spearmint-leaf candies. With white icing in pastry bag fitted with number-19 tip, pipe snow over top of spearmint-leaf "tree" and icicles on pretzel trees; while icing is wet, attach a leaf-shaped candy for tree-top on spearmint-leaf tree.

12. With 1 cup icing and green food color, tint icing green; place in pastry bag fitted with number-352 tip. Using photograph as a guide, pipe leaves around base of windows, above door and around vestibule, on pretzel trees and on seams of cottage. While icing is wet, arrange the cinnamon-candy "berries" on leaves and attach chocolate candy sprinkles. Let stand 2 hours, or until all icing is dry.

13. Finish scene: Arrange trees near cottage. Arrange sugar to make snowdrifts around cottage. With icing in pastry bag with number-19 tip, using photograph as a guide, attach end of pumpernickel cracker stick to center of another cracker stick forming right angle; when icing hardens, attach remaining end of cracker stick to center of another cracker stick to form an H. Repeat to make two fences with 5 cracker-stick posts each; arrange in snowdrifts. With icing, pile cracker sticks to make a log pile; arrange in snowdrift. With gumdrops, arrange a path in snow to cottage door. Place Red Riding Hood in snow near path.

Holiday Dinner-Party Recipes

The rituals of Christmas range from large festive gatherings to intimate dinner parties. Here are some of Jaclyn Smith's favorites.

Herb-Cheese Pimiento Dip

2 jars (4-ounce size) pimientos,
   drained
2 cups sour cream
2 packages (3-ounce size)
   cream cheese, softened
2 packages (.056-ounce size)
   green-onion dip mix
Chopped chives
Crudités

In food processor, puree pimientos. Blend in sour cream, cream cheese and dip mix. Spoon into serving bowl; sprinkle with chives. Cover; chill several hours to allow flavors to mellow. Serve dip with crudités.

Makes 2½ cups.

Mustard 'n' Sweet Baby Spareribs

3 pounds spareribs, split
   lengthwise through the
   bones into 2-inch-wide pieces
1 cup cider vinegar
1 cup boiling water

*Cornish Hens With
Raspberry-Sesame Sauce.*

Glaze
1 jar (12 ounces) currant jelly
1 jar (7 ounces) sweet-and-sour
   sauce
¼ cup Dijon-style mustard
¼ cup prepared horseradish
2 tablespoons salad oil

1. Preheat oven to 500°F. Place spareribs in large roasting pan. Pour vinegar and water over ribs. Cover pan tightly with aluminum foil. Bake 30 minutes.

2. Meanwhile, make glaze: In medium saucepan, combine glaze ingredients. Bring to boiling, stirring; simmer 10 minutes.

3. Reduce oven temperature to 375°F. Remove pan from oven; carefully remove foil. Drain ribs; brush with glaze. Bake 15 minutes; turn ribs over. Brush with glaze; bake 15 minutes longer. Cut ribs into 1-rib widths for appetizers, or into 3- or 4-rib-wide pieces for entrée servings. Use remaining glaze as dipping sauce for ribs.

Makes 8 appetizer servings or 4 entrée servings.

Cornish Hens With Raspberry-Sesame Sauce

8 (1¼ pounds each) Cornish
   hens
4 tablespoons butter or
   margarine
½ cup lime juice
1½ teaspoons salt
¼ teaspoon white pepper
⅔ cup sesame seeds, toasted
2 jars (10-ounce size) raspberry
   jelly
Fresh bay leaves
Peach slices
Raspberries

Herb-Cheese Pimiento Dip.

1. Preheat oven to 350°F. Remove giblets and rinse hens; pat dry.

2. In saucepan, melt butter. Add ¼ cup lime juice, the salt and pepper. Brush hens inside and out with mixture. Tie legs together. Place on rack in roasting pan. Roast hens, basting often, 1 hour and 15 minutes, or until tender.

3. Meanwhile, in small saucepan, combine sesame seeds, jelly and remaining ¼ cup lime juice. Heat, stirring, until blended; brush over hens last 5 minutes of cooking time. Remove string from hens; garnish with bay leaves, peach slices and raspberries; pass remaining raspberry-sesame sauce separately.

Makes 8 servings.

Holiday Dinner-Party Recipes

Fusilli With Creamy Spinach Sauce

1 package (16 ounces) fusilli (curly spaghetti)
1 pound mushrooms, thinly sliced
½ cup butter or margarine
2 packages (10-ounce size) frozen leaf spinach, thawed and drained
½ pound boiled ham, cut into thin strips
1 cup slivered sun-dried tomatoes
½ cup chopped parsley
2 medium cloves garlic, crushed
2 cups heavy cream
1 teaspoon salt
¼ teaspoon ground nutmeg
¼ teaspoon pepper
½ cup grated Parmesan cheese

Cook fusilli as package label directs. Drain; set aside. Meanwhile, in large skillet, over medium heat, sauté mushrooms in butter 3 minutes, or until golden. Add spinach, ham, tomatoes, parsley and garlic; cook 3 minutes. Add cream, salt, nutmeg and pepper; cook until slightly thickened. Add fusilli and cheese; toss to coat.

Makes 8 servings.

Mixed Leaf Salad With Smoky Parmesan Walnuts

2 large heads Boston lettuce, torn into large pieces
1 large head radicchio, torn into pieces
1 large bunch watercress, large stems removed
Smoky Parmesan Walnuts (recipe follows)

Strawberry Glacé Pie.

Balsamic Vinaigrette
1 small clove garlic, crushed
½ teaspoon freshly ground black pepper
½ teaspoon salt
¼ cup olive oil
¼ cup balsamic vinegar
2 teaspoons cold water
1 teaspoon Dijon-style mustard

1. In large bowl, combine greens and half the walnuts. Set aside.

2. In jar, combine dressing ingredients. Shake to blend. Pour over salad; toss to coat evenly. Sprinkle with remaining walnuts.

Makes 8 servings.

Smoky Parmesan Walnuts

1 tablespoon unsalted butter or margarine
1 cup walnut pieces
¼ teaspoon hickory-flavored salt
2 tablespoons grated Parmesan cheese

Preheat oven to 350°F. Melt butter in shallow baking dish in oven. Stir in walnuts and salt. Bake 5 minutes. Stir in cheese. Bake 4 minutes, or until cheese is lightly browned. Cool mixture.

Makes 1 cup.

■ Planning a Christmas party? Here's one of our favorite holiday appetizers. It's delicious and, best of all, it's created in a jiffy. Simply combine equal parts brown sugar and pecans or walnuts, and sprinkle over a partially heated round Brie. Heat at 350°F until sugar is melted and cheese is warm. Serve spread on very thin slices of toasted French bread. It's sure to be a hit with holiday guests.

Strawberry Glacé Pie

3 pints strawberries
3 tablespoons granulated sugar
5 teaspoons cornstarch
2 tablespoons lemon juice
1 tablespoon water
1 tablespoon almond-flavored liqueur
1 package (8 ounces) cream cheese
⅓ cup (4 ounces) almond paste, crumbled
½ cup confectioners' sugar
2 teaspoons grated lemon peel
9-inch baked pie shell (see *Note*)

1. In saucepan, with potato masher, crush ½ pint strawberries. Stir in granulated sugar, cornstarch, lemon juice and water. Cook, stirring, until thickened and translucent. Remove from heat; stir in liqueur. If desired, pass mixture through sieve into small bowl. Place plastic wrap directly on surface; refrigerate.

2. In food processor, blend cream cheese, almond paste, confectioners' sugar and lemon peel. Spread mixture over bottom of pie shell; arrange whole strawberries on top. Spoon crushed-strawberry mixture over top to coat completely. Refrigerate 3 hours.

Makes 8 servings.

Note: If desired, when making pie shell, cut out leaves from extra pastry. Brush edge of pie shell with mixture of beaten egg and 1 tablespoon water; attach pastry leaves to edge. Brush leaves lightly with egg mixture. Bake as pastry recipe directs; cover with foil if pastry browns too quickly.

Get to the Punch Line

Spiced Black-Currant Punch

12 black-currant tea bags

2 (3-inch) cinnamon sticks

3 cups boiling water

1 bottle (1 liter) ginger ale, chilled

1 bottle (1 liter) club soda, chilled

3 cups ice-cold water

2 cups vodka

1 can (12 ounces) frozen orange juice concentrate, thawed

1 can (12 ounces) frozen lemonade concentrate, thawed

1 cup crème de cassis

1 cup grenadine syrup

Place tea bags and cinnamon sticks in large glass measure. Add boiling water; steep 4 minutes. Meanwhile, combine remaining ingredients in a punch bowl. Discard tea bags and cinnamon sticks; pour tea into punch bowl. Mix until blended. Chill until ready to serve. If desired, with short lengths of wooden picks, attach assorted whole fruits, lime slices, cinnamon sticks and bay leaves to pineapple half (with frond attached); freeze until firm. Use to garnish punch.

Makes 48 (½-cup) servings.

Spiced Black-Currant Punch.

■ Don't throw away that half-empty bottle of ginger ale or lemon-lime-flavored soda. Instead, pour the beverage into an ice-cube tray and freeze. Keep on hand and later use the ice cubes to chill and to add flavor to a party punch.

Luscious Last-Minute Hors d'Oeuvres

Zucchini Tempters

1 cup buttermilk baking mix
¾ cup grated Parmesan cheese
1 tablespoon chopped parsley
½ teaspoon salt
⅛ teaspoon pepper
3 cups thinly sliced zucchini
 (2 medium)
1 cup shredded carrot
1 small onion, chopped
1 medium clove garlic,
 crushed
4 large eggs
½ cup salad oil

Preheat oven to 350°F. Grease 13-by-9-by-2-inch baking dish; set aside. In bowl, combine ingredients. Spoon into prepared dish; bake 35 minutes. Cut into 1½-inch pieces; serve warm or at room temperature.
Makes 3½ dozen.

Caviar-Stuffed Eggs

8 large hard-cooked eggs
6 tablespoons mayonnaise or
 salad dressing
2 tablespoons minced chives or
 green onion
1 tablespoon salmon caviar
Dash of pepper
Additional caviar and chives

Halve eggs crosswise. Put yolks in bowl; with fork, mash. Stir in next 4 ingredients. Put in pastry bag with star tip; fill egg whites. Garnish with caviar and chives.
Makes 16 servings.

Cheese-Stuffed Mushrooms

1 pound medium mushrooms
1 container (4 ounces) garlic-and-herb semisoft cheese
2 tablespoons chopped
 parsley
3 cups water
1 tablespoon lemon juice

Preheat oven to 400°F. Remove mushroom stems, reserving caps. Chop enough stems to measure 1 cup; place in bowl. (Reserve remaining stems for another use.) Stir in cheese and parsley. In saucepan, bring water and lemon juice to boiling. Add mushroom caps; cook 1 minute. Drain. Spoon cheese mixture into caps. Arrange in shallow baking pan. Bake 8 minutes.
Makes about 2 dozen.

Clockwise from top: Herb-Cheese Dip, Zucchini Tempters, Caviar-Stuffed Eggs, Cheese-Stuffed Mushrooms.

Herb-Cheese Dip

1 cup cottage cheese
1 package (3 ounces) cream
 cheese
1 package (1 ounce)
 ranch-dressing mix
½ cup heavy cream
Salt-free herb blend
Assorted crackers and crudités

In food processor, puree cottage cheese. Blend in next two ingredients. With processor running, add cream. Pour into serving dish; top with herb blend. Serve with crackers and crudités.
Makes about 2 cups.

A Hanukkah Dinner for All

Although this menu was planned for Hanukkah, the Jewish Festival of Lights, it's a luscious meal for any gathering.

CHOPPED LIVER WITH
TOASTED CHALLAH
MATZO-BALL SOUP
*APRICOT ROAST CHICKEN
*POTATO-ZUCCHINI LATKES
TSIMMES (GLAZED CARROTS)
*COCOA-HONEY CAKE

*recipe given

Apricot Roast Chicken

Stuffing
¼ cup parve margarine
2 medium celery stalks,
  chopped
1 medium apple, chopped
1 medium onion, chopped
3 cups whole-wheat bread cubes
½ cup dried apricots, coarsely
  chopped
½ cup pecan pieces
½ cup raisins
¼ cup chopped parsley
1 teaspoon poultry seasoning

7- to 8-pound roasting chicken
½ cup apricot preserves, melted

1. Preheat oven to 325°F. Make stuffing: In skillet, over medium-high heat, melt margarine; add celery, apple and onion. Sauté 3 minutes; place in bowl. Add remaining stuffing ingredients; mix well. Loosely fill cavity of chicken with some stuffing; secure with poultry pins. Tie legs together. Place remaining stuffing in small casserole. Cover; bake last 30 minutes chicken is in oven.

2. Place chicken, breast side up, in large roasting pan. Roast 2 hours, or until meat thermometer inserted in leg registers 170°F, brushing occasionally with preserves during last 30 minutes of cooking time.
Makes 6 to 8 servings.

Potato-Zucchini Latkes

2 large eggs
¼ cup unsifted all-purpose
  flour
¼ teaspoon baking powder
½ teaspoon salt
⅛ teaspoon pepper
Dash of ground nutmeg
1 small onion, grated
1½ pounds baking potatoes,
  unpared
½ pound zucchini
¼ cup salad oil
Additional salad oil
Applesauce

1. Line baking sheet with paper towels. Preheat oven to 250°F. In bowl, mix eggs, flour, baking powder, salt, pepper and nutmeg. Add onion. Shred potatoes and zucchini; stir into egg mixture.

2. Heat oil in 12-inch skillet over medium heat. Drop potato mixture, ¼ cup at a time, into hot oil; flatten into 3-inch rounds. Cook until golden, about 3 minutes on each side, adding more oil if necessary. Remove to baking sheet. Keep warm while frying remaining pancakes. Transfer to serving dish; if desired, garnish with parsley sprigs. Serve with applesauce.
Makes about 16 pancakes.

Cocoa-Honey Cake

2½ cups unsifted all-purpose
  flour
½ cup unsweetened cocoa
  powder
1 teaspoon baking powder
1 teaspoon baking soda
½ teaspoon ground cinnamon
¼ teaspoon ground cloves
1 cup strong tea
1 cup honey
3 large eggs
⅔ cup sugar
⅓ cup salad oil
1 small banana, mashed
1 tablespoon grated orange
  peel

1. Preheat oven to 350°F. Generously grease and flour 10-inch Bundt pan. In bowl, combine flour, cocoa, baking powder, baking soda and spices. In glass measure, mix tea and honey.

2. In bowl of electric mixer, at medium speed, beat eggs with sugar 5 minutes, or until thickened. Gradually add oil, the banana and orange peel. Alternately beat in flour and honey mixtures, beginning and ending with flour mixture, until

blended. Pour into pan; bake 55 minutes, or until cake tester inserted in center comes out clean. Cool in pan on wire rack 5 minutes; invert cake onto rack. Cool. Garnish as desired.

Makes 16 servings.

■ The number of candles placed in the Hanukkah menorah increases each night—one the first, two the second, etc., for a total of eight candles (plus the shamash, used to light the others). Candles are put in the menorah from right to left (as Hebrew is read) but lit from the left, so the one put in last is lit first.

Clockwise from top: Cocoa-Honey Cake, Potato-Zucchini Latkes, Apricot Roast Chicken.

Compliments of the California Prune Board and the Walnut Marketing Board.

Holiday Fantasies

Add a festive touch to your table or mantel with one of our very special Noël creations.

Bountiful Basket

PROPS AND SUPPORTS
Cutting board; X-acto knife; ruler; eight 36-inch-long, ⅛-inch-thick wooden dowels; five 11-inch-long wooden skewers; 1 (2-by-20-inch) sheet, ¼-inch-thick foam-core board; glue; scissors; 60 small stamens; 8 medium stamens; five ½-inch-wide artificial red berries; hammer; thin nail; 7-foot-length, 18-gauge green florist's wire; wire cutters; small metal spatula; rolling pin; about 4 large baking sheets; pastry brush; wire rack; 2 disposable pastry bags; pastry tips: Nos. 3 and 18; about 9 kitchen towels; waxed paper; tweezers; oasis; basket with handle; Styrofoam blocks; assorted seasonal greenery or green silk leaves; decorative straw or moss; red-ribbon bow

1 recipe Royal Icing, page 220

A bountiful basket, blooming with dainty prune-and-walnut flowers decorated with frosting centers.

DECORATIONS
4 whole unshelled walnuts; flour; ½ package (17¼-ounce size) frozen puff pastry, thawed (1 sheet); 1 large egg white, beaten; 50 walnut halves; 37 unpitted prunes

1. On cutting board, with X-acto knife and ruler, cut one 19-inch, one 17-inch, one 16-inch, four 15-inch, two 14-inch, one 9-inch, one 6½-inch, two 6-inch and one 5¾-inch lengths from dowels and two 10-inch, one 8-inch and two 7-inch lengths from wooden skewers. Trim one end of each dowel and skewer length to a point; set aside. With X-acto knife and ruler, cut thirteen 1½-inch-diameter rounds from foam-core board; set aside.

2. Set aside one 19-inch, one 17-inch, one 16-inch, two 15-inch and one 14-inch dowel. Glue blunt end of remaining dowels and the skewers to one flat side of each foam-core round; let stand until glue dries, about 1 hour.

3. Meanwhile, with scissors, trim wire of each small stamen to ⅝-inch length and wire of each medium stamen and berry to ¼-inch length. Set aside. With hammer and nail, make a small hole in shell at flat end of each whole walnut. Insert florist's wire in one hole; with wire cutters, trim wire to 5½ inches. Set aside. Repeat with remaining walnuts and wire, making one 8-inch wire length and two 13-inch wire lengths; set lengths aside.

4. With spatula, spread enough icing over each dowel and skewer to cover glue and portion of wood on foam-core rounds, spreading icing to make a smooth mound. Let stand until icing dries, about 6 hours.

5. Meanwhile, preheat oven to 375°F. On floured surface, with floured rolling pin, roll out puff pastry to 12-inch square. With X-acto knife and ruler, cut pastry to make four 12-by-½-inch strips; reserve remaining pastry for another use. Twist one pastry strip around each of one 19-inch, one 16-inch and two 15-inch reserved dowels to cover the length of each dowel. Place prepared pastry twists on baking sheet; brush with egg white. Bake 20 minutes, until golden brown. Cool on baking sheet on wire rack. With metal spatula, transfer twists to wire rack; cool.

6. On cutting board, with X-acto knife, cut 10 walnut halves in half lengthwise; set aside. Slice 25 prunes lengthwise, cutting through fruit to the pit but being careful not to cut prune in half. With X-acto knife, using photograph as a guide, spread prune open to expose pit, scraping pit clean with knife blade (be careful not to dislodge pit). Pinch ends of prune to resemble petal. Set aside.

7. Make walnut and prune "buds": Using photograph as a guide, thread 5 uncut prunes onto one 14-inch dowel and 7 uncut prunes onto one 17-inch dowel, pushing pointed

(Continued on page 236)

end of each dowel through each prune at an angle so ends of prunes point in alternate directions on each "side" of dowel. With ½ cup icing in pastry bag fitted with number-18 tip, using photograph as a guide, attach walnut quarters between prunes. Pipe icing stars over place where walnuts join. With ½ cup icing in pastry bag fitted with number-3 tip, pipe thin, tall spikes of icing over each star. Place several kitchen towels on each of several baking sheets; place a sheet of waxed paper over towels. Place prepared buds on waxed paper on one baking sheet; let stand 2 hours, or until icing dries.

8. Meanwhile, make walnut flowers: With icing in pastry bag fitted with number-18 tip, using photograph as a guide, attach 5 walnut halves onto foam-core round, ¼ inch from outside edge of each, on remaining dowels. With icing in pastry bag fitted with number-18 tip, pipe icing stars over center of foam-core rounds. With icing in pastry bag fitted with number-3 tip, pipe thin, tall spikes of icing around edge of icing center. While icing is wet, using photograph as a guide, with tweezers, insert 1 medium stamen into center of icing on each round. Surround with small stamens, dividing evenly. Place flowers, stamen side up, on waxed paper on prepared baking sheets; let stand until icing dries, about 6 hours.

9. Onto each foam-core round on remaining skewers, with icing, using photograph as a guide, attach 5 prune petals, joining prunes at center of round. With icing in pastry bag with number-18 tip, pipe a star where prunes join. While icing is still wet, attach an artificial berry to each star. With icing in pastry bag

with number-3 tip, pipe thin, tall icing spikes around berry. Place on waxed paper on baking sheets; let stand until dry, about 6 hours.

10. Finish basket: Place oasis in basket, using Styrofoam blocks as necessary to raise top of oasis to level of edge of basket. Using photograph as a guide, arrange greenery, walnut and prune buds and flowers, pastry spikes and whole walnuts in oasis in basket. Arrange straw over oasis. Tie bow on handle.

Santa's Stable

(pictured, pages 234 and 235)

PATTERN PIECES
(pages 245 through 248)

A, B, C, D, E, E1, F, F1, G, G1, G2, G3, H, I, J, J1, J2, K, K1, K2, L

PROPS AND SUPPORTS
Marker; ruler; tracing paper; scissors; X-acto knife; 1 (40-by-32-inch) sheet foam-core board; parchment paper or aluminum foil; rolling pin; baking sheets; wire racks; small metal spatula; 7 disposable pastry bags; pastry tips: Nos. 1 (four), 3 (two) and 46; custard cup; small paintbrush; wooden pick; glue; tape; tall juice cans; short cans; wire cutters; thin green florist's wire
1 recipe Gingerbread Dough, page 241
4 recipes Royal Icing, page 220 (make in separate batches before using)
Food paste colors: True brown, Christmas red, leaf green, black

DECORATIONS
Flour; about 8 whole cinnamon graham crackers; about 3 packs cinnamon-flavored stick chewing gum; about 3 packs spearmint-flavored stick chewing gum; about 24 silver candy-coated almonds; 1 (½-inch-thick) licorice candy; 9 (about 7-inch) pretzel rods; about 4 large shredded-wheat-cereal biscuits; 1 pack pink stick bubble gum; about 20 pieces milk-chocolate twig-shaped candy; small multicolored candy balls; small white candy balls; chocolate sprinkles; 3 small black jelly beans; 1 bear-shaped animal cracker; multicolored candy sprinkles; 1 sugar cone; 2 double-stuffed chocolate sandwich cookies; silver dragées; 4 licorice wheel-shaped candies or chocolate sandwich cookies; 1 (2- or 3-inch) peppermint stick; about 7 (4-inch-wide) twist pretzels; granulated sugar; peppermint candies; round oat cereal; candy jellied rock-shaped candies

1. With marker, ruler and tracing paper, trace pattern pieces; enlarge to scale. Label all pieces; cut out with scissors. With X-acto knife and ruler, cut out 20-by-25-inch piece foam-core board for base; set aside. On remaining foam-core board, outline patterns A, G1, G3 and H; cut out with X-acto knife. Set aside. Reserve remaining foam-core board.

2. Make gingerbread pieces: On floured 22-by-12-inch sheet parchment paper or aluminum foil, with floured rolling pin, roll 1 piece of dough to ¼-inch thickness. Place rolled dough and paper on baking sheet; chill 15 minutes. Roll out and chill remaining dough as above. Flour reverse side of all patterns except C, G1, G3, H and I. Lay as many

---

Pages 234 and 235: Here's a reindeer residence that would do Santa and his flying herd proud! The one-dimensional gingerbread barn comes complete with shredded-cereal haystacks and a Santa-cookie weathervane. Instructions begin on this page.

Santa's Stable designed by Steven Vordenberg and executed by Holly Sheppard.

floured patterns as possible on the chilled rolled dough, ½-inch apart. With X-acto knife, cut out around patterns. Carefully remove patterns and excess dough. (Save trimmings in plastic bag; chill to reroll later.)

3. Preheat oven to 350°F. Bake gingerbread pieces 15 to 25 minutes, or until very firm and dark brown. (Soft gingerbread is not advised for use in this construction.) Remove small pieces as they brown to wire racks, since they bake faster; cool completely. Store in airtight container until ready to use.

4. Make roof: Place pattern piece C on graham cracker. With X-acto knife, score around edges. Repeat to make 2 outlines. Cut out pieces; set aside. With brown food color (or, if desired, unsweetened cocoa powder) tint 2 recipes icing gingerbread brown. On work surface, place foam-core piece A. With small metal spatula, spread some brown icing on roof area. Cover with gingerbread piece B. Attach one graham-cracker C piece to cutout area in rooftop; spread with icing. Top with second graham-cracker C piece. With X-acto knife, cut ¾-inch squares of cinnamon- and spearmint-flavored sticks chewing gum, about 40 of each. With brown icing in pastry bag fitted with number-3 tip, using photograph as a guide, attach gum to roof, trimming gum squares to fit roof edges; attach silver-coated almonds to roof edges.

5. With X-acto knife and ruler, using barn pattern as a guide, lightly score gingerbread to make outline of door, loft and windows, including frames; outline boards, spaced ⅛-inch apart. With red food color, tint 1 recipe icing red. With ⅓ cup red icing in pastry bag fitted with number-1 tip, pipe icing over scored board marks on gingerbread. With remaining red icing in pastry bag fitted with number-3 tip, fill in icing outlines of boards. With small metal spatula, spread icing to give weathered, painted wood look.

6. With brown food color, tint ¼-cup gingerbread-brown icing dark brown. Cover 1 tablespoon icing with plastic wrap; set aside. With small metal spatula, spread icing to cover stall windows and loft, adding water to icing, ¾ teaspoon at a time, if icing is too stiff to spread easily. With X-acto knife, cut licorice in half to make 2 (¼-inch-thick) pieces. While icing is wet, attach a licorice piece to center of 2 stall windows closest to door (these will raise the reindeer heads away from the barn.) Let stand 2 hours, until icing dries.

7. Make barn doors: With X-acto knife, halve whole graham cracker lengthwise along division in cracker. Cut another graham cracker into quarters along divisions in cracker; cut 1 more quarter from another whole cracker. Place pattern piece I on a graham-cracker quarter. With X-acto knife, score around pattern. Repeat with pattern reversed for second outline; cut out pieces. With red icing in pastry bag with number-1 tip, using photograph as a guide, outline cinnamon-sugar side of cut crackers; pipe an X over length of each cracker piece and on top and bottom halves of whole crackers. Let stand 2 hours, until dry.

8. With ¼ cup white icing in pastry bag fitted with number-46 tip, using photograph as a guide, outline barn doors and windows. With 2 tablespoons white icing in pastry bag fitted with number-1 tip, pipe an X where lines overlap. Let stand 2 hours, until icing dries.

9. Make oat bin: With gingerbread-brown icing in pastry bag fitted with number-3 tip, attach a short side of each gingerbread piece F1 to wide V end of a gingerbread piece F to make a V shape of F1 pieces, with flat sides of gingerbread inside. Attach remaining gingerbread piece F to pieces. Let stand 2 hours, until icing dries.

10. Make water trough: With gingerbread-brown icing in pastry bag

fitted with number-3 tip, attach each short side of a gingerbread piece E1 to a long side of a gingerbread piece E to make a box with flat sides of gingerbread inside; attach each short side of E1 pieces to remaining gingerbread piece E. With ruler, measure dimensions of trough opening; with marker, outline rectangle with trough opening dimensions onto a piece of remaining foam-core board. With X-acto knife, cut out rectangle. With gingerbread-brown icing in pastry bag fitted with number-3 tip, piping icing from hollow end of trough so that icing does not show on outside, attach foam-core rectangle to one end of trough. Let stand 2 hours, until icing dries.

11. Make cart: With gingerbread-brown icing in pastry bag fitted with number-3 tip, attach each short side of a gingerbread piece G to a short side of a gingerbread piece G2 to make a box with flat sides of gingerbread inside. With gingerbread-brown icing in pastry bag fitted with number-3 tip, attach each short side of G2 pieces to remaining gingerbread piece G. Let stand 2 hours, until icing dries. With gingerbread-brown icing in pastry bag fitted with number-3 tip, attach each foam-core piece G3 (½ inch) from short end of foam-core piece G1. Let stand 2 hours, until icing dries; when dry, with gingerbread-brown icing in pastry bag fitted with number-3 tip, attach cart bottom to cart. With X-acto knife, cut a 4-inch length from each of 2 pretzel rods. With gingerbread-brown icing in pastry bag fitted with number-3 tip, attach each rod crosswise and on underside of foam-core cart bottom so that pretzel is next to each G3 piece for wheel supports. Let stand 2 hours, until icing dries.

12. With gingerbread-brown icing in pastry bag fitted with number-3 tip, attach sign (D) to 2 whole pretzel rods. Let stand 2 hours, until icing dries.

(Continued on page 238)

13. With small metal spatula, spread reserved dark-brown icing over lower half of loft window and at sides of window. While icing is wet, using photograph as a guide, gently attach some shredded wheat cereal; attach loft doors. With spatula and dark-brown icing, attach stall doors under stall windows.

14. With X-acto knife, cut sticks of bubble gum into ear-shaped pieces for each reindeer and milk-chocolate twigs for antlers; set aside. With ¼ cup gingerbread-brown icing in pastry bag fitted with number-1 tip, outline reindeer. In custard cup, thin 2 tablespoons gingerbread-brown icing to painting consistency, adding ½ teaspoon water at a time. With paintbrush, cover reindeer within icing border. While icing is still wet, attach colored candies for collars, white candies for eyes, the bubble-gum ears and chocolate sprinkles for fur texture. With X-acto knife, cut 3 black jelly beans in half. With gingerbread-brown icing in pastry bag fitted with number-1 tip, attach jelly-bean noses and milk-chocolate antlers. With red icing in pastry bag fitted with number-3 tip, pipe nose on red-nosed reindeer. Let stand 2 hours, until dry.

15. With dark-brown icing thinned to painting consistency, paint red-nosed reindeer's reflection in water trough. With green food color, tint 2 tablespoons icing green. With green icing in pastry bag fitted with number-1 tip, pipe scarf and hat on elf; scarf on bear cracker, and "North Pole Corral" on sign. With 2 tablespoons red icing in pastry bag fitted with number-1 tip, pipe Santa suit and hat on bear cracker, nose on red-nosed reindeer's reflection in water trough, and overalls, mittens and cap decorations on elf. With 2 tablespoons white icing in pastry bag fitted with number-1 tip, pipe beard on Santa and fur trim on Santa suit, snowflakes on sign, "oat bran" on oat bin and shirt, button and boot

laces on elf. While icing is wet, decorate shirt with colored sprinkles. With X-acto knife, cut stick of bubble gum for elf's face. With white icing in pastry bag with number-1 tip, attach face on elf and white candy eye on elf face. With tip of paintbrush and black food color, color pupil on all eyes, and paint belt and eye on Santa cracker. With X-acto knife, trim wide end of sugar cone to make a 2-inch-high cone. With white icing in pastry bag with number-1 tip, attach open end of sugar cone to flat side of 1 chocolate-sandwich cookie; attach dragées around cone edge on cookie; attach decorated cookie to flat side of another chocolate-sandwich cookie. With gingerbread-brown icing in pastry bag with number-3 tip, attach licorice wheels and peppermint-stick handle to cart. Let stand 2 hours, until icing dries.

16. With gingerbread-brown icing in pastry bag with number-3 tip, attach J reindeer to stall near end of barn and J1 and J2 reindeer to licorice pieces in stalls; attach wooden pick to back side of Santa cracker. Let stand 2 hours, until icing dries.

17. With glue and tape, attach foam-core H pieces to back of barn and to foam-core base, placing 8-inch side of H pieces against barn and 1-inch side of support on base. Support with tall juice cans until glue dries. Meanwhile, using photograph as a guide, with gingerbread-brown icing in pastry bag fitted with number-3 tip, attach doors to barn; attach Santa-cracker weathervane to graham-cracker-weathervane base on rooftop.

18. Make fence: With X-acto knife, cut 4 pretzel-rods crosswise in half; set aside. With gingerbread-brown icing in pastry bag fitted with number-3 tip, attach pretzel-rods with sign to foam-core base, using tall juice cans to support pretzels. With icing, attach one wide loop of pretzel to each rod and small loop to

foam-core base, using cans to support pretzels until icing dries; attach one cut pretzel-rod to other wide loop and foam-core base, using short cans for support. Repeat with remaining pretzels and pretzel rods.

19. Make wire supports for reindeer and elf: With wire cutters, cut 5 (2½-foot) lengths of florist's wire. Curve each wire to make one circle of 3 (3-inch-diameter) loops; bend remaining wire around loops several times; extend wire across circle and around loops several times; and, with remaining wire, extend a loop that extends up if remaining loops are flat. Wrap end of wire around outstanding loop for support.

20. Finish scene: Using photograph as a guide, arrange wire supports around corral and in barn; place corresponding reindeer or elf on each support. Pile sugar in drifts. Place cart near elf so handle extends to elf's hand. Fill cart with peppermint candies. Fill oat bin with oat cereal. Arrange trough so red-nosed reindeer and his reflection correspond. Pile candy rocks around corral and bales of shredded wheat cereal in barn.

Spaniel Surprise Puppy

PROPS AND SUPPORT
1 tin (32 ounces) bittersweet almond-flavored Italian cookies (128 cookie pairs); small metal spatula; 3 disposable pastry bags; pastry tips: Nos. 3, 4 and 4B; 1 roll (25-foot) heavy-duty aluminum foil; tape; scissors; bowl; 4 yards red velvet floral ribbon (wired ribbon); 4 sheets red tissue paper

4 recipes Decorating Icing, (recipe follows; make in separate batches before using)

Food paste colors: black, cocoa brown (or use unsweetened cocoa powder), leaf green

Our playful spaniel puppy is made from cocoa icing over a foil figure.

Compliments of Lazzaroni Amarettini Di Sarranno.

DECORATIONS
Reserved cookies from tin (above); 2 large marshmallows; 1 red (strawberry or cherry) roll-up fruit candy; additional wrapped bittersweet almond-flavored Italian cookies

1. Remove lid and cookies from tin; set lid aside. Unwrap cookies; set aside. With green food color, tint two recipes icing green. With metal spatula, spread enough green icing over outside of tin to cover. While icing is still wet, attach flat side of enough cookies to cover tin, placing cookies in rows. With remaining green icing in pastry bag fitted with number-4B tip, using photograph as a guide, pipe a star in each gap between cookies, keeping icing stars in rows spaced between cookie rows. Pipe icing over top edges of tin. Set decorated tin aside until icing dries, about 4 hours.

2. Make spaniel: Crumple several 3-foot lengths of aluminum foil; pack lightly in bottom of tin. Crumple more foil, packing loosely and shaping for base portion of dog; stuff form in tin. Wrap and crumple more foil, taping and wrapping foil around body to form head, ears, mouth and nose. Roll up one 3-foot length of foil; arrange roll crosswise in front of dog for paws. Tape and wrap with strips of foil to hold in place. Using photograph as a guide, bend foil to form paws.

3. With cocoa powder or brown food color, tint remaining icing brown. With metal spatula, spread about half the icing over shaped foil. Press marshmallows in place for eyes. With scissors, cut fruit roll to make tongue in dog's mouth; press

in place. Let stand until icing dries, about 4 hours.

4. Set aside ¼ cup brown icing. With remaining brown icing in pastry bag fitted with number-4 tip, pipe shaggy icing "fur" over icing on dog.

5. In small bowl, with black food color, tint reserved ¼ cup brown icing black. With black icing in pastry bag fitted with number-3 tip, pipe nose on dog's muzzle, outline mouth and eyes, and make pupils on (marshmallow) eyes. Let stand until icing dries, about 2 hours.

6. With a 2-yard length of ribbon, using photograph as a guide, wrap icing-covered tin as for a package, taping sides of ribbon on inside of tin and letting ends fall back over sides. With additional ribbon, make large bow; attach to ribbon trim on tin. Lightly pack red tissue paper and additional unwrapped cookies around dog. Tape a wrapped cookie in dog's mouth.

Note: Different breeds of dogs can be styled from foil; color icing as desired. Vary pastry tips for different fur texture.

Decorating Icing

3 large egg whites, at room temperature
1 to 1½ packages (1-pound size) confectioners' sugar (sift if lumpy)
½ teaspoon cream of tartar
Unsweetened cocoa powder (see *Note*)

In small bowl of electric mixer, combine egg whites, 1 package sugar and the cream of tartar. Beat at high speed until icing is stiff enough to hold its shape when beaters are raised. If icing is not stiff, add more sugar. Place a sheet of plastic wrap directly on icing surface to keep from drying out; if icing is in pastry bags, wrap tips with plastic wrap.

Makes about 2 cups.

Note: When icing is used as mortar, the stiffer it is, the faster it will dry. To match icing color with gingerbread, add cocoa powder by tablespoonfuls to icing while beating.

To prepare icing for decoration, use wooden picks to add dots of paste colors to icing until desired color is achieved.

Twelve-Days-of-Christmas Tree

1 recipe Gingerbread Dough (recipe follows)
Royal Icing recipe, page 220
Molded Chocolates (recipe follows)

PROPS AND SUPPORT
Marker; tracing paper; the 12 Days of Christmas Kit (see *Note*); scissors; cooking parchment paper or aluminum foil; X-acto knife; 4 disposable pastry bags; pastry tips Nos. 2, 101 and 102 (two); 1 package (16 ounces) sugar cubes; 12-inch diameter aluminum-foil-covered Styrofoam round

Food paste colors: leaf green, Christmas red

1. With marker and tracing paper, trace pattern pieces from kit or make one round each: 1¼-inch, 2-inch, 2¾-inch, 3½-inch, 4½-inch, 5-inch, 6-inch, 7-inch, 8-inch, 9-inch, 10-inch diameter. Cut out with scissors.

2. On floured 15-by-12-inch sheet of parchment paper or aluminum foil, roll 1 piece of gingerbread dough to ¼-inch thickness. Place rolled dough and paper on baking sheet; chill 15 minutes. Meanwhile, roll out and chill remaining dough as above.

3. Flour reverse sides of patterns; lay as many patterns as possible on chilled rolled dough, ½ inch apart. With X-acto knife, cut out around patterns. Carefully remove paper patterns and excess dough. (Save dough trimmings in plastic bag; chill to reroll later.)

4. Preheat oven to 350°F. Bake gingerbread rounds 6 to 15 minutes, or until firm and browned. Using paper to lift rounds, carefully remove small rounds as they brown to wire rack, since they bake faster; cool completely. Store in airtight container until ready to decorate.

5. With food colors, tint half of the icing red and the other half green. Place one-third of red icing in pastry bag fitted with number-2 tip; place half of remaining red icing in pastry bag fitted with number-101 tip; place remaining red icing in pastry bag fitted with number-102 tip. Place green icing in pastry bag fitted with number-102 tip. With either icing, attach about 12 sugar cubes to Styrofoam round, placing cubes in a ring about 2 inches inside edge of round. Pipe a dot of icing on top of each cube; center largest gingerbread round over cubes. Repeat, stacking remaining gingerbread rounds in decreasing sizes and placing sugar cubes between layers. Let gingerbread stand until icing dries, about 3 hours.

6. With additional icing, using photograph as a guide, attach molded chocolates to gingerbread, starting at top with partridge, and arranging pears, turtledoves, French hens, calling birds, gold rings, geese and eggs, swans, maids, drums, notes, ladies and lords in descending order. Let gingerbread stand until icing dries, about 1 hour.

7. Using photograph as a guide, with green icing in pastry bag, pipe ruffled leaves onto gingerbread rounds between all molded chocolates; with red icing in pastry bag fitted with number-2 tip, pipe berries onto leaves. With red icing in pastry bag fitted with number-101 tip, make a bow on partridge, extending ends in a curling trail over height of tree. With red icing in pastry bag fitted with number-102 tip, make a ruffle around side of

This edible evergreen centerpiece doubles as dessert.

Compliments of Wilton Enterprises.

base. Let stand until icing dries, about 1 hour. Store in cool place.

Note: Kit is available from Wilton Enterprises, Inc., 312-963-7100, or your local Wilton dealer.

Gingerbread Dough

8½ to 9 cups unsifted all-purpose flour
1 tablespoon ground ginger
2 teaspoons ground cinnamon
½ teaspoon salt
1 cup butter-flavored shortening
1 bottle (16 ounces) dark corn syrup
1½ cups lightly packed brown sugar

1. In large bowl of heavy-duty electric mixer, mix together 4 cups flour, the spices and salt. Set aside.

2. In medium saucepan, over low heat, melt shortening. Add corn syrup and sugar; stir until sugar dissolves. Remove from heat.

3. With mixer at low speed, gradually beat syrup mixture into flour mixture. At medium speed, beat in 2 cups flour. With wooden spoon or hands, mix in remaining flour until stiff dough forms. (Dough should be firm, not sticky.) Divide dough into four parts; if not using immediately, wrap in plastic wrap and refrigerate up to a week. If dough is refrigerated, let it come to room temperature before rolling (about 3 hours).

Molded Chocolates

1 package (12 ounces) semisweet chocolate
Chocolate molds (see *Note*): 1 partridge, 4 pears, 2 turtledoves, 3 French hens, 4 calling birds, 5 rings, 6 geese and eggs, 7 swans, 8 maids, 9 drums, 10 notes, 11 ladies, 12 lords

1. In top of double boiler, over hot, not boiling, water, melt chocolate, stirring. Or place chocolate in large glass bowl. Cook in microwave on HIGH 1 minute; stir. Cook on MEDIUM for 30-second intervals, until melted. Do not overheat, or chocolate will harden and scorch.

2. Spoon some melted chocolate into each mold. (Do not hold molds directly over hot chocolate. This will cause condensation and will dull and spot the chocolate.)

3. Place molds in freezer 2 to 3 minutes or until chocolate hardens. (Bottom of molds will look frosty.) Unmold by gently pressing around edges of mold to release chocolate. Place unmolded chocolates on baking sheet; keep in cool place.

Note: Molds are available from Wilton Enterprises, Inc., 312-963-7100, or your local Wilton dealer. Or use other molded chocolates.

■ Trimmings from gingerbread dough make stunning (and fragrant!) tree ornaments, gift tags and place cards. Reroll trimmings and chill dough as for gingerbread houses, except roll dough to ⅛-inch thickness. To make ornaments: With ¼-inch round cutter or metal tip from a pastry bag or plastic drinking straw, cut a hole near the top of each cookie. Make holes about ½-inch inside edges so when cookies soften by the heat of tree lights they will not tear through. To make tags and cards: Cut holes all around edges of cookies to lace tags and cards with ribbons. Decorate cookies with decorating icing, and "paint" them with thinned icing. (Liquid food colors may be used to tint icing, but paste colors will be more intense.) Do not use too much icing, as this will soak through the cookies, softening them and adding to their weight. Store in an airtight container.

Patterns for Holiday Centerpieces

Grandma's Cottage

(pictured, page 219; instructions begin on page 222.)

Cottage patterns are one-fourth actual size.

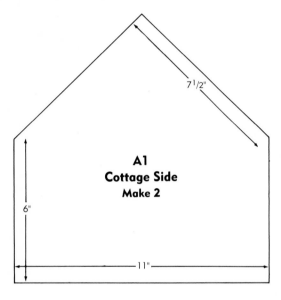

7¹/₂"

6"

11"

A1
Cottage Side
Make 2

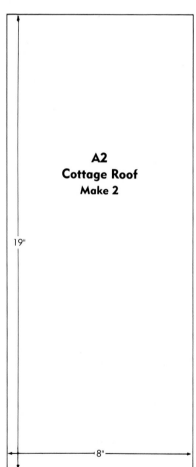

19"

8"

A2
Cottage Roof
Make 2

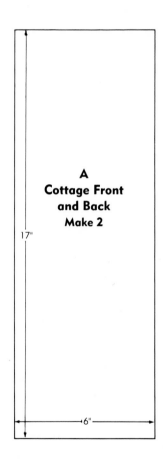

17"

6"

A
Cottage Front
and Back
Make 2

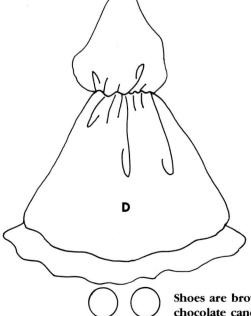

D

Red Riding Hood pattern is three-fourths actual size.

Shoes are brown candy-coated chocolate candies.

Grandma's Cottage

Cottage patterns are one-fourth actual size.

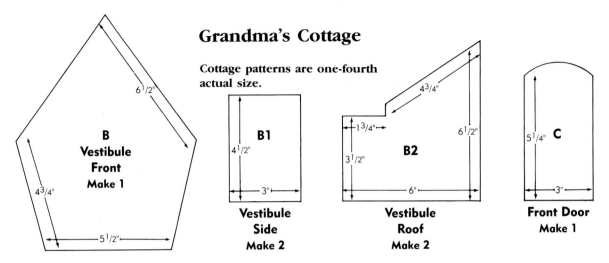

B Vestibule Front Make 1

6½"

4¾"

5½"

B1 4½" 3"

Vestibule Side Make 2

B2 4¾" 1¾" 3½" 6¼" 6"

Vestibule Roof Make 2

C 5¼" 3"

Front Door Make 1

Rapunzel's Tower

(pictured, pages 214 and 215; instructions begin on page 214.)

Castle patterns are one-fourth actual size.

Rapunzel and dove patterns are three-fourths actual size.

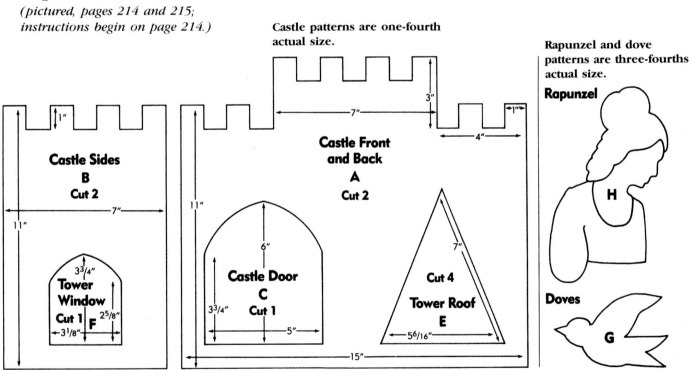

Castle Sides B Cut 2

1" 7" 11"

Tower Window Cut 1 3¾" 2⅝" 3⅛" **F**

7" 3" 4" 1"

Castle Front and Back A Cut 2

11"

Castle Door C Cut 1 6" 3¾" 5"

15"

Cut 4 Tower Roof E 7" 5⁶⁄₁₆"

Rapunzel

H

Doves

G

Cinderella's Castle

(pictured, pages 216 and 217;
instructions begin on page 220.)

Cinderella pattern is
three-fourths actual size.

Castle patterns are one-fourth
actual size.

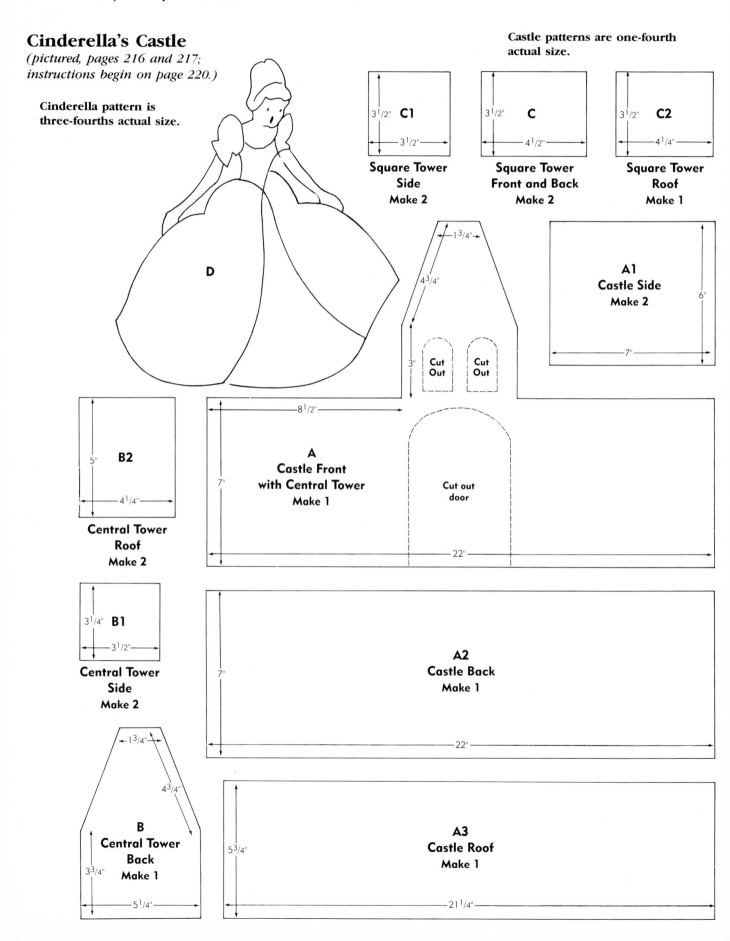

D

C1 3 1/2" 3 1/2"
Square Tower
Side
Make 2

C 3 1/2" 4 1/2"
Square Tower
Front and Back
Make 2

C2 3 1/2" 4 1/4"
Square Tower
Roof
Make 1

1 3/4"
4 3/4"
3"
Cut Out   Cut Out

A1
Castle Side
Make 2
6"
7"

B2 5" 4 1/4"
Central Tower
Roof
Make 2

8 1/2"
A
Castle Front
with Central Tower
Make 1
7"
Cut out door
22"

B1 3 1/4" 3 1/2"
Central Tower
Side
Make 2

A2
Castle Back
Make 1
7"
22"

1 3/4"
4 3/4"
B
Central Tower
Back
Make 1
3 3/4"
5 1/4"

A3
Castle Roof
Make 1
5 3/4"
21 1/4"

Santa's Stable

(pictured, pages 234 and 235;
instructions begin on page 236.)

Patterns are one-half actual size.

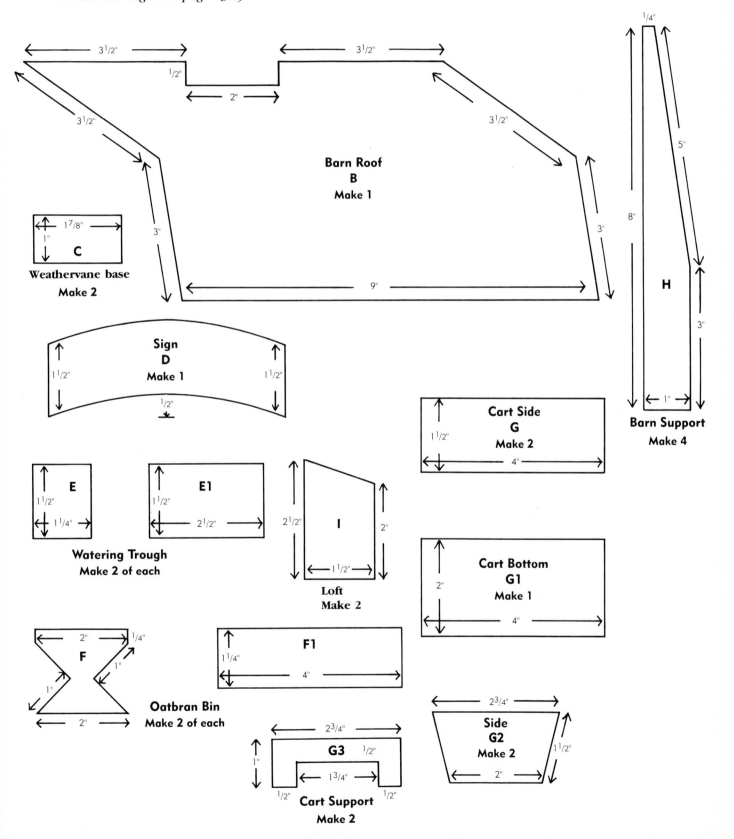

Barn Roof
B
Make 1

1⁷/₈"
1"
C
Weathervane base
Make 2

Sign
D
Make 1

E
1¹/₂"
1¹/₄"

E1
1¹/₂"
2¹/₂"

Watering Trough
Make 2 of each

I
2¹/₂"
2"
1¹/₂"

Loft
Make 2

Cart Side
G
Make 2
1¹/₂"
4"

Cart Bottom
G1
Make 1
2"
4"

H
1/4"
5"
8"
3"
1"

Barn Support
Make 4

F
2"
1/4"
1"
1"
2"

Oatbran Bin
Make 2 of each

F1
1¹/₄"
4"

G3
2³/₄"
1/2"
1"
1³/₄"
1/2"
1/2"

Cart Support
Make 2

Side
G2
Make 2
2³/₄"
2"
1¹/₂"

Santa's Stable

Barn pattern is one-half actual size.

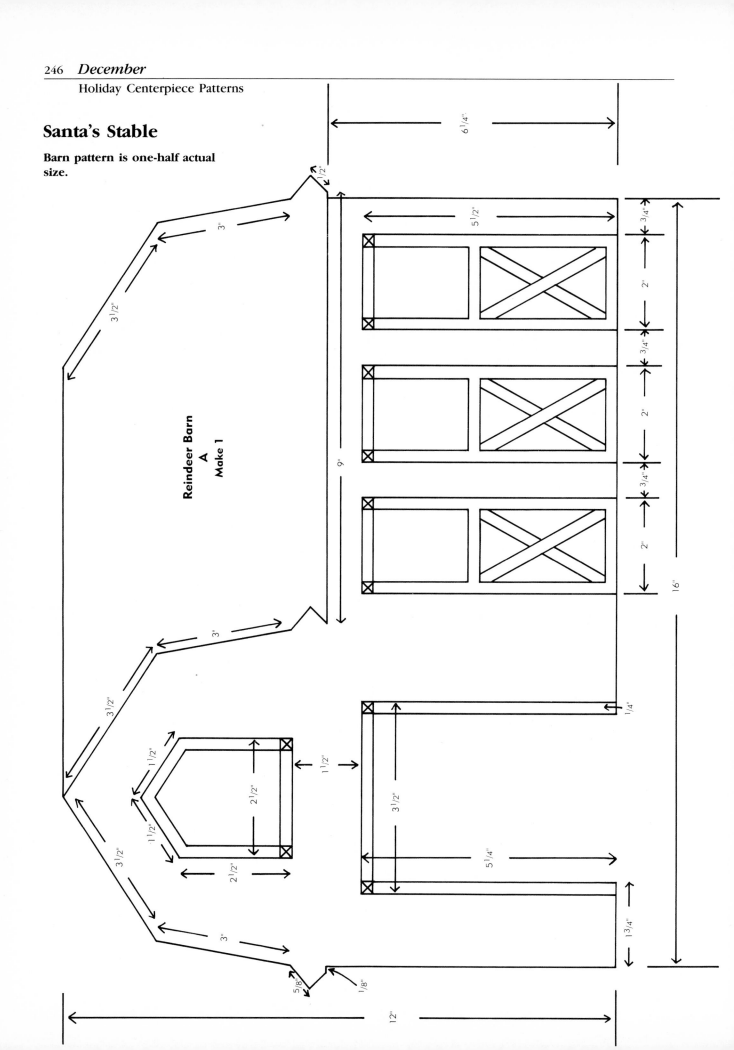

Reindeer Barn
A
Make 1

Santa's Stable

Figure patterns are actual size.

Reindeer Head
J2
Make 1

Reindeer Head
J
Make 1

Elf
L
Make 1

Grazing Reindeer
K
Make 2

Reindeer Head
J1
Make 1

Santa's Stable

Figure patterns are actual size.

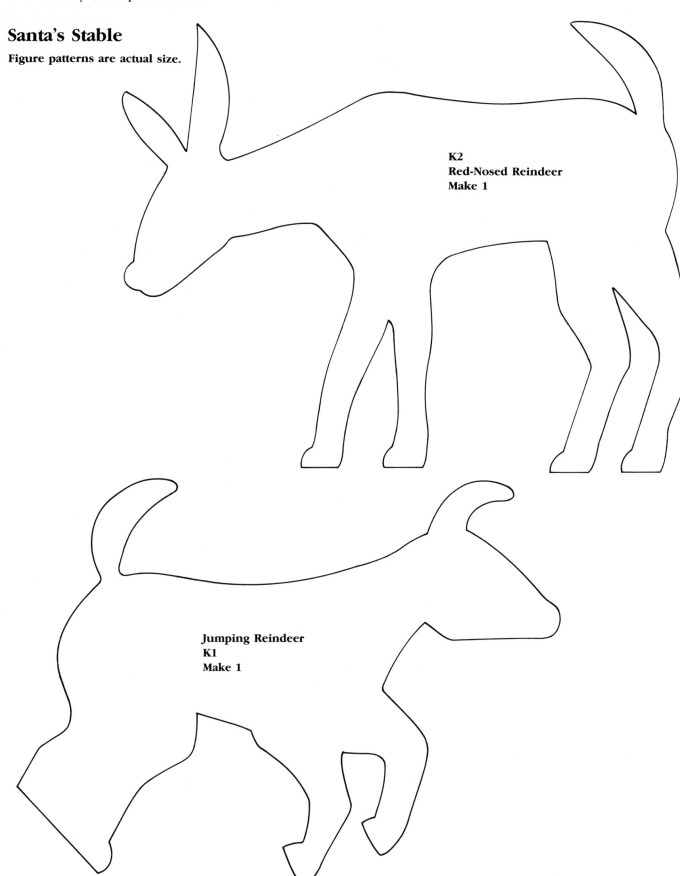

**K2
Red-Nosed Reindeer
Make 1**

**Jumping Reindeer
K1
Make 1**

General Recipe Index

General Recipe Index

Recipe Title Index